The Indigenous Biography of Cleo Kelley

Ancestry

Genealogy

Heritage

Legacy

Expanded Edition

By

Sibyl D. Kelley

Copyright 2025 Sibyl D. Kelley

All rights reserved. This book cannot be reproduced or duplicated without the expressed consent of the author and or publisher. All events are historical products of eyewitness attestation, narrated to the author by individuals credited in the acknowledgement or published references.

ISBN: 9798218703769 Paperback

ISBN: 9798218877088 Hardcover

LCCN: 2025925020

Library of Congress

U.S. Programs, Law, and Literature Division

Cataloging in Publication Program

101 Independence Avenue, S.E.

Washington, DC 20540

Table of Contents

Acknowledgment . . . . Page iv
Introduction . . . . Page v
Preface . . . . Page vi
The Ancient World and the Origin of Royalty. . . . . Page viii
The Reconstruction Era for the Blount, Garrer, and Wilson Families. . Page xi

Chapter 1   The Progressive Era . . . . Page 1
Chapter 2   The Age of Consent 1918. . . . . Page 5
Chapter 3   The 1920s and the Prohibition of John Wesley Garrer   Page 9
Chapter 4   The 1930s Cleo's Migration . . . . Page 14
Chapter 5   The 1940s Our Home in Lawtey . . . . Page 23
Chapter 6   The 1950s A Personal Vision . . . . Page 39
Chapter 7   1960s Welcome to Schoolboy's and the Era of Kelly's Nite Limit. . . . . Page 82
Chapter 8   The 1970s: Margurie W. Kelly vs The Florida Division of Beverage. . . . . Page 193
Chapter 9   The 1980s: The Kellys Standing Together . . . . Page 280
Chapter 10   The 1990s: The Kelly's 50th Anniversary . . . . Page 315
Chapter 11   Y2Ks: Kelly's Nite Limit and the Digital Blues. . . . . Page 345
Chapter 12   A Personal Heritage and Legacy . . . . Page 351

References . . . . Page 358
Index. . . . . Page 363

Acknowledgment

The Indigenous Biography of Cleo Kelly (Expanded Edition) meticulously chronicles the ancestry, genealogy, history and enduring legacy of Clifford Kelly Sr of Lawtey, Florida. Elaborated with 70 additional pages, the book was authored by his eldest granddaughter. Memories and narratives were shared by his extended family, friends, and longtime business associates, enriching the tapestry of his life story with heartfelt reflections and lived experiences. On January 1, 2020, at Ben and Emma Strong's home in Lawtey, Florida, the family came together to reflect on the cherished memories about the roster of recording artists who once graced the stage at Kelly's Nite Limit—a once lively juke joint nightclub founded by our ancestor Clifford Kelly Sr. With gratitude, I would like to extend a special thank you to Clifford Kelly Jr., Marylou Kelly Williams, Bobby Kelly Sr., Emma Kelly Strong, and Benjamin Strong.

Additional narratives were contributed by Willie Mae Jordan, Donna Garrer Miller, Eva J. Evans, Jerry West, Lee Parker, Ulysee Muff Sr., Robert Austin Jr., Chuck Roberson, Beverly Drummond Turner, and Mrs. Harridelle Taylor Bright (whose insights were drawn from her University of Florida oral history program notes).

The Book Cover: The paperback cover was inspired by the dance floor at Kelly's Nite Limit. The railroad track pays homage to Cleo Kelly's journey into Florida. The hard cover design was inspired by a 1947 Kelly family photograph.

Introduction

The Indigenous Biography of Cleo Kelly (Expanded Edition) offers a vivid portrait of Clifford Kelly Sr of Lawtey, Florida capturing key moments that shaped his life. Born in 1918 in Blythe, Georgia, he was named Cleosie Daniel by his teenage mother, Emma Kate Daniel. In time, young Emma entrusted her son to adoption. He was renamed Cleo Kelley by his adoptive parents, John and Nellie Kelley of Burke County, Georgia. The child's father, John Wesley Garrer, had been entrained for service in World War I (WWI).

In the midst of the Great Migration, 18-year-old Cleo Kelly boarded a train with his uncle Grady Lee Daniel, leaving Augusta, Georgia, behind as they headed toward North Florida. Amid the backdrop of World War II (WWII), he secured work as a Laborer for Seaboard Airline Railway—and it was then that Cleo Kelley became Clifford Kelly. In 1954, he imagined owning a night club, similar to the one owned by his father John Wesley Garrer in Louisville, Georgia. By 1957, with the support of his wife, Mrs. Margurie Williams Kelly, the place became a juke joint nightclub known as Kelly's Nite Limit. During the Rock 'n Roll Era, with raw intuition, Clifford Kelly Sr, booked and promoted over 125 recording artists to perform at his nightclub.

The first recording artists to perform live at Kelly's Nite Limit were Larry Birdsong, B.B. King, The Platters, Chuck Willis, Roy Gaines, Dinah Washington, The 5 Royals, The Drifters, and Muddy Waters. By 1964, the venue was expanded to host an audience of 700–1000 people. Tucked within the small rural town of Lawtey, Bradford County, Florida, the business remained open for five decades (1954–2004). From the sacred sands of ancient Kemet to the trials of precolonial and postcolonial America, this is the ancestry, genealogy, history, and enduring legacy of Clifford "Schoolboy" Kelly—a self-made blues music Artist Promoter and Master Concrete Finisher.

Preface

You share an ancient paternal lineage with Pharaoh Ramesses III.

Image and narrative for King Ramses III provided by 23&Me.

Pharaoh Ramesses III, who reigned for nearly thirty years, defended Egypt in three consecutive wars, yet his rule stirred dissent within his own administration. Driven by rising internal discord, Tiye, a lesser wife of Ramesses III, conspired to install her son, Pentawer, on the throne by orchestrating the assassination of the pharaoh and his appointed heir. A surviving papyrus from the trial records that the conspiracy failed and all the participants involved were tried and convicted. However, a modern CT scan of Ramesses III's mummy exposed a deep slit to the pharaoh's throat, reigniting debate over a conspiracy once thought conclusively resolved. The embalmers went to great lengths to conceal his other wounds, including crafting a resin replica to replace Ramesses's severed toe, which is likely lost during the fatal attack.

For millennia, the burial adornments of Ramesses III veiled the violent secrets of one of history's most infamous royal conspiracies. Ramesses III's paternal lineage traces to haplogroup E-V38—the same ancestral lineage from which your own bloodline descends. You and Ramesses III share an ancient paternal ancestor who probably lived in North Africa or Western Asia.

The Ancient World and the Origin of Royalty

Knowing the name of the land of your origin is vital for your identity. *Alkebulan* is the oldest word of indigenous origin. It means Eden, or "Garden of Eden." Adam was created from the dust of the ground in Eden. There are twenty paternal generations from Adam to Abram and forty-two paternal generations from Abram (Abraham) to Yeshua outlined in *The Biblia (The Book)*. The Biotechnology Company 23 & Me traced—via DNA analysis—the paternal-line ancestry of Clifford Kelly Jr. back to the ancient indigenous lineage of Pharaoh Ramses III.

In 1217 BC, Ramses III was born to King Setnakhte and Queen Tiye Merenese in Alkebulan in the city of Waset, Kemet. King Ramses III reigned for thirty-one years during Kemet's Third Golden Age. He had three wives—Tyti, Isis, and Tiye—and was father to one daughter and ten sons. The King's DNA haplogroup, E-V38 (E1b1a), represents Bantu Israelite lineages originating from North East Alkebulan. Although ancient borders have been realigned, some of the Bantu-speaking families are indigenous to East Alkebulan in the ancient land of Cush, which is modern-day Ethiopia (Abyssinia).

During the reign of Ramses III (1186–1155 BC), the land of Kemet encompassed ancient Nubia (NUBA), a region located in what is now modern-day Sudan. NUBA was renowned for its abundant gold mineral deposits. Under islamic rulership, the word Sudan means

Land of the Blacks. After thousands of years of cultural and political heritage in Kemet, the land eventually came under the control of other kingdoms. Persia started ruling Kemet in 525 BC. The Macedonians conquered Kemet in 332 BC and named the land Aegyptus (Egypt). A Roman territory was established in 146 BC along the northern coast of Alkebulan. This Roman province was named Afar/Afri/Africae/Africa. For centuries, thousands of indigenous citizens of Kemet perished or were scattered throughout Alkebulan. DNA testing revealed that the paternal ancestors of Clifford Kelly Jr. settled

Pre Colonial Map of Africa 1858

bilād as-sūdān (Soudan)

Land of the Blacks

in Northeast, Central, and West Africa. The ancestors migrated within the precolonial states of Buganda (Uganda), Kirinyaga (Kenya), Cross River State (Nigeria, Benin, and Kingdom of Judah), Ndongo (Angola), and Kongo (Republic of Congo). The paternal bloodline origin for Clifford Kelly Jr., tracing from the fifth to eighth generation into antiquity, is rooted in Indigenous American ancestry (Ta Meri: ancient America) and Sudanese heritage (Ta-Seti, Ta-Nehisi: ancient Nubia). Clifford Kelly Jr. is the firstborn son of Clifford Kelly Sr., in whose honor this ancestral and genealogy book is written.

There are historians who believe King Ramses III and his royal Navy sailed to ancient America (Ta Meri) and built cities as far west as the Grand Canyon. So how did the (Y)-chromosome of ancient royal Kemet's Third Golden Age arrive in the Southeast United States? From The Nile Valley to the Peach State of Georgia? The Act Prohibiting the Importation of Slaves was enacted by Congress in 1807. On January 1, 1808, federal law prohibiting the transportation of enslaved people into the United States was effectively mandated. For Clifford Kelly Sr., there's no known family narrative nor folklore indicating that any direct male paternal bloodline ancestors were enslaved and brought to America—not by first name, surname, nickname, or identification number. There is no family narrative or oral history of a plantation or plantation owner associated with any direct male ancestors in the paternal bloodline of Clifford Kelly Sr. After thousands of years of heritage in North America, the paternal bloodline of Clifford Kelly Sr. survived major historical events, including the Yamassee Indian War of 1715, Black Code Laws of 1740, the Cherokee War of 1759, Battle of Brier Creek 1779, Battle at Burke County Jail in 1779, Siege of Augusta in 1781, War of 1812, Battle of Waynesboro in 1864, and the Civil War 1861–1865.

The Reconstruction Era for the Blount, Garrer, and Wilson Families

The Blunt-Blount Family of Richmond County, Georgia

Prior to the establishment for the colony of Georgia in 1732, the original settlers of the region were Creek and Cherokee Tribes. From 1865 to 1877, the Reconstruction Era marked the period after the American Civil War. During this time, efforts were made to grant formerly enslaved people full equality, including citizenship, the right to vote for men, and other civil provisions. The paternal bloodline of Clifford Kelly Sr. was traced to three men bearing the surname of Blunt or Blount: John Blount Sr. (1835), John Blount Jr. (1874), and John Blunt III (1895). There's no known history of enslavement associated with any of them. John Blount Sr. was born in Columbia County, Georgia, and his wife, Emma Jones, was born in Green County, Georgia, in 1854. They were married on October 20, 1872, in Richmond, Georgia. Their union produced nine children. John Blount Sr. was a farmer and laborer, while his wife Emma was a homemaker. In 1879, the Jones family established Jones Chapel AME Zion Church in Blythe, Georgia. John Blount Sr. and Emma Jones Blount are the paternal great grandparents of Clifford Kelly Sr.

The Garrer Family of Richmond County, Georgia After the Civil War

Prince Garrer was born in 1841 in Richmond, Georgia. His wife, Elizabeth Garrer, was born in 1844 in Virginia. They were married in 1864 in Augusta, Richmond County, Georgia. Together, they had eleven children. Prince was a farmer, while Lizzie worked as a dorm servant. The Civil War ended in 1865 and caused thousands of people to migrate into Richmond County. Although the South was war torn, the City of Augusta was practically untouched by the violence of the battle.

On July 21, 1867, Prince Garrer was listed in the Georgia U.S. Returns of Qualified Voters and Reconstruction Oath Books. In 1890, he owned 101 acres of land in Richmond County, as listed in the Georgia U.S. Property Digest. Prince Garrer was a landowner and a registered voter in Augusta, Richmond County, Georgia two years after the Civil War.

In 1880, the families of Prince Garrer and John Blount Sr. resided just a few homes apart in the same region of Richmond County, Georgia. Prince and Elizabeth Garrer are the paternal great grandparents of Clifford Kelly Sr. as well.

The Wilson Family of Peetsville, Florida

East Florida was the original homeland of the ancient Yamassee Indians. Florida became the twenty-seventh state of the United States on March 3, 1845. New River County was established in 1858 by the Florida Legislature. In 1861, New River County was renamed Bradford County. The City of Lake Butler, Florida, was the designated County Seat for Bradford County, Florida.

With ancestry into the 1600s of Dunfermline, Fife, Scotland, the extended Wilson family resided in Lee County and Sumter County South Carolina. Pastor Samuel Wilson, migrated from South Carolina, into the Florida Territory. His parents Dave Wilson and Margaret Dixon Wison, were residents of Charleston, Berkeley, County South Carolina. The extended Wilson family resided in Lee County and Sumter County, South Carolina. Catherine Wilson, the wife of Samuel Wilson, was born in the State of Florida. Her parents also migrated from South Carolina into the Florida Territory. The Wilson family was among the original settlers and farmers of a region in Bradford County known as Peetsville, Florida. The region was named after one of the original settlers, Mr. Peter Tisdale. He and his wife Mrs. Mollie Davis Tisdale migrated into Bradford County, Florida from Charleston Berkeley County, South Carolina as well.

In 1870, the first congregation of St. John Baptist Church was established in Peetsville, Florida. From 1870 to 1874, Pastor John Cox served as the minister and overseer. Located in a small frame building near the railroad, the settlers of Peetsville held church services and operated a school until 1880. A new rectangular frame structure, featuring a belfry and bell, was built and dedicated after the turn of the century, in 1906.

Unfortunately, during the Reconstruction Era, the Bradford County Courthouse burned down in 1865 and again in 1875, resulting in the loss of a vast portion of historical records. Nevertheless, there were nineteen African Americans serving in the Florida Legislature. Peetsville and Lawtey were adjacent communities of Bradford County, Florida. The region of Peetsville was located east of Lawtey. The individuals credited with the founding Lawtey, Florida, are Captain Thomas J. Burrin, Mr. William Lawtey, and Colonel Volney Job Shipman. In 1877, Captain Burrin donated land in Bradford County for the establishment the City of Lawtey. On February 4, 1879, Col. V.J. Shipman was appointed the postmaster of a region known as Burrin, Florida. On October 27, 1884, the Burrin, Florida, post office was changed to Lawtey, Florida.

The U.S. Federal Census of 1900 lists Catherine Wilson, born in 1867, as a resident of Bradford County, Florida. She was indigenous to the land later referred to as East Lawtey (Peetsville), residing there ten years before the Township of Lawtey was officially established. According to Wilson family history, Samuel Wilson was 54 and his wife Catherine was 39 when she gave birth to their daughter Martha Wilson on May 22, 1902. This would place Catherine Wilson's actual year of birth at 1863. Mrs. Catherine Wilson was born in Bradford County Florida in 1863 before the American Civil War (Battle of Estelusti or Battle of Olustee) that was fought in North Florida on February 20, 1864. Sam and Catherine Wilson were married in 1887 and continued to reside in East Lawtey. Seven of their children survived to adulthood. The details of their daughters' marriages are as follows: Mary Wilson married Fred Johnson of Lawtey, Florida; Josephine Wilson married Samuel Jackson of Baldwin, Florida; Martha Wilson married Sinclair Robinson of Jacksonville, Florida; Susie Wilson

Marriage license for Eddie Brown and Susie Wilson provided by Ancestry.com

married Eddie Brown of Lawtey, Florida.

On August 7, 1922, Eddie Brown and Susie Wilson were married at the Bradford County Courthouse in Starke, Florida. Before marriage, Susie Wilson attended the Lawtey Training School. At age 16, she had a child born on January 16, 1921. Her infant daughter was named Margurie Williams. The child's father was a 25-year-old farmer named Clarence Williams, born in Lawtey on May 15, 1896. He was the son of Charles H. Williams and Lizzie Stuart Williams of Lawtey. Charles H. Williams, a farmer, was born in Hilliard, Nassau County, Florida, in 1865. His wife, Lizzie, was a homemaker and was born in Traders Hill, Charlton County, Georgia, in 1873. They had twelve children. Charles and Lizzie Stuart Williams are the paternal grandparents of Margurie Williams. Samuel and Catherine Wilson are the maternal grandparents of Margurie Williams Kelly, who became the wife of Clifford Kelly Sr.

CHAPTER 1

The Progressive Era

The Blunt, Garrer, and Scott Families (1890–1917)

For nearly a decade, the Progressive Era was marked by widespread campaigns against organized corruption in the United States. The Georgia counties of Richmond, Burke, and Jefferson were no exception, as indigenous families continued to navigate their daily lives in the American South.

John Blunt III was born on January 29, 1895, in Blythe, Georgia. His biological parents were never married to each other. His father John Blount Jr. born in 1874, lived in Richmond Georgia. He was the son of John Blount Sr and Emma Jones Blount of Burke County Georgia.

John Blount III's mother, Tamer Garrer, was born on January 27, 1877, in Richmond, Georgia, also. Tamer Garrer was the daughter of Prince and Elizabeth Garrer. Tamer Garrer married Madison Scott on October 30, 1897, more than two years after her son John Blunt III, was born. The child was raised by her parents Prince and Elizabeth Garrer, in Richmond, Georgia.

Madison Scott was the son of Samuel Scott and Harriett Parker Scott. Madison was employed as a farmer and an undertaker, while his wife, Tamer, was a homemaker for their children, Ina Bell, Maggie, Abbie, and Agnes. The details of the marriages of the adult children of Madison and Tamer Garrer Scott are as follows: Ina Belle Scott married Ernest Harris of Louisville, Georgia. Maggie Scott married John Christon in Detroit, Michigan. Abbie E. Scott married Pearl Barnes of Hephzibah, Georgia. Agnes Scott married Jerry Brown of Blythe, Georgia.

In 1900, John Blunt III resided in the care and custody of his maternal grandparents, Prince and Lizzie Garrer, in Augusta, Georgia. He was 5 years old and ready for kindergarten. The Haines Normal and Industrial Institute (est 1886) was a school founded by Lucy Craft Laney to educate African American children in the town of Augusta. The Institute was a kindergarten–college preparatory school that employed thirty-four teachers and had over nine hundred students.

In 1910, by age 16, John Blunt III was no longer attending school, but he was able to read and write. He worked on the family's one hundred–acre farm, just like both of his grandfathers. Most residents in the region were all employed as farmers and laborers. John Blunt III continued to reside with his maternal grandparents at their new home on New McDuffie Road in Richmond County. He was raised with his maternal uncle Warner Garrer and his maternal aunts Eva Garrer and Lillie Belle Garrer. Eva Garrer, age 22, was now married to a farmer named Charlie Jones of Blythe, Georgia. His family were among the original settlers and founders of Jones Chapel AME in Blythe. Lillie Belle Garrer, age 29, was now married to military veteran Ellie Peterson Blount of Augusta. He was also the younger brother of John Blunt Jr.

THE PROGRESSIVE ERA

Years later, Warner Garrer registered for WWI, married Sarah Garrer, and relocated to Jersey City, Hudson County, New Jersey.

Children grow up to follow their own path, yet it was still rather common and traditional for families to live close to one another in order to provide support. After marriage, many of the adult children from the Blount, Garrer, and Scott families lived next door, down the road, or in the same home as their aging parents or grandparents. Charlie and Eva Jones lived with Eva's older parents, Prince Garrer, now aged 75, and his wife, Lizzie, aged 74. Eva and her husband, Charlie, worked on her father's family-owned farm. During the Progressive Era, the next generation of the extended Blunt, Blount, Garrer, Scott, and Jones families remained in the same neighborhood, their homes separated only by a small creek. One day late in May 1911, 16-year-old John Blunt III went to check on his mother, Tamer Scott, who lived close by. Tamer was not feeling well that day and asked her son John III to help her use the bathroom. Although the Scott family had substantial resources, indoor plumbing was still limited—or nonexistent—for most American families. John III helped his mother sit down on the chamber pot or pee-pot, as she requested. Afterward, John helped his mother get back into her bed. Next, John left his mother's bedroom and went outside. John immediately noticed that his mother, Tamer Scott, was standing outside with him. Tamer walked with her son all the way down to the creek. Then suddenly, Tamer was gone. She was nowhere to be found. Tamer simply vanished. John ran to his grandmother's nearby home to tell her what had just happened. When John arrived at his grandmother's house, Grandma Lizzie simply looked at him and said, "I know, she just left here." It would be years before John Blunt III spoke about this incident again. His mother, Mrs. Tamer Garrer Scott, passed away on May 28, 1911, in

Augusta, Georgia, at age 34. She was laid to rest at Fort Eisenhower, Richmond County, Georgia.

A few years after his mother passed away, for reasons unknown, John Blunt III changed his last name to Garrer. The surname Garrer was his mother's maiden name. On May 18, 1917, the United States Congress enacted the Selective Service Act, authorizing the federal government to expand the military via conscription. On June 5, 1917, at age 22, John Blunt III registered for the U.S. World War I Draft under the name John Garrer in Richmond, Georgia. By July 5, 1917, over 700,000 Black Americans had registered for military duty. Although they were barred from serving in the Marine Corps and relegated to subordinate roles in the U.S. Navy, Black Americans were permitted to serve all branches of the U.S. Army. The Army Air Corps, the predecessor to the U.S. Air Force, barred African Americans from serving in uniform. Despite facing racial discrimination and exclusionary laws, joining the U.S. military represented a pivotal milestone toward the pursuit of full citizenship for Black American men.

Eventually, John Garrer's stepfather, Madison Scott, relocated to Harlem in Columbia County, Georgia, where he fathered another son named Harold Scott. The child's mother was Gertrude Palmer of Burke County, Georgia. Madison Scott and Gertrude Palmer were married and had more children: Freddy Scott and Odessa Scott. Their father, Madison Scott, registered for WWI on July 12, 1918, in Richmond, Georgia. He was not on active duty and continued to live in Columbia County, Georgia, where he worked as a farmer and self-employed undertaker. The marriages of the children of Madison Scott and Gertrude Palmer Scott are as follows: Harold Scott married Willie Mae Robertson of Harlem, Georgia. Odessa Scott married Spencer Mims of Augusta, Georgia.

CHAPTER 2

The Age of Consent 1918

During the Progressive Era, Georgia was the most resistant state to raising its age of consent (AOC). In 1918, the State of Georgia's AOC was 10 years, meaning that a person could legally consent to marriage or premarital intercourse as early as 10 years of age. During that same year, the State of Georgia increased the age of consent to 14 years. As a result, Georgia was the only state in America with an age of consent for children less than 16 years of age.

John Wesley Garrer, age 23, had premarital relations with an incredibly young teenage girl named Emma Kate Daniel. She was the daughter of Joshua and Lula Daniel of Blythe, Burke County, Georgia. Emma was born on April 4, 1904. On March 25, 1918, Emma Daniel, age 13, gave birth to a son named Cleosie Daniel. John Wesley Garrer and Emma Kate Daniel were never legally married to each other.

Emma Daniel gave her son Cleosie Daniel up for adoption to John Kelley Jr and his wife Mrs. Nellie H. Kelley. They were the parents of three other sons named Willie Mack Kelley, Solomon Kelley and Lee Kelley. John Kelley Sr also resided with the family. Cleosie Daniel was given the name of Cleo Kelley by his new adoptive parents. The Kelley family resided in the community of Tarvers Branch in Burke County,

Photograph of John Kelley Jr., the adoptive father of Cleo Kelly, provided from the collection of Margurie Williams Kelly

Georgia. John Kelley was a farmer. His wife, Nellie, was a homemaker. Their adopted son, Cleo Kelley, was raised with the full knowledge of his biological mother (Emma Kate Daniel), his father (John Wesley Garrer), and the extended Daniel, Garrer, Scott, and Jones family.

In April 1918, one month after she gave birth to her son, 14 year old Emma Daniel continued to reside with her father and younger brother Prophet Issac Daniel. Her father, Joshua Daniel, was now married to a woman named Cornelia Walker Garrer. She was the mother of seven children and the widow of Mr. James Garrer, who passed away on February 11, 1917.

The following year, on June 28, 1918, Mrs. Cornelia Walker Daniel, age 38, gave birth to a son named Grady Lee Daniel. Cleo Kelley and his uncle, Grady Lee Daniel, were born three months apart in the same year. Despite their uncle-nephew relationship, Cleo and Grady Lee were raised remarkably close—more like siblings or first cousins.

The Daniel family moved forward as Josh Daniel, age 40, was a farmer who registered for WWI on September 12, 1918. He never saw active duty because the war ended abruptly in November that same year. Within a few years, the Daniel family relocated from Blythe, Georgia, to 2583 East 50th Street Cleveland, Cuyahoga County, Ohio.

Joshua Daniel always maintained employment as a laborer in farming or manufacturing for the steel industry. One day, Joshua returned home to find his wife, Corneilia lying in bed, unresponsive and still. No one was aware that Corneilia had any medical issues, making the discovery of her unresponsive condition all the more shocking and distressing. Corneilia Daniel passed away on March 8, 1924, due to complications from Pleurisy. Joshua Daniel arranged for his wife's memorial service to be held in her home State of Georgia. On March 11, 1924, Mrs. Corneilia Walker Daniel was laid to rest in Harlem, Georgia.

WWI registration card for Joshua Daniel, provided by Ancestry.com

THE AGE OF CONSENT 1918

There were many Black communities flourishing all over America. Yet, the hope for more opportunities and advancement inspired numerous Black Americans to register for military service in WWI. On August 5, 1918, John Garrer was inducted as an alternate and reported for duty at Camp Wheeler in Macon, Georgia. On August 24, 1918, he was selected and entrained for Camp Jackson in Columbia, South Carolina. Although he had a 5-month-old infant son, John Wesley Garrer stood ready to serve his country, answering the call to military duty with resolve and commitment. Unexpectedly, the war ended three months later, on November 11, 1918. Germany formally surrendered, and all nations agreed to lay down their arms as the terms of peace were negotiated.

Military registration card for John Garrer, provided by Ancestry.com

CHAPTER 3

The 1920s and the Prohibition of John Wesley Garrer

Prohibition, as defined by the 18th Amendment, banned the sale, manufacture, and transportation of alcoholic beverages. In January 1920, America was dry. Yet the government did not prohibit the consumption of any alcoholic products whatsoever. The Prohibition era saw a rise in organized crime related to the production and smuggling of alcoholic beverages—a practice known as "bootlegging." In 1925, John Garrer, a 30-year-old generational farmer and military veteran, was caught selling moonshine in Burke County, Georgia—a region that was dry at that time. On June 25th, 1925, he was charged with a misdemeanor of violating Prohibition Law. He was sentenced up to twelve months and a $100 fine by the State Prison and Parole Commission. After his release, John Garrer returned to his family in Keysville, Georgia. However, easy money and old habits die hard, and John Wesley Garrer would soon return to his familiar vices of bootlegging whiskey. The residents of Burke County were not immune to the economic downturn that swept across the United States. The lingering aftershocks of WWI and the stock market crash of 1929 would affect the United States for the next decade. Regardless of the financial repercussions and social challenges of living in the American South, John Wesley Garrer was prosperous and a true ladies' man. At age 32, he met the lovely Mamie Key Taylor of Keysville, Georgia. She was a widow, as her husband, Mr. Bill Taylor, passed away in 1926. John Garrer and Mamie Key Taylor had two daughters. The first daughter was named Willie Belle Taylor born on December 5, 1927. The second daughter was named Harridelle Taylor born on November 25, 1929. Unfortunately, the marriage was short lived, and the couple parted ways while their daughters were still very young. John moved on but for a while, he continued to live in Keysville, where he worked as an Undertaker. Mrs. Mamie Taylor and the children continued to live in Keysville. She had several resources including a farm to support the family. The children attended Palmers Elementary School in Burke County. They also attended Key's Grove School in Jefferson County. After their mother remarried, the family moved to Augusta, Georgia where Willie Belle and Harridelle attended Catholic school. Both daughters became assertive young women, living productive lives. Meanwhile, their father, John Wesley Garrer—the consummate ladies' man—became romantically involved with Mrs. Desmer Bostick. On October 1, 1932, Desmer Bostick Allen of Burke County Georgia gave birth to a son and named him Peter Allen Jr. The child was named after Desmer's husband Deacon Peter Allen Sr. The Allen family were farmers who lived in Hephzibah, Richmond County, Georgia. John Wesley Garrer and Desmer Bostick Allen were never legally married to each other. At age 21 Peter Allen Jr enlisted in the U.S. Army where he served honorably for twenty six years. He was a decorated soldier who was promoted to Sergeant First Class and received the Purple Heart. He later married Georgie Allen, a native of Burke County, Georgia. He was the father of four children: Kenny Allen, Tracy Allen, Carla Allen, and Peter Shanks.

The Adolescence of Cleo Kelley

Although he was adopted, and moved around within the extended family, Cleo Kelley knew who his parents were and where they lived. The families of Cleo Kelley (adoptive and biological) all continued to live closely in the Georgia counties of Burke, Jefferson, and Richmond. There were a lot of children in all of the families. Sometimes there were so many children in the home that little Cleo Kelley had to sleep outside on the porch. Even during the cold winters of Northeast

The Fifteenth Census of the United States.

Tarvers, Burke County, Georgia.

April 25, 1930.

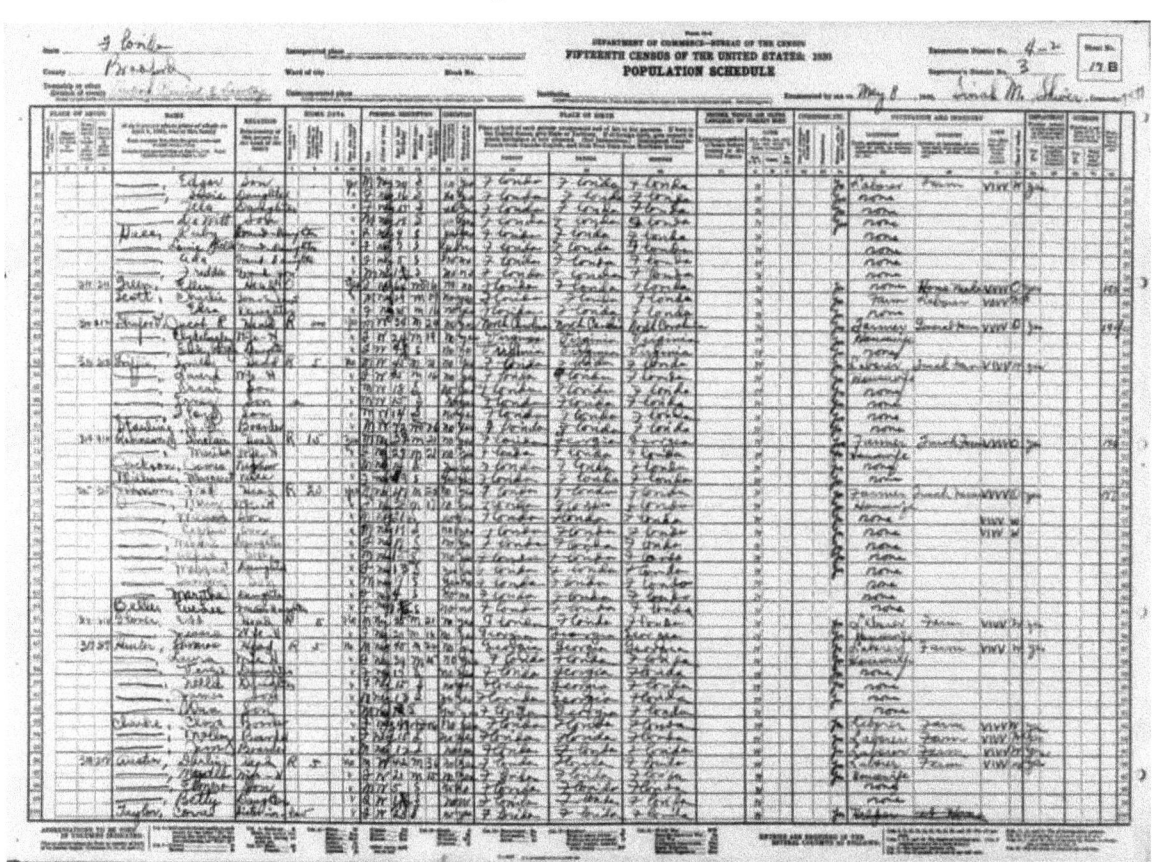

*The Kelley Family: John Kelley Jr., Nellie Kelley, Lee Kelley, **Cleo Kelley**, and John Kelley Sr. (Lines 24–28). Provided by Ancestry.com*

Georgia, this sleeping arrangement remained unchanged. The families were not poor. During the Great Depression Era, the homes were often overcrowded due to the needs of multiple children and widowed members of the extended family.

The Cradle of Education

In many rural towns of Georgia, it was common for Black Americans to use churches both as places of worship and as schools to educate their children. In Burke County, Georgia, Black American children also had the opportunity to attend the Boggs Academy, a boarding school founded in 1906 by Minister Dr. John Lawrence Phelps in the town of Keysville. The school was under the direction of the Presbyterian Board of Missions for Freedmen. The Kelley family lived in Tarvers Branch, and to attend the school at Boggs Academy in Keysville, children had to walk nearly three miles one way each day. The Daniel family lived in Blythe. The children from Blythe walked over five miles one way to attend the academy. However, due to the financial pitfalls of the Great Depression, many children, like Cleo and Grady Lee, had to work instead of going to school. Many family members also succumbed to respiratory ailments, leaving a substantial void of able-bodied adults to plant and harvest crops on the family farms. Cleo started working when he was 9 years old , while Grady Lee, also age 9, could complete only the 2nd grade. Due to his open adoption, Cleo maintained a close bond with his younger uncle, Grady Lee, and his younger brother, Robert Willie Jordan. The three of them—Cleo (age 14), Grady Lee (age 14), and 10-year-old "Rah-Willie" (as Cleo would say)—were always supportive of one another. The young boys were raised in an era when children did not question the actions of their parents—adults in general—nor the authorities. They all understood that if you saw or overheard something unusual, you kept quiet—no matter what. Children simply did not divulge themselves into the affairs of an adult or what was commonly known as "grown folks business" among the Black population in the South. Emma Daniel was the mother of Cleo Kelley and Robert Willie Jordan. She was also the older sister of Grady Lee Daniel. Emma Daniel, age 27, was now married to John Willie Jordan, a laborer for the Sikes Coal and Wood Company. Their family lived on Magnolia Alley in Augusta, Georgia. However, the biological father of Emma Daniel's son, Robert Willie Jordan, was a gentleman named Prince Jones of Richmond County. Emma Daniel had two children, but was never legally married to the biological father of either of her now teenage sons. Cleo Kelley (birth name: Cleosie Daniel), the child Emma gave up for adoption when she was 13, remained a part of her life.

CHAPTER 4

The 1930s Cleo's Migration

During the Great Migration, over six million African Americans from the Southern United States relocated to the Midwest and northern states. Since the Civil War, Black Americans founded over a thousand towns, municipalities, and settlements throughout the nation. They migrated heavily into New York, Chicago, Detroit, Cleveland, and Philadelphia. Millions of single men and whole families moved away from the South in search of a better livelihood, seeking economic opportunities and relief from racial disparities. Midway through the Great Depression, the Social Security Administration was founded. On August 14, 1935, President Franklin D. Roosevelt signed the Social Security Act into law. As part of President Roosevelt's New Deal, additional federal agencies were established to control agriculture, stabilize wages, prices, and inflation. As part of the New Deal, the federal government also launched a tremendous public works program for the construction of the interstate highway, national and state parks, and public buildings, transforming the American landscape and architecture. During WWI, the railway system was under control of the U.S. Government to ensure the orderly transport of the American Troops and military supplies. Although children under age 16 could legally work for their parents, federal law established the age of majority for adulthood and employment in the United States at age 21.

In 1936, Cleo and Grady Lee (both aged 18) and Rob Willie (age 14) had seen enough racial hatred and cruelty in their community of Burke County. The young teenagers became fearful of living anywhere in the State of Georgia. One day, they devised a plan to run away from home and start a new life. In 1937, when that long awaited day to carry out their plan arrived, all three of them set out on foot to begin their journey. After a short time, Rob Willie, the youngest of the group, became fearful and ran back home to his mother, Mrs. Emma Daniel Jordan, seeking the comfort and safety he had just left behind. Nevertheless, while millions of Americans were migrating to the north, Cleo Kelley and Grady Lee Daniel hopped a train from Augusta, Georgia and made their way further south into the State of Florida.

Schoolboy and the New Deal

After WWI and the Great Depression, the National Industrial Recovery Act was passed by Congress. This legislation authorized President Roosevelt to regulate industry for fair wages. During this time, in the absence of fair wages, it was common and widespread for children and teens to work on farms or perform manual labor to help support their families. Under the Fair Labor Standards Act of 1938, the federal minimum wage was established at $0.25 per hour or $2 per day. Nonetheless, Clifford Kelly was hired as a laborer and was paid only $1 dollar per day. Moreover, under this Act, no one under age 18 may be employed in any occupation that the Secretary of Labor has declared as hazardous, such as manufacturing or mining. Anyone under age 21 was still considered legally a minor in the United States. Cleo Kelley, age 19, made it to Northeast Florida, where he worked odd jobs such as harvesting melons, selling scrap metal, picking up trash, or clearing out garbage. "Boy you need to be in school," one field hand said to Cleo

Kelley. The adult workers thought that young Cleo should be in the classroom instead of working in the field all day. They all started referring to him as "Schoolboy" because he was a young smart kid who saved his money. As Cleo got a little older, the Assistant Foreman in Starke for Seaboard Air Railway called Cleo by his nickname "Schoolboy" because the young man would come back daily to ask for work. Cleo Kelley, who was still legally a minor, accepted any form of menial manual labor he could find until he was old enough to work for the railroad. At night, Cleo and Grady Lee slept in box cars off the railway.

Thousands of young men sought employment with the railroad industry expanding along the East Coast. The main airline track extended from Richmond, Virginia to Jacksonville, Florida. Passengers entering the Sunshine State at Jacksonville utilized connector routes to Orlando, Tampa, and St. Petersburg. Cleo was eager and ready to work. However, it would be a couple of years before Cleo "Schoolboy" Kelley reached legal age to work for the railroad.

Unfortunately, while he was still living in Florida, Grady Lee Daniel, around age 19, got into an argument that led into a fight. The altercation ended tragically and fatally. Allegedly, the homicide occurred over a card game. Reportedly, authorities concluded it was an act of self-defense. Nevertheless, Grady Lee Daniel was ordered by the authorities to get out of town and leave the State of Florida for good. He left as ordered and returned to Richmond County, Georgia. In 1938, Grady Lee, now age 20, resided at 315 Twiggs Avenue in Augusta, Georgia with his sister Mrs. Emma Williams, who was now married to a gentleman named Fred Williams. Emma's first husband John Jordan passed away a few years prior. Meanwhile, Cleo Kelley remained in North Florida. On March 25, 1939, Cleo Kelley, age 21, reached the legal age to work

Photograph of Emma Daniel Williams, provided by the Collection of Margurie Kelley

for the railroad. In addition, during the month of March, he applied for a social security number utilizing the name Clifford Kelly. Soon afterward, he was hired as a laborer by the Seaboard Airline Railway in Jacksonville, Florida. Despite his new job and growing reputation, those who knew him best still called him Cleo Kelley. One day, Cleo Kelley decided to get off the train in Lawtey to get something to eat. It was in Lawtey that Cleo Kelley first laid eyes on a petite, dark-skinned girl with a distinct unibrow and with long hair all the way down her back. That 5-foot-2-inch tall, 120-pound girl, was 17-year-old Margurie Williams. She was at the store with her cousins, Margaret and Martha Johnson of Lawtey. The girls were all first cousins, as their mothers, Mary Wilson Johnson and Susie Wilson Brown, were sisters. Margurie lived in the home with their maternal aunt, Martha Wilson Robinson and her husband Sinclair Robinson. Martha Robinson was a homemaker. Her husband Sinclair Robinson was employed as a farmer and truck driver. Margurie's mother, Susie Wilson Brown, passed away when Margurie was about 3 years old. Margurie's stepfather Eddie, Brown of Lawtey, moved to St. Augustine, became a minister, and married Mildred Bagley. Although Margurie Williams and Mildred Bagley were born during the same year, Margurie always referred to her step father's new wife as mother Mildred. Sinclair and Martha Robinson were also the legal guardians for their nephews, James Jackson Sr. and James Jackson Jr.

James Jackson Sr. was the son of Samuel Jackson and Josephine Wilson Jackson. Martha Wilson Robinson, Josephine Wilson Jackson, Mary Wilson Johnson, Evelena Wilson Taylor and Susie Wilson Brown are the daughters of Samuel and Catherine Wilson of Lawtey.

The Fifteenth Census of the United States.
Lawtey, Bradford County Florida.
May 8, 1930.

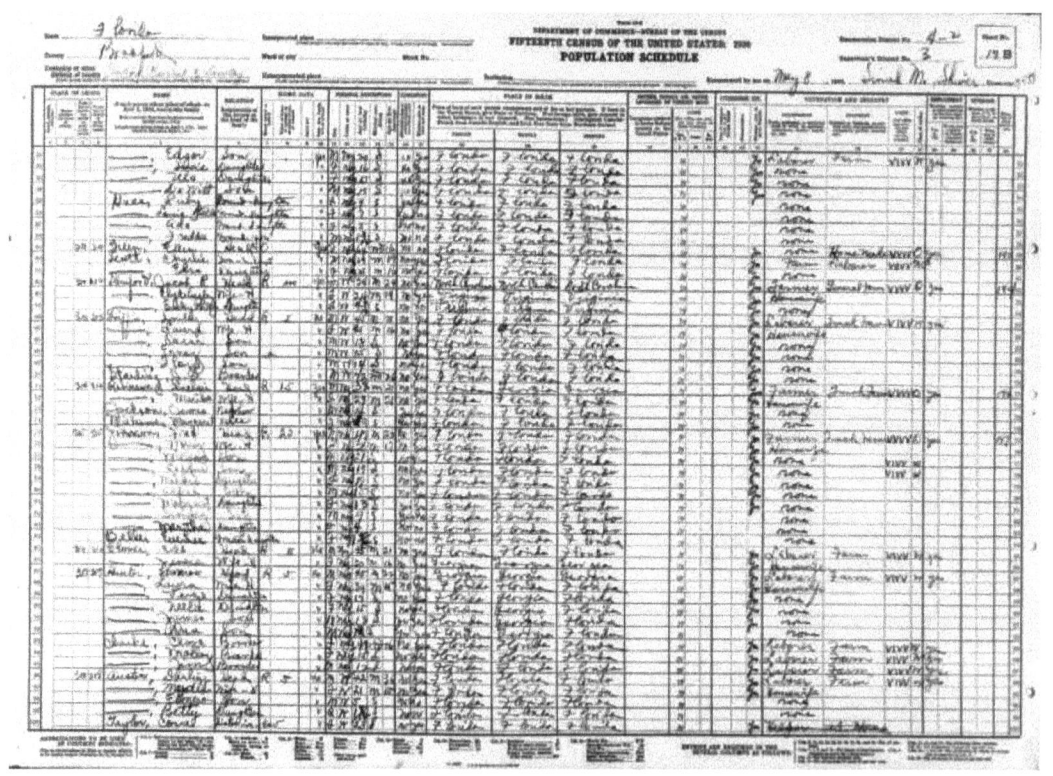

*The Robinson Family: Sinclair Robinson, Martha Robinson, James Jackson (age 15) and **Margurie Williams (age 9)**. Lines 71-74. Provided by Ancestry.com*

Martha Robinson, also known as aunt Maude, did not want young Cleo Kelley coming over to the house. Aunt Maude was adamant and wanted her niece Margurie to finish high school first. Cleo, however, was very persistent in pursuing Margurie. Cleo was very good at earning and saving his wages. Afterall, the federal minimum wage was twenty five cents per hour. Cleo believed that he made a good living

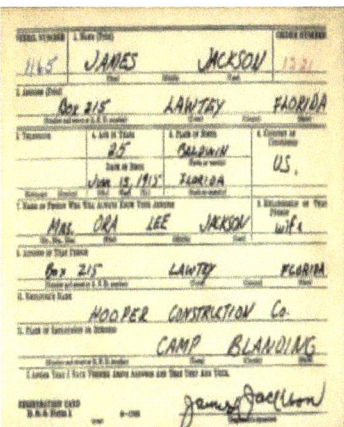

Photograph of James Jackson Sr., provided by the collection of Margurie Williams Kelley

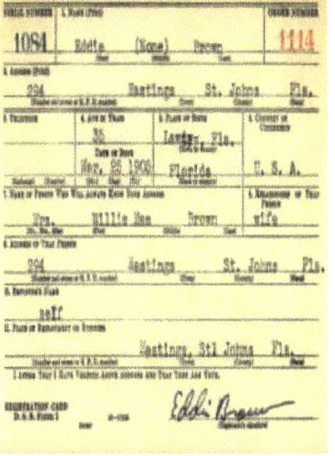

Photograph of Pastor Eddie Brown provided by the collection of Margurie Williams Kelley

(WWII Registration Cards, provided by Ancestry.com)

and that he was a rather good catch too. After Cleo and Margurie met, he once said, "I was working for a dollar a day and I had $80 when I met her." No matter how many times aunt Maude insisted that Cleo go away and stay away, it did not deter him from trying to establish a courtship with Margurie.

It was now Christmas time, and Cleo bought Margurie an engagement ring. Aunt Maude said "NO" to the engagement. Cleo would later return to aunt Maude's house with a mink stole for Margurie instead. Cleo was proud and pleased with the gift he selected for Margurie. He thought it was the nicest gift Margurie ever had. Despite aunt Maude's resistance to their relationship, Cleo Kelly and Margurie Williams remained in contact.

While Cleo was employed by Seaboard Air Line Railway, Margurie was a student at Robinson Jenkins Ellerson (RJE) High School in Starke, Florida. The school was founded in 1909 by Pastor James Robinson, Professor A.O. Jenkins Sr., and Mr. Robert Ellerson. In 1936, RJE increased its credentials and curriculum to become a high school by adding grades 9 and 10. In 1939, Margurie Williams graduated as the first Valedictorian of RJE High School.

Class of 1939
Margurie Williams (Valedictorian) and Elizabeth Miller (Salutatorian)
Robinson Jenkins Ellerson High School
Starke, Florida

The Lawtey Training School

Training Schools were created from 1900 to 1910 in the United States. Initially due to Black code laws, Black Americans were not permitted to attend a public high school. Students enrolled at a training school were taught skills to become teachers, nurses, or blue-collar workers for the manufacturing industry. Only vocational courses were taught, with no emphasis on a curriculum of arts and letters. In August 1900, the Bradford county school board appointed W.H. Hampton as

Margurie Williams (Valedictorian) with Elizabeth Miller (Salutatorian)

Robinson Jenkins Ellerson High School

Class of 1939

Starke, Florida

the Teacher for the colored children of Lawtey. Mr. Hampton also boarded with Pastor Samuel Wilson and his wife Catherine Wilson, at their home in Lawtey. Sam and Catherine Wilson are the maternal grandparents of Margurie Williams.

In 1939, Mr. Charles C. Anderson—a former U.S. Army Veteran from Madison County, Florida—moved to Lawtey, Florida. He earned an associate's degree as a licensed Instructor from Florida Normal College in St. Augustine, Florida. After which he obtained employment at the Lawtey Training School as a Teacher-Principal. In 1939, the federal minimum wage increased to $0.30 per hour, amounting to $48 per month for a teacher. With a student body of 120 children, for a salary of

$65 per month, he taught grades six, seven, and eight in one classroom. Within the next fifteen years, utilizing the GI Bill, Mr. Anderson obtained a bachelor's degree in education from Tuskegee Institute in Alabama. He also obtained a master's degree in administration and supervision at the Teachers College of Columbia University in New York. Soon afterward, another building was constructed, and the school was renamed in his honor as Charles C. Anderson Junior High School. Along with several teachers and support staff from East Lawtey, his wife Mrs. Alice Strong Anderson and his sister Annie B. Anderson were also employed as Teachers at the school. Mr. Charles C. Anderson was known as "C.C. Anderson," "Professor Anderson," or "Proff," as he was often referred to by his indigenous peers.

Over the course of fifty years, both the families of East Lawtey and the school's student body grew substantially. The family surnames are: Allen, Anderson, Austin, Barber, Bell, Berry, Brown, Bright, Britt, Bullock, Clark, Crawford, Cromity, Davis, Demps, Denefield, Diggs, Fayson, Felton, Floyd, Franklin, Green, Hamilton, Hampton, Heath, Henderson, Hendrieth, Hollis, Houston, Hudson, Jackson, Jenkins, Jennings, Johnson, Kelly, King, Kittles, Lee, Mack, McNeal, Miller, Moody, Moore, Myers, Newsome, Nichols, Perkins, Pittman, Randolph, Robinson, Ross, Scott, Sherman, Simmons, Slocum, Smith, Strong, Thompkins, Tisdale, Tucker, Watkins, Wiggins, Williams, and White.

Professor Anderson was always sharp, attentive, and well dressed on campus. Generations of indigenous children of East Lawtey-Peetsville attended the school under his leadership. Prior to its closure, the school was known as Anderson Elementary School. Mr. Charles C. Anderson served as an Educator and Administrator for the Bradford County School District for forty years. For seventy years, the school served as the epicenter of the East Lawtey-Peetsville community.

CHAPTER 5

The 1940s Our Home in Lawtey

Meanwhile, after his uncle's court ordered departure, Cleo Kelley moved forward with his life and remained in North Florida. In May 1940, Cleo Kelley signed an Application for Marriage License as Clifford Kelly. Margurie Williams (age 19) and Clifford Kelly (age 22) were united in marriage on May 25, 1940 at the Bradford County Courthouse in Starke, Florida. Aunt Maude did not attend the ceremony. It was aunt Maude's older sister Mary Wilson Johnson and family friend Edward Denefield who attended the nuptials and signed the marriage certificate as witnesses.

Photograph of Edward R. Denefield, Areatha Lee Denefield, and James E. Denefield (age 10), provided by Valerie Daniels

While their home was under construction, the newlyweds lived temporarily with Edward and Areatha Lee Denefield in Lawtey. Edward Denefield and Clifford Kelly were very good friends who invested in buying rental properties together in Brevard County, Florida. Edward Denefield was also a skilled Cement Finisher. He was employed by Sears Roebuck and served five years in the U.S. Army. By the time the Kellys moved into their home, Edward Denefield was deployed for WWII and was stationed at Fort Bragg, North Carolina. His wife, Areatha Denefield, was a homemaker and businesswoman overseeing their various rental properties.

The marriage license copy of Clifford and Margurie Kelly, provided by Ancestry.com

Clifford Kelly and the Peacetime Draft (WWII)

The Selective Training and Service Act of 1940 required all men between the ages of 21 and 45 to register for the military draft. This marked the first peacetime draft in the history of the United States. Under this act, two million Black Americans registered for Selective Service, and approximately one million were selected for active duty.

Photograph of Grady Lee Daniel, provided by Marylou Kelly

As federally mandated, Grady Lee Daniel (age 22) registered for military duty on October 16, 1940, in Savannah, Georgia. He was entrained by the U.S. Navy in Cleveland, Ohio. His nephew Clifford Kelly (also age 22) registered in Starke, Florida. Due to his flat feet, Clifford Kelly was disqualified for military duty. He continued employment as a Laborer for Seaboard Airline Railway layering crossties and wooden planks. Clifford later accepted civilian employment at Camp Blanding, Florida, serving as a supervisor in production of shoes for the U.S. Army. The military base was located approximately six miles east of Lawtey off Highway 16 near Kingsley Lake. During WWII, Camp Blanding became Florida's fourth largest city, spanning a massive one hundred eighty-thousand acres and accommodating one hundred seventy-five thousand soldiers and other personnel.

WWII Draft Registration Cards for Clifford Kelly and Grady Lee Daniel, provided by Ancestry.com

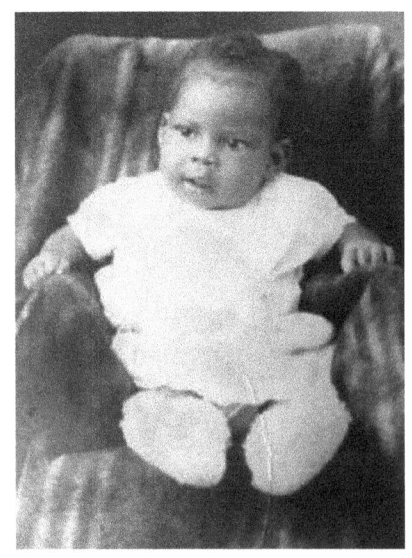

Photograph of Emma Louise Kelly, provided by the Collection of Margurie Williams Kelly

In January 1941, Clifford and Margurie Kelly welcomed their firstborn child, a daughter named Emma, in honor of his mother, Emma Daniel Williams. Little Miss Emma Louise Kelly was the first grandchild of John Wesley Garrer and Emma Kate Daniel Williams.

The year 1941 was a busy year for the family in Georgia as well. With all of his extramarital liaisons, John Garrer continued to engage openly in Burke County, Jefferson County, and Richmond County, Georgia. He was still selling alcohol in Burke County, which was a "dry" county. The sale of alcohol was strictly prohibited. John Garrer was well known in his community for bootlegging moonshine or "selling shine." The authorities would come after him, and he would get away for the most part, but not for long. On Sept 8, 1941, John Wesley Garrer (age 46) was arrested again on three counts for violation of the Prohibition Law.

Ready to Serve (Registration Day WWII)

In November 1942, Congress lowered the minimum draft age for men down to age eighteen. The war effort may have been in dire condition as Joshua Daniel registered again for Selective Service on April 25, 1942. Joshua Daniel, who was born on February 15, 1882, was the father of Grady Lee Daniel and Emma Daniel Williams. He was the maternal grandfather of Clifford Kelly Sr. and Robert Willie Jordan. Like millions of black Americans, during the past thirty years,

Josh Daniel left the South during the Great Migration. Six million African Americans migrated from the Southern United States to find employment and to escape racial hatred and discrimination. The American automobile industry was growing along with the expansion of the railway system and interstate highway. Jobs at every level needed to be filled. However, Joshua Daniel was over age 60 at that time. He was employed in the Sanitation Dept for the City of Cleveland. He was also married to his third wife, Annie Bell Daniel, a woman twenty years his junior.

Photograph of Robert Willie Jordan, provided by Willie Mae Jordan

On June 30, 1942, 20-year-old Robert Willie Jordan registered for WWII in Richmond County Georgia. Three years earlier, he married the love of his life, Hazel Turner, in Edgefield, South Carolina. To their union, two children were born. The first daughter was named Willie Mae Jordan, born in 1939, and the second daughter was named Alwena Jordan, born in 1941. The family made their home in Augusta, Georgia. Even though the war effort was ongoing, Robert W. Jordan was not selected for active duty. He maintained employment as an upholsterer and driver for the Continental Can Company (Federal Paper Board) in Augusta. Although their plan to run away together as teenagers did not pan out as they hoped, Clifford Kelly, Grady Lee Daniel, and Rob Willie were always actively involved in one another's lives. The extended family of Clifford Kelly was growing with complexities, yet over the decades, he traveled to Georgia and Ohio to visit them and vice versa.

Photograph of Emma (age 3) and Clifford Jr. (age 3 months), provided by Emma Kelly Strong

While serving time for prohibition violation, John Garrer became a grandfather again. His son and daughter in law Clifford and Margurie Kelly became the parents of their firstborn son named Clifford Lee Kelley Jr born on July 19, 1943. The Kellys moved into their new home in Lawtey in October 1944. Mr. and Mrs. Kelly soon became the parents of another son named Vernon Lee Kelly, in November 1945. Sadly, the infant did not survive (November 15, 1945 to January 8, 1946) due to respiratory complications when he was 8 weeks old. The death of the baby hurt so deeply that Mrs. Kelly took a pair of scissors and cut herself off from the only family photograph in which she was holding her newborn son. After grieving the loss of their baby, the family began to move forward. Clifford Kelly continued working for the railroad while his wife made a home for the family and worked as a hairdresser and seamstress.

In Georgia, after serving his sentence for prohibition violation, Clifford Kelly's father, John Wesley Garrer decided to become a more legitimate businessman. John Garrer opened a funeral home in Blythe, Georgia. It was not too long afterward that John met the love of his life, the former Alavan Walker Bell. They were married in Edgefield, South Carolina, when he was 49 years old.

After WWII ended on September 2, 1945, Clifford Kelly's maternal uncle Grady Lee Daniel received an honorable discharge from the U.S. Navy on March 4, 1946. He made his home permanently in Cleveland, Ohio with his wife, the former Miss Ella Morris. The extended family of John Wesley Garrer was growing as his daughter, the former Willie Belle Taylor, married U.S. Army veteran Luther Henry Jones Sr. He was the son of Lewis and Emily Jones of Richmond County, Georgia. Luther Jones Sr. and his wife Willie Belle Taylor Jones welcomed their first daughter named Peggy Ann Jones in March 1947. Clifford Kelly and his wife Margurie welcomed another daughter named Marylou Kelly in October of 1947 as well.

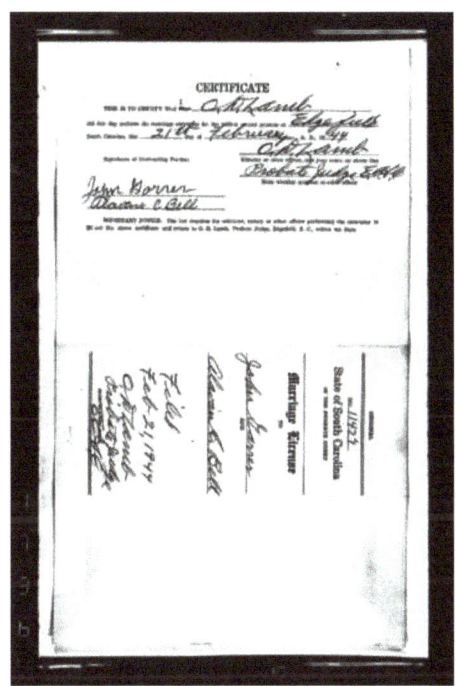 

Photograph of Alavan Walker Bell and John Garrer, provided by Donna Garrer Miller. Marriage Certificate dated February 21, 1944 provided by Ancestry.com

Clifford Kelly, Willie Belle Taylor Jones, and Harridelle Taylor all have the same father, Mr. John Wesley Garrer of Louisville, Georgia. Harridelle was now 18 years old. After the birth of her niece, Marylou Kelly, Harridelle Taylor wanted to move to Lawtey, Florida to help take care of her sister-in-law Margurie Kelly. Clifford Kelly made a promise to Harridelle's mother Mrs. Mamie Key Holmes that he would protect Harridelle if she moved to Florida with him. Due to his word, Mrs. Holmes agreed to allow her daughter Harridelle to leave their Georgia home. Harridelle moved to Lawtey, Florida and lived with her older brother Clifford Kelly and his young family.

Like so many young indigenous women of the era, Harridelle Taylor was employed in domestics and food services. She had an innate gift for decorative crafts, baking, and fashion. Lovely, elegant, and simply exquisite are synonymous to describe the physical beauty of Miss Harridelle Taylor. Whether she was working or not, Harridelle Taylor was so stunningly beautiful to look at, that all the guys wanted to date her. Miss Taylor was a stylish classy young woman who carried herself so very well. She turned heads everywhere with her beauty, style, class, and grace.

Harridelle Tayor

Photograph provided by

The Collection of Margurie Williams Kelley

Mrs. Willie Belle Taylor Jones

Photograph provided by Marylou Kelly Williams

THE 1940S OUR HOME IN LAWTEY

The Kelly Family at home in 1947

Clifford Sr. (age 29), Clifford Jr. (age 4), Emma (age 6),
Marylou (age 2 months), Margurie (age 26)

Photograph provided by Emma Kelly Strong

John Wesley Garrer: Expanding the Family Business

For decades after the Civil War and WWI, Black Americans were overwhelmingly successful in their own established municipalities and communities. As more grandchildren were born in Florida, John Garrer and his wife Alavan opened additional businesses in the State of Georgia. In total, John Garrer owned five funeral homes. A parlor was located in the towns of Blythe, Louisville, Keysville, Gough, and Sardis. He owned a clothing and accessories store named VAN's Five and Ten in Gough, Georgia. The store was named after his wife, Alavan Garrer. The department store was stocked with goods for the whole family. After shopping, customers could enjoy a meal at the café located adjacent to the store. John Garrer and his wife Alavan owned City Limit Barbeque Grill located at 1437 Twiggs Street in Augusta, Georgia. They also owned a "package store" (code for liquor store) in Augusta as well as a jukebox vending machine business. He owned two nightclubs in Georgia: one in Louisville and the other in Sardis. His most popular nightclub was called Garrer's Blue Flame in Louisville, where B.B. King and other blues artists performed. All of John Garrer's businesses were headquartered at his residence in Louisville, Georgia.

John Garrer was a very shrewd businessman. He had prestige, a status of prominence, and financial success in all of his business endeavors. He always carried a $1,000 bill in his money belt for emergencies. If he had to use the money, he would simply go back to the bank and replace it with another $1,000 bill. John Garrer was happily married to his beautiful wife Alavan, yet he still managed to have an eye for the ladies. One such lady would be the alluring Geraldine Cunningham of Jefferson County, Georgia. Everyone knew her as "Gerrie." She was employed at

John Wesley Garrer

Garrer's Blue Flame and Garrer's Mortuary in Louisville. In 1949, John Garrer and Geraldine Cunningham had a romantic interlude. Their daughter Eva Jean Cunningham was born later that year during the month of September. John Garrer and Geraldine Cunningham were never legally married to each other. Their daughter Eva Jean was raised by her mother in Louisville, Georgia, where she was acknowledged by her father and paternal relatives.

Mrs. Alavan Garrer was a confident woman who once implied, "John can have all the women he wants, as long as he brings that money home." Which he did, as John Garrer had another wife named Ida Belle Garrer. She was a housekeeper who lived at 572 Linden Avenue in Augusta. Alavan Garrer lived her comfortable lifestyle 45 miles away down in Louisville. For years, Alavan Garrer did not lift a finger at home. Alavan (or "Miss Van"), as she was often referred to, hired a personal hairdresser to style her hair at the Garrer home. As the years passed, and responsibilities increased, Mrs. Alavan Garrer had a more active role with her husband's businesses and finances. It was a lot of work but eventually, she learned how to effectively manage all of the businesses headquartered at their residence in Louisville, Georgia.

As John Garrer increased his offspring in Georgia, so did his son Clifford Kelly down in Florida. Clifford Kelly and his wife Margurie had another daughter named Margaret Jean Kelly, who was born on November 26, 1950. Roughly six months later, in 1951, 3-year-old

Photograph of Jean Kelly (age 6 months) and Marylou Kelly (age 3 years) in 1951

Marylou Kelly and her 9-year-old sister Emma Kelly were outside having fun, playing, and riding a bike. It wasn't often that Emma was allowed to go outside and play after being diagnosed with childhood asthma. Her mother simply believed Emma should remain indoors and relax to reduce any respiratory triggers. Yet on this day, while Emma and Marylou were outside, somehow, Marylou's foot was caught in the bicycle chain and severely injured one of her toes. The child was taken to the doctor, but her toe could not be reattached. For whatever reason, the physician decided to remove the child's toe by simply snatching it off. Marylou screamed from the pain. Her father Clifford Kelly Sr. was so mad and enraged at the doctor that he balled his fist and hit the doctor in the head. Clifford Kelly stormed out of the doctor's office with his daughter trying to comfort her. Although Marylou suffered a childhood trauma with the loss of her toe, the incident did not hinder her for long. One day, her mother Margurie Kelly noticed the child bouncing up and down on the sofa while watching The Howdy Doody Show. Marylou thoroughly enjoyed her daily TV adventure to Doodyville. While sitting on the sofa, the child would sing, jump, and bounce every day during the program. So much so until the family sofa finally crashed and broke down in the living room. Little Marylou Kelly was unharmed.

As the 1950s progressed, more children, nieces, nephews, and cousins were born for the extended family in Georgia. Clifford Kelly's younger sister Willie Bell Jones and her husband Army veteran Luther Henry Jones had more children. The couple welcomed another daughter named

Mrs. Margurie Kelly at home in Lawtey, Florida 1952, she was expecting her sixth child. Photograph provided by Marylou Kelly Williams

Margot Jones in June 1951 as well as beautiful twin daughters named Rhodia Jones and Rosemary Jones, born two years later. After the birth of a son named Luther Jones Jr. and youngest daughter Pamela Jones, their family continued to reside in Augusta, Georgia.

On December 2, 1952, Clifford and Margurie Kelly had their sixth child, another son named Jerome Sims Kelly. The child grew up with the nickname of Ronnie Kelly. He was a handsome boy with a cheerful countenance.

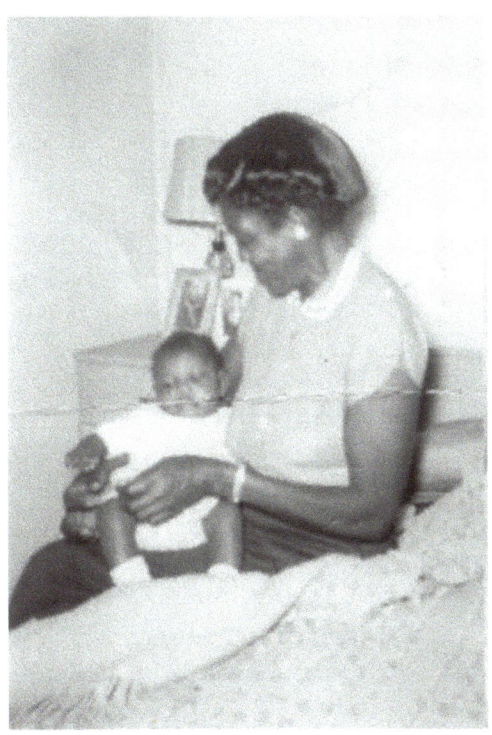
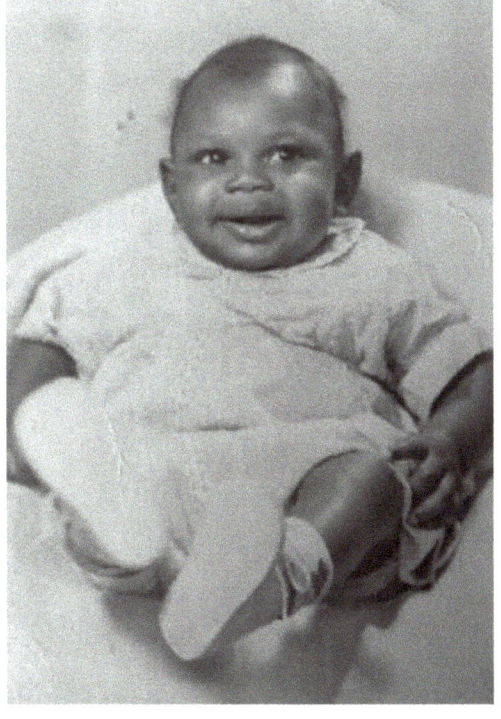

Photograph: Jerome Sims Kelly at 6 months old. Martha Wilson Robinson "Aunt Maude" holding her grandnephew Jerome in June 1953

John Wesley Garrer (age 52) and his wife Alavan (age 54) did not have biological children together. In 1952, the couple adopted their grandniece and grandnephew who were siblings. Donna Jean Anderson (age 3) and Raymond Anderson (age 12 months) were officially adopted in Waynesboro, Georgia. The couple raised Donna and Ray Garrer together and loved them as their very own.

As the Garrer extended family grew, their businesses continued to thrive. John Garrer would not step outside his front door unless he was wearing a tailored suit and tie, a diamond ring, and diamond tie clip. Along with all of his businesses, John Garrer owned a beautiful home, three Cadillacs, and a Ford Station Wagon. He also owned two hearses for transport between all five of his funeral parlors. John Wesley Garrer was a prosperous businessman while living in a small southern town during the Jim Crow era. John Garrer loved life and wanted to travel. His dream was to visit Europe one day. It would be about five years later before his dream vacation took place.

As time permitted, Clifford Kelly Sr. remained in contact with his father and would visit with him in Georgia. Clifford and Margurie Kelly would bring their children along to meet their relatives. Even though their biological grandparents were not all married to each other, the children simply adapted within the family dynamics. With every visit, the children were becoming more aware of the unique circumstances and the degree of relationship of their extended family.

CHAPTER 6

The 1950s A Personal Vision

Clifford Kelly was still employed as a Laborer for Seaboard Airline Railway in Florida. Yet, he wanted to know more as to how his father obtained all of those businesses in Georgia. Clifford Kelly would ask questions whenever he visited family in Georgia and Ohio. Clifford was outgoing and very talkative with anyone he met. He would talk and mingle with African American business owners at grocery stores, barbershops, juke joints, clothing stores, nightclubs, diners, and cafés. Clifford would take the information he learned from various business owners to implement his ideas for success. Soon afterward, Clifford Kelly bought a wood frame shed-like cabin structure in Lawtey. The cabin used to be someone's home. The empty structure was located off the muddy, murky, and swampy Kingsley Road, which was still a dirt road at the time.

The acreage was located next to the home of Mr. Joseph Britt Sr. and his wife Mrs. Willie Mae Britt. Everyone referred to her as Mother Mae Britt or Mother Britt, a very devout woman of faith and kindness. Everyone knew her husband simply as "Joe Britt," a skilled licensed barber who helped serve the needs of the indigenous men of East Lawtey.

Clifford Kelly and Joseph Britt in Lawtey (1952)

(James Jackson Jr. sitting in Mr. Kelly's Cadillac)

Photograph provided by the Collection of Margurie Williams Kelley

Mae Bell and Elizabeth Miller at Kelly's (The Shed) in 1952

Clifford Kelly utilized the cabin as a juke joint. He bought tables and chairs for the building and added a jukebox. Customers could buy drinks and listen to music. The only problem for Clifford Kelly was regulated business hours by the county and prohibition. The building was located inside the city limit; therefore, Clifford Kelly had to close his doors by 2:00 a.m. As a result in 1952, Clifford Kelly purchased 7 acres of land approximately 1,000 yards east of the juke joint cabin on Kingsley Road. It was his wife Margurie Kelly that wanted a restaurant-café, not a juke joint, bar, or nightclub. Nevertheless, the land was located outside the Lawtey City Limit, making it the perfect location for Clifford's idea.

Next, Clifford Kelly hired a company to transport his house from the pathway off Middleburg Road for about 2 miles east to his newly purchased land. It was on this land that Clifford Kelly started construction for a new cinder block-style building that became Kelly's Restaurant.

It's Time to Turn the Corner

Photograph and Memorial for James Jackson Jr., provided by Emma Kelly Strong

The year was 1954 when Mrs. Margurie Kelly became pregnant with her seventh child. While construction for Kelly's Restaurant was underway, she continued working from home as a hairdresser and seamstress. Although he was prosperous and settled, Clifford Kelly Sr., had wandering eyes. Just like his father John Garrer, Clifford Kelly Sr. was a ladies' man too.

On one occasion, this ugly faced woman—nicknamed "Turn-the-Corner" or "Turn-nah-kona"—who had a beautiful shape and figure was walking down Kingsley Road in Lawtey. It was often said, she was so fine that the men would literally turn the corner to get a good look at her. Yet she was so ugly in the face that some of them would turn the corner to get away from her instead.

One day in the Spring of 1954, "Miss Turn-the-Corner" came strolling herself down Kingsley Road in front of the Kelly home singing the words "I'm In Love With A Married Man and I Don't Know What to Do." Although Margurie Kelly was about three months pregnant, that did not stop her from attacking Turn-the-Corner in public. Margurie Kelly (age 33) and her younger cousin James Jackson Jr., who was known as Junior Jackson (age 20) confronted the woman face to face. Cousin Junior was the son of James Jackson Sr., and Lillie Belle Hampton of Lawtey. Margurie Kelly and Junior Jackson were raised together by their maternal aunt Mrs. Martha Wilson Robinson (Aunt Maude) in Lawtey.

Therefore, it begins: Margurie took a board that had nails in it and literally beat "Turn the Corner's rump" while Cousin Junior held the woman down on the ground. Margurie beat "Turn-the-Corner" until the woman's dress was torn and shredded at the buttocks. Next, Margurie grabbed Turn-the-Corner by the throat. Margurie choked the poor woman until Turn-the-Corner's eyes rolled back, her tongue came out and temporarily stopped breathing. Turn the Corner never walked down Kingsley Lake Road singing another note in front of the Kelly home ever again. Although it was the end of Turn-the-Corner, it was not the only time Margurie Williams Kelly took matters into her own hands when it came to Clifford Kelly Sr. and his wandering eyes.

Later that same year of 1954, James Jackson Jr. enlisted with the U.S. military. He was stationed at Fort Bragg, North Carolina. The Vietnam War began on November 1, 1955. He served three years in the Army and two years in the Army Reserve. On March 23, 1957, he married the love of his life Mary Gilmore. She is the daughter of Taft and Odessa Gilmore of Brooker, Bradford County, Florida.

After an honorable discharge, James Jackson Jr. was hired by the U.S. Postal Service, where he worked for the next thirty-two years. Eventually the couple made their home in Gainesville, Florida, with their daughter Jennifer Jackson and son James Jackson III. Years later, after Mary Gilmore Jackson passed away, James Jackson Jr. married Ferniece Williams of Williston, Levy County, Florida.

East Lawtey and the Bradford County School System

The Lawtey Training School continued to excel under the leadership of its Principal Mr. Charles C. Anderson. He earned a masters degree in Administration and Supervision from Columbia University. In 1954, the Lawtey Training School was officially renamed Charles C. Anderson Junior High School in his honor.

A couple of years later, a 6-year-old student named Margaret Jean Kelly had a speech impediment. Nonetheless, she was still an outgoing child. Due to her young age, little Jean Kelly surprised everyone when she went on stage at Charles C. Anderson Jr. High School and performed the 1954 hit "Tweedlee Dee" by Lavern Baker in front of the entire school. Bradford County had segregated schools in all its municipalities. Anderson Junior High in Lawtey met the needs of the students with two major exceptions. The indigenous students of East Lawtey received old, outdated, used-up textbooks. The school bus provided for them was old and raggedy as well. The indigenous citizens and parents of East Lawtey contributed to the economy as taxpayers and proudly served in the armed forces. Yet, their tax dollars were not utilized to fully benefit their children's education. Public schools were segregated across America and unequally funded. On May 17, 1954,

U.S. Supreme Court Justice E. Warren delivered the unanimous ruling in the civil rights case *Brown v. Board of Education of Topeka Kansas*. The ruling initiated the end of segregation in public education. In Bradford County, Florida, the ruling marked the beginning of the end for both RJE High School in Starke and Anderson Jr. High School in Lawtey. Rather than shutting down any schools, Bradford County officials voted to allow its citizens—including teachers and students—to enroll, register, or work at any school of their choosing. The plan worked for the next fifteen years.

Fourth graders Marylou Kelly, Milton Floyd, and Minnie Pearl Moore at Charles C. Anderson Junior High School Lawtey, Florida, (1955-1956). Photograph provided by Marylou Kelly Williams

Welcome to Kelly's Restaurant

Photograph of Clifford Kelly Sr. behind the counter at Kelly's Restaurant, provided from the Collection of Margruie Williams Kelly.

Also in 1954, the construction of Kelly's Restaurant was almost complete. A young 15-year-old artistic and talented Earl Barber of Lawtey was commissioned to paint the walls of the new building. Earl created a mural of painted green palm trees with coconuts along a blue waterfront. He added two golden lions, with one leaping lion in the air. A black panther was painted on the wall between the men's and ladies' restrooms. Numbers painted in white were strategically aligned for designated seating for customers. To alleviate the constant aroma of beer, bbq, tobacco, perfume, and pork chop, a commercial exhaust fan with a shutter was installed in the ceiling to circulate and extract the air. The kitchen and dining area resembled a classic 1950s café-style eatery, featuring a lunch counter equipped with countertop jukeboxes. The checkered floor was layered with hunter green and canary yellow tiles.

Out on the flat, beneath the marquee, Mr. Kelly had six steel-bar high chairs installed so customers could sit outside while waiting for their food at either of the service order windows. Five of the steel chairs were designed for adults, and one was intended for a child or a person of smaller stature. Mrs. Kelly had a green thumb, so her husband built two custom flower pots on the flat—one triangular and the other rectangular—so that she could plant Colocasia, commonly known as Elephant Ears.

In August of 1954, Kelly's Restaurant opened its door for business. Mrs. Margruie Kelly prepared the delicious grilled burgers, seasoned fried fish, chicken, pork chops, shrimp, french fries, and potato salad. Lawtey resident Richard Allen was the pit master who prepared savory "falling-off-the-bone" barbeque to perfection. Customers could also purchase coffee, tea, sodas, chewing gum, cookies, candy, pickled products, chips, pork rinds, ice cream, headache powder, cigars, cigarettes, handkerchiefs, breath fresheners, combs, shaving powder, shoe polish, beer, and wine like a five and dime store within a café setting. The restaurant was an immediate success in East Lawtey.

A Road Trip for the Kellys

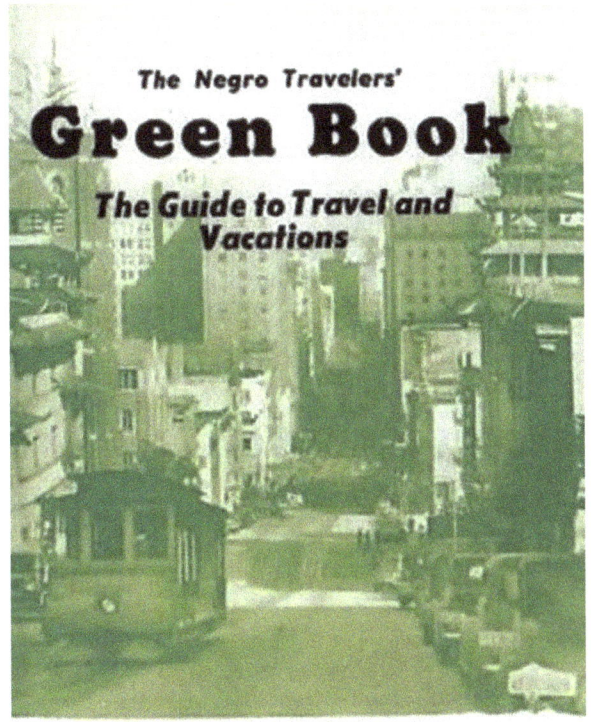

The Negro Travelers' Green Book was first published in 1936, by Victor Green, a Postman from Harlem, New York. The book was a detailed reference guide of stores, hotels, restaurants, and other services offered by Black entrepreneurs in the U.S. Black Americans utilized this resource to ensure their safety while traveling throughout the United States.

Although they were expecting their seventh child, Clifford and Margruie Kelly continued with frequent road trips to visit their extended family. Clifford Kelly's grandfather, Joshua Daniel, who lived at 10103 Ostend Avenue, and his uncle, Grady L. Daniel, who lived at 6557 Pau Court, both continued to reside in Ohio with their wives. In late September 1954, the Kellys traveled to Cleveland, Ohio with their children. Mrs. Kelly always packed enough food such as sandwiches, boiled eggs, fruit, and soft drinks for the family just in case a Black American restaurant was not available while traveling up North. Clifford and Margurie Kelly looked forward to road trips and always acquainted their growing family with as many relatives as possible.

While in Cleveland, Jean (age 3) and Marylou (age 6) enjoyed playing in the hills and rolling ridges of Bedford Heights, a predominantly Black American district of Cuyahoga County, Ohio.

While visiting with their extended family in Cleveland, Major League Baseball season finals were also underway. Clifford Kelly was fortunate to obtain tickets to the 1954 World Series. On October 1, 1954, Game Three of the World Series between the Cleveland Indians and the New York Giants was played at Cleveland Stadium. The following day, the Giants completed a series sweep with a 7–4 triumph in Game Four, in Cleveland.

*Clifford and Margurie Kelly outside
Cleveland Stadium in October 1954*

After the Kellys returned home to Florida, a few weeks later in November, Mrs. Margurie Kelly gave birth to her seventh child, a son named Bobby King Kelly. It was an exceedingly difficult birth because the child was born breech. Mrs. Margurie Kelly described the eleven-hour ordeal of giving birth as "like having kittens." Mrs. Aretha Lee of Lawtey was the Midwife. Mrs. Lee delivered all the indigenous children of Lawtey for years and years. Nevertheless, this birth was too problematic and traumatic for Mrs. Kelly. Her husband Clifford Kelly Sr. wanted to ensure that his wife never experienced that level of agonizing pain ever again. Out of concern for his wife, Clifford Kelly Sr. underwent a vasectomy. His son Bobby King Kelly was the last child born to their union.

Wedding Bells for Harridelle Taylor

Photograph of Harridelle Taylor, provided by Marylou Kelly Williams

The year was 1955, when the beautiful and statuesque, 25-year-old Harridelle Taylor was again on the radar in Lawtey. She resided in Detroit, Michigan for a while but returned to East Lawtey to help take care of her sister-in-law, Margurie Kelly. After the birth of her last child, Margurie Kelly suffered tremendously. Her recovery was difficult, so having Harridelle in her life was like a gift from above. Harridelle, the younger sister of Clifford Kelly Sr., also worked at Kelly's Restaurant, where all the guys had eyes for her. Margurie was a good cook, but her expertise was as a licensed hairdresser and seamstress. Harridelle, on the other hand, was an excellent cook who had a background in foodservice and hospitality. Harridelle would often provide Margurie with ideas for food prep and presentation, including the use of carryout boxes.

It was at Kelly's Restaurant where Harridelle Taylor met 21-year-old Emmett Bright Jr. He was the son of Emmett Bright Sr. and Mrs. Florence Jackson Bright of Lawtey. Harridelle was fashionable, stylish, and popular with the guys. It was rumoured that Harridelle met a very wealthy man in Michigan, who loved and wanted to marry her. As fate would have it, Harridelle married a much younger man. The beautiful Harridelle Taylor and the handsome Emmett Bright Jr. celebrated their wedding reception at Kelly's Restaurant in June 1955. The couple welcomed their firstborn child, a daughter named Deborah S. Bright two years later. The Brights made their home in Lawtey and had three more children: Emmett Warren Bright Jr., Judith Maria Bright (known as Judy), and Mischel Lucretia Bright. The couple founded two businesses in Bradford County. Emmett Bright Jr. founded Bright's Construction Company, which was in operation for over thirty-five years.

Mr. and Mrs. Emmett Bright Jr.

June 18, 1955

Photograph provided by the Collection of Margurie Williams Kelly

Mrs. Margurie Williams Kelly on December 25, 1955 Lawtey, Florida. Adorned wearing the mink stole given to her by Cleo Kelley after her aunt Maude Robinson objected to their engagement in 1939. Photograph provided by Emma Kelly Strong

A Whale of an Idea

Photograph of The Whalers at Kelly's Nite Limit, provided by Emma Kelly Strong

Prohibition ended in the United States after the 21st Amendment was ratified. Alcoholic policy was delegated to the states and frequently transitioned to the county and city level. For years, Bradford County, Florida, was dry. In 1956, after two years of business at Kelly's Restaurant, Clifford Kelly received his first beverage license. The sale of alcoholic beverages was legal in Bradford County, Florida.

During the late summer of 1957, while cutting pulpwood, Clifford Kelly Sr. accidentally sliced through his ring finger. His 14-year-old son Clifford Kelly Jr. got behind the steering wheel of the family vehicle to drive his father to the doctor. They traveled the back road of Highway 16 to Starke because Clifford Jr. did not have a driver's license. It was unfortunate for Clifford Sr. because the doctor could not save his finger entirely. Due to the severity of his injury, the first joint of Clifford Sr's left ring finger was amputated.

Not long after the pulpwood accident, Clifford Sr. had an idea and started a music group called The Whalers. Members of the band were Enoch Allen, Otto Williams, Jessie Hamilton, Louis Henderson, and Clifford Kelly Jr. The teenage musicians were all residents of East Lawtey. Surprisingly, shows for the band were promoted at the University of Florida on fraternity row in Gainesville. Clifford Kelly Sr. would convince students at the college that he could book an artist to perform live at their fraternity parties. Normally the fee would be a few hundred dollars and a handshake. There was only one problem, instead of an actual recording artist performing, Clifford Sr. brought in his own house band of musicians "The Whalers" to perform the show. The students had no idea that they were being hustled. Radio was still the king of media during this time, so no one really knew what the recording artists looked like. The students simply wanted to hear some live blues music that was now spreading rapidly across mainstream USA under a new banner titled Rock 'n Roll.

Moreover, during this time in 1957, Clifford Kelly Sr. was getting into trouble with law enforcement for bootlegging just like his father John Garrer in Georgia. Even though he had a beverage license, it was for only the sale of beer and wine. Clifford Kelly Sr. did not have a liquor license. Clifford Sr. would carry five or six big blue kegs in the trunk of his car. He transported and sold his special bootleg formula in towns such as Starke, Alachua, Penny Farms, Green Cove Springs, McClenny, Lake City, and more secluded regions throughout the area. Clifford Kelly had the authorities on his back for trafficking bootleg alcohol in Bradford County for years to come. Clifford Sr. would constantly try to outrun the police with his car. Sometimes he would jump out of his car and take off running even if he were dressed in a tailored suit and hard bottom shoes. There were times Clifford Kelly would simply burn the car up to hide the evidence or abandon the car whenever authorities pulled him over. If Clifford Kelly were arrested and released, he would simply buy another car, month after month after month, without hesitation. The local auto dealer, Mr. Craft in Starke, did not seem to mind—he knew that Mr. Kelly would return with cash in hand for another purchase.

Mr. Schoolboy Kelly: "I'm Havin' A Dance Saturday Night!"

From 1954 to 1957, the federal minimum wage increased from $0.75 to $1 per hour. The Whalers performed on fraternity row at the University of Florida as well as the new Kelly's Nite Limit. The nightclub atmosphere with live entertainers was highly successful, attracting hundreds of people from several counties. Kelly's was a booming business every night of the week. Customers who frequented the nightclub worked hard for their money. The ticket price for a show at Kelly's was $2 advance and $2.50 on the night of the show. With everything he learned from his father and other business owners, Clifford Kelly contacted ABC Booking Corporation in New York. The agency was co-founded in 1944 by legendary jazz trumpeter Louis Armstrong from New Orleans. Other agencies contacted were Shaw Artists Corp, Universal Attractions Inc., and The Gale Agency all of New York. The booking agencies forwarded a press kit of their recording artists to Mr. Kelly. Assisted by his wife Margurie Kelly, he selected, booked and promoted recording artists to perform at his new juke joint nightclub named Kelly's Nite Limit.

Clifford Kelly would place placards throughout North Florida to advertise and promote his upcoming shows. He nailed placards at every night club, juke joint, corner store, and telegraph pole he could use in the surrounding counties. For each show, Clifford Kelly always placed the promotional portrait of the artists he booked on the wall inside Kelly's Nite Limit. Most business owners would frame the first dollar they earned for their new establishment. Clifford and Margurie Kelly framed the promotional photographs of the first recording artists to perform at their namesake venue, Kelly's Nite

Limit. Customers also enjoyed playing their favorite records on the floor model Tomaster Arietta Piccolo Jukebox inside of Kelly's. Beginning 1958, the first recording artists to perform at Kelly's Nite Limit are: Larry Birdsong, The Platters, B.B. King, Chuck Willis, Roy Gaines, Dinah Washington, The 5 Royales, The Drifters, Muddy Waters, Little Richard, and James Brown. There was not enough space within the picture frame to include the images of Little Richard and James Brown. Their photographs were placed unframed on a separate wall where customers entered the dance hall area. In a area near the ceiling, Little Richard's image was placed at the far left corner, while James Brown's image was placed at the far right corner. Over the years more and more promotional portraits of recording artists were added to the display.

Larry Birdsong   Recording Artist   Excello Records

Memorabilia: "Pleading for Love" by Larry Birdsong reached number #11 on Billboard's R&B chart in 1956. He was professionally managed at Excello Records by Theodore R. Jarrett 177 Third Avenue North Nashville, Tennessee. Promotional portrait provided by Kelly's Nite Limit.

    Author: Theodore R. Jarrett (Excello Records)

THE 1950S A PERSONAL VISION

BB King   RPM Records   Shaw Artist Corporation

Memorabilia: BB King's first album titled "Singing the Blues" was released by Crown Records in 1957. It was a compilation for some of his Billboard Top Ten singles released from 1951-1956 by RPM Records. He was professionally managed by Shaw Artists Corporation 565 Fifth Avenue New York, NY. Promotional portrait provided by Kelly's Nite Limit.

Author: Shaw Artists Corporation

THE 1950S A PERSONAL VISION

![The Platters promotional portrait]

THE PLATTERS

Memorabilia: Beginning in 1955: "Smoke Gets In Your Eye", "The Great Pretender", "My Prayer" and "Twilight Time" by the Platters all reached number one on Billboard's Pop Chart. The vocal group had 40 Billboard Pop and R&B hits over a ten year period. The Platters were professionally managed by ABC Associated Booking Corporation 745 Fifth Avenue New York, NY. Promotional portrait provided by Kelly's Nite Limit.

Author: Personality Productions Inc.

Memorabilia: Chuck Willis was known as The King of the Stroll. His biggest hits, "C. C. Rider" (1957) and "What Am I Living For" (1958), both reached No. 1 on Billboard's R&B chart. Along with his band leader and guitarist Roy Gaines, the duo were professionally managed by The Shaw Agency 565 Fifth Avenue New York, N.Y. Promotional portrait provided by Kelly's Nite Limit.

Author: Shaw Artists Corporation

Memorabilia: Her hit recording "What A Difference a Day Makes" went to number #1 on Billboard's R&B Chart. She won a Grammy Award for the recording in 1959 for Best Rhythm and Blues Performance. Dinah Washington was professionally managed by Universal Attractions 200 West 57th Street New York NY. Promotional portrait provided by Kelly's Nite Limit.

Author: RCA Radio Corporation of America

THE 5 ROYALES
Exclusive Apollo
Recording Artists

UNIVERSAL ATTRACTIONS
2 PARK AVE., NEW YORK 16, N.Y.

Memorabilia: Their hit recordings "Baby Don't Do It" and "Somebody Help Me Please" both went to number one on Billboard's R&B Chart in 1952 & 1953. The 5 Royales had a total of nine Billboard R&B Top Ten hits from 1952-1957. The group was professionally managed by Universal Attractions 2 Park Avenue New York, NY. Promotional portrait provided by Kelly's Nite Limit.

Author: Universal Attractions Inc.

THE 1950S A PERSONAL VISION

Memorabilia: In the 1950s, the group had four number-one Billboard R&B hits: "Money Honey" (1953), "Honey Love" (1954), "Adorable" (1955), "There Goes My Baby" (1959). The Drifters were professionally managed by The Gale Agency 48 West 48th Street New York, NY. Promotional portrait provided by Kelly's Nite Limit.

Author: The Gale Agency Inc.

MUDDY WATERS   CHESS RECORDING ARTIST

Memorabilia: Known for his recordings "Got My Mojo Working", and "Mannish Boys" He scored fourteen (14) Billboard R&B Top Ten hits from 1950–1958. Muddy Waters was professionally managed by The Shaw Agency 565 Fifth Avenue New York, NY. Promotional portrait provided by Kelly's Nite Limit.

Author: Shaw Artists Corporation

Exclusive Recording Artist Little Richard Exclusive Management
Specialty Records HERALD ATTRACTIONS INC.

Memorabilia: "Good Golly Miss Molly", "Keep A Knockin" and "Lucille" sold millions of copies around the world during the 1950s. He scored seven Billboard Hot 100 hits. Little Richard was professionally managed by Herald Attractions INC , 4066 ½ One Central Avenue Suite #3 Los Angeles, California. Promotional portrait provided by Kelly's Nite Limit.

Author: Herald Attractions Inc.

Memorabilia: Promotional portrait for James Brown provided by the Collection of Mrs. Margurie Williams Kelly. On Billboard's R&B Chart, "Try Me" was the first number one (#1) recording for James Brown & The Famous Flames in 1958. His recording "Please, Please, Please" charted at number six (#6) in 1956. James Brown was professionally managed by Universal Attractions 200 West 57th Street New York NY. Promotional portrait provided by the Collection of Mrs. Margurie Williams Kelly

Author: Universal Attractions Inc.

Memorabilia: Sonny Boy and Schoolboy

Clifford "Schoolboy" Kelly is seated on the right, next to the sloped wall of his Lawtey, Florida home with blues music pioneer Eugene Powell also known as Sonny Boy Nelson. In 1936, Sonny Boy Nelson from Utica, Mississippi was a delta blues recording artist for Bluebird Records in New Orleans, Louisiana. Photograph provided from the Collection of Mrs. Margurie Williams Kelly.

The Runner

Although Clifford Kelly had a beverage license for only beer and wine, he began selling liquor at the nightclub. He did not have a liquor license for Kelly's Nite Limit. Bootlegging alcohol was a risky endeavor that his father John Garrer committed repeatedly in the mid-1920s to 1940s in Georgia. Clifford Sr. would ask his son Clifford Jr. to carry some half pints of liquor over to the juke joint (Kelly's Nite Limit) often referred to as "The Place". Clifford Jr., age 14, officially became "The Runner." As instructed by his parents, he would carry five or six half pints of liquor in a brown paper bag to the nightclub. Clifford Jr. would be up all night walking back and forth between the juke joint and the Kelly home, carrying bags of liquor. Even on school nights, the process was nonstop.

Mrs. Kelly would pour the liquor into a cup over ice and serve it to the customers. Due to his prolonged bootleg activity, Clifford Sr. would be arrested and his wife Margurie would bail him out of jail. Each time Clifford Sr. was arrested for selling bootleg alcohol, the fines would increase. This conduct by Clifford Kelly Sr. continued for years. He owned a restaurant juke joint in the Jim Crow South. Laws of ethnic bias governed the American South from Reconstruction to the mid-twentieth century. For the next decade, Clifford Kelly Sr. bent and broke the rules with blatant disregard in a society of double standards, unfair treatment, and unjust laws.

Clifford Kelly's stature was over 6-feet tall, weighing more than 230 pounds. At Kelly's Nite Limit, he was the founder, owner, and bouncer guarding the front entrance and the cash box. If anybody got out of line or had one too many drinks, Clifford Kelly Sr. would grab and toss anyone out of the venue into the clay-covered parking lot. As his juke joint grew in popularity, Clifford Kelly Sr. played the game, greased palms, looked the other way, made a lot of money, and enjoyed himself immensely.

Many of the recording artists that were booked to perform at Kelly's Nite Limit were from small rural towns just like Lawtey where there was very little to do. On one occasion, in 1958, Clifford Kelly booked the young and buxom Miss Etta James to perform at his juke joint. She, on the other hand, was from Los Angeles, California. On the day of the show, Ms. James and her band arrived early in Lawtey. There was nothing for them to do except sit on the bus until show time.

At 14 years old, Clifford Kelly Jr., who owned a Harley motorcycle, suggested that they all go fishing at the Clora Hole across the road. The Clora Hole was a creek located near the property of Mrs. Clora Davis or "Other Mama," as she was often referred to in East Lawtey. Etta James and her musicians agreed to go fishing to occupy their time. There was only one problem though, they did not have any bait to fish with. Clifford Jr. had an idea. He got on his motorcycle and drove home to get some sliced bread. In lieu of live bait, they placed small chunks of clumped bread onto the fishing hook instead. The fish, however, were not fooled by the fake bait. Nobody caught any fish. Yet for a little pastime, Miss. Etta James, her musicians, and Clifford Kelly Jr. enjoyed themselves as they tried to catch some fish at the Clora Hole in Lawtey. Afterward, for the first time, Etta James performed live at Kelly's Nite Limit. Her hit record titled "The Wallflower (Dance with Me Henry)," released on Modern Records, reached #1 on Billboard's R&B Chart back in February 1955.

Emma Kelly Captures the Moment with Shirley and Lee

They were billed professionally as The Sweethearts of the Blues, "Shirley and Lee." Their debut single titled "I'm Gone" hit #2 on Billboard's R&B Chart in 1953. Their hit record titled "Let the Good Times Roll" ranked #1 on Billboard's R&B Chart in 1956 on Aladdin Records. The recording sold over a million copies and was certified gold by the RIAA. Shirley Goodman and Leonard Lee from New Orleans performed at Kelly's Nite Limit in 1958. It was a special evening for 17-year-old Emma Kelly and her good friend Rosebud Kittles. The young teens met with the soul singing duo and were photographed on stage with them after the show.

Photographed from left to right: Rosebud Kittles, Shirley & Lee, Emma Kelly and a friend on the Kelly's Nite Limit stage in 1957.

In 1958, Emma Kelly was nearing her high school graduation. Her mother Mrs. Margurie Kelly chaperoned the RJE High School Prom earlier that year. Since the school's gymnasium was under construction at the time, the formal event was held at Kelly's Nite Limit. Although Emma was invited to the Prom, she was not allowed to date. Nevertheless, Emma was allowed to attend the event. Mother and daughter both wore white evening dresses. Emma wore a dainty white sweetheart dress. Mrs. Kelly wore a white, ruffled, off-the-shoulder chiffon evening dress with matching gloves. Mrs. Kelly was so overprotective that Emma's date was not permitted to pick her up from home for the Prom. Therefore, Emma's parents escorted her to the Prom themselves. Marylou, Jean, Ronnie, and Bobby watched closely as their big sister Emma and their parents walked down the front porch steps wearing their formal attire. Emma's date waited for her over at Kelly's Nite Limit.

Mrs. Margurie Williams Kelly
(The Chaperone)

RJE Prom Night 1958, Lawtey, Florida

Photograph provided by Marylou Kelly

Emma Kelley

RJE High School 1958

In late Spring of 1958, Emma Louise Kelly graduated from RJE High School in Starke, Florida. As a graduation gift, her parents took her to the dentist to have a gold tooth implanted. After graduating high school, Emma Kelly enrolled at Florida Normal and Industrial College in St. Augustine, Florida, where she majored in Education.

THE 1950S A PERSONAL VISION

RJE High School

Class of 1958

Starke, Bradford County, Florida

From left to right: (Back row): Mrs. Edna Kennedy (Teacher), Jimmie Green, John Diggs, Simon Mitchell, William Reddish, Ben McDougald, Clemintine Williams, Mary Alice Roberts. Front row: Shirley Hamilton, Mildred Heath, Emma Kelly, Genell Lewis, Roberta Scott, Mary Johnson, Pauline Clark, Flossie Dell, and Fannie Bell Morris

Photograph provided by Emma Kelly Strong

Photographer: Bullington Supply and Gift Shop, Starke, Florida

Robinson Jenkins Ellerson (RJE) High School

Class of 1958

Starke, Florida

Formal Attire

From left to right (seated): Mildred Heath, Genell Lewis, Mary Lee Johnson, Roberta Scott, Shirley Hamilton, Fannie Bell Morris, Pauline Clarke, and Flossie Dell. Standing: Mrs. Edna Kennedy (Teacher), Emma Kelly, Jimmie Green, John Diggs, Simon Mitchell, Ben McDougal, Leroy Fraizer, William Reddish, Clementine Williams, and Mary Alice Roberts

Photograph provided by Emma Kelly Strong

Photographer: Bullington Supply and Gift Shop, Starke, Florida

Rosa Lee Moore

Miss RJE 1958–1959

*Photograph provided from the collection of
Mrs. Margurie Williams Kelly*

During the 1950s, it was very common for indigenous high school graduates of East Lawtey to further their education at Florida Normal and Industrial College (est 1892), and Edward Waters College (est 1866). Edward Waters College was the very first private college established in the State of Florida. There were two other colleges in Florida for indigenous students to attend: Florida A&M University (est 1887) and Bethune Cookman College (est 1904).

The tiny town of Lawtey (East Lawtey/Peetsville) was producing a generation of accomplished college graduates. There were many large families of indigenous people who were educated, productive, and gainfully employed. Numerous citizens of East Lawtey contributed to the economy for decades as career employees. They were employed in construction, education, dentistry, health care, military sciences, medicine, Christian ministry as well as those who vested themselves as entrepreneurs of lawn services, moving and hauling, licensed barbers, licensed beauticians, carpentry, cooks, seamstresses, farmers, midwives, and a few mom and pop stores.

John Garrer Goes to Europe

Photographs of John Wesley Garrer, provided by the Collection of Margurie Williams Kelley

Mr. Robert R. Reed of Illinois, the organizer of the National Negro Funeral Directors Association, visited the State of Georgia with the intention of organizing the Negro funeral homes of Georgia into a state association. Founded in 1926, The Georgia association was composed of licensed Black American Funeral Directors and Embalmers. In 1939, the name of the association was changed to The Georgia Funeral Service Practitioners Association. The organization was incorporated in July of 1959 as a nonprofit without capital stock. John Garrer, the owner of five funeral homes, was a member of the association for 27 years.

Photograph of Donna Garrer and friend provided by Donna J. Garrer Miller

In addition, in 1959, John W. Garrer (the father of Clifford Kelly Sr.) fulfilled his dream of traveling to Europe. It was his dream come true vacation, as well as a business trip for the Undertaker's and Mortician Convention. The convention consisted of meetings, consultations, educational sessions, and exhibits of interest for funeral services providers. While in Europe, John Garrer visited the cities of Venice, London, Pisa,

Amsterdam, and Paris. John Garrer was known for wearing a fancy suit and tie everywhere he went. He was photographed in a like manner with his hat in hand standing near the Leaning Tower of Pisa in Italy. After the convention, he returned to the USA on September 15, 1959. Life was good for the owner of a 1956 Ford Station Wagon, three Cadillacs (1955, 1957, 1959), five funeral homes, two night clubs, and two restaurants.

Yet sadly, due to a house fire, John Garrer lost his home. After the fire incident, many of the family's photographs and possessions were destroyed. The photograph of him vacationing in Pisa, Italy became a treasured family heirloom. John Garrer once told his children that with an education they could go further than him. He quoted: "Here I am, an uneducated man but I saw the world." John Garrer did not have a complete education, but he learned to read and write. He was exceptionally good with numbers and could determine facts and figures like a calculator. He was very alert and always aware if someone was trying to scam him with a bogus business offer. He was a wealthy man with resources to rebuild and continue a lifestyle he worked so very hard to achieve.

Kelly's Curb Masters Construction Company

Clifford Kelly Jr. graduated from RJE High School in 1960 at age 16. He was popular in the community because he once owned a Harley and loved to race cars. He burned out the engines of three of his father's cars due to drag racing in Lawtey. It was also very trendy for indigenous people to wear gold caps on their teeth. Just like both of his parents and his sister Emma, Clifford Kelly Jr. followed the trend as well. Clifford Sr. had plans for his son to attend mortuary school in Chicago. After which Clifford Jr. would be prepared to take over the five funeral homes owned by his grandfather, John Garrer, in Georgia. Children do not always grow up to follow their parent's dreams or visions. In 1961, Clifford Kelly Jr. moved to Cocoa, Florida and got a job at Cape Canaveral as a laborer. His father worked as a Concrete Finisher in Cocoa and Orlando. It soon dawned on Clifford Sr. that he could bid for construction contracts personally. Therefore, he hired a crew of laborers, and began to negotiate in bidding. Due to Central Florida's massive residential and commercial development, construction contracts were plentiful. As a result, Clifford Kelly and his very own subcontracting company, Kelly's Curb Master Construction, were well established for the next three decades.

CHAPTER 7

1960s Welcome to Schoolboy's and the Era of Kelly's Nite Limit

In the 1960s, Globe Posters of Baltimore, Maryland, became known for their creative process of vivid colors, combining letter pressed forms with day-glow screen-printed backgrounds. For decades, Clifford Kelly selected Globe Posters to create the placards for the live shows he promoted.

During the 1960s, as Kelly's Nite Limit rose in popularity, Clifford "Schoolboy" Kelly booked and promoted a wide array of recording artists to perform live at his nightclub. As the previous decade came to an end, some of the greatest recording artists in blues and jazz were promoted at Kelly's Nite Limit. All recording artists were booked through their agents. Some artists were scheduled for repeat performances, beginning in 1958 and continuing throughout the 1960s. Listed with their respective record labels and booking agencies, the recording stars are:

Fats Domino (Imperial Records), Agency: Shaw Artists Corporation, 565 Fifth Avenue, New York, NY.

The Midnighters (King Records), Agency: Universal Attractions, 200 West 57th St., New York, NY.

Little Walter (Chess Records), Agency: Shaw Artists Corporation, 565 Fifth Avenue, New York, NY.

Little Willie John (King Records), Agency: Ben Waller's Enterprises, 8919 Melrose Avenue West, Hollywood, California.

The Famous Flames (King-Federal Records), Agency: Universal Attractions, 100 West 57th Street, New York, NY.

Shirley and Lee (Aladdin Records), Agent: Cosimo Matassa. Agency: The Gale Agency, 48 West 48th Street, New York, NY.

Clyde McPhatter (Atlantic Records), Agency: General Artist Corporation, 640 Fifth Avenue, New York, NY. Manager: Irvin Feld, 1110 7th St, N.W. Washington D.C.

Ray Charles (Atlantic Records), Agency: Shaw Artists Corporation, 565 Fifth Avenue, New York, NY.

Big Maybelle (Savoy Records), Agent/Manager: Freddie Mendelsohn. Agency: The Gale Agency, 48 West 48th Street, New York, NY.

Etta James (Modern Records), Agency: Ben Waller's Enterprises, 8919 Melrose Avenue, West Hollywood, California.

Sam Cooke (RCA Records), Agent:/Manager: Jess Rand. Agency: The William Morris Agency, 151 El Camino Beverly Hills, California.

Charles Brown (King Records), Agency: Shaw Artists Corporation, 565 Fifth Avenue, New York, NY.

Ruth Brown (Atlantic Records) Agency: The Shaw Agency 565 Fifth Avenue New York, NY.

Chubby Checker (Parkway Records), Agency: (GAC) General Artists Corporation, 640 Fifth Avenue, New York, NY.

The Dells (Cadet-Chess Records), Agency: Queen Booking Corporation, 1650 Broadway Suite 1410, New York, NY.

Ivory Joe Hunter (Atlantic Records), Agent/Manager: Bettye Berger, 305 South Bellevue Suite 105, Memphis, Tennessee.

Little Anthony (END Records), Agency: Shaw Artists Corporation 565 Fifth Avenue, New York, NY.

Barrett Strong (Anna-Tamla Records) Agency: International Talent Management 2652 West Grand Boulevard, Detroit, Michigan. Agent/Manager: Berry Gordy Jr.

Ike and Tina Turner (SUE Records), Agency: Sullivan Enterprises 919 Grove Street San Francisco, California.

Dionne Warrick (Scepter Records), Agent/Manager: Phil Cantor, Agency: William Morris Agency Inc., 9601 Wilshire Boulevard Beverly Hills, CA 90219.

Peaches & Herb (Date Records), Agency: ABC Booking Corporation, 445 Park Avenue, New York, NY 10022.

Gene Chandler (VeeJay Records), Agency: Shaw Artists Corporation, 565 Fifth Avenue, New York, NY.

Bobby Blue Bland (Duke Records), Agent: Evelyn Johnson, Agency: Buffalo Booking Agency, 2807 Erastus Street Houston, Texas 77026.

Bo Diddley (Chess Records), Agency: Shaw Artists Corp, 565 Fifth Avenue, New York, NY. Personal Management: Komac Enterprises.

Solomon Burke (Atlantic Records), Agency: Universal Attractions Inc., 200 West 57th Street New York, NY.

Carla Thomas (Stax Records), Agency: Phil Walden Artists and Promotions, 1019 Walnut Street, Macon, Georgia.

Dee Dee Sharp (Cameo/Parkway Records), Agency: Paramount Artists Group, 1203 N.W. 28th Street, Washington, D.C.

Pattie LaBelle & The Bluebelles (Atlantic Records), Agency: William Morris Agency New York, NY. Agent: Bernard Montague 6229 Ellsworth Street Philadelphia, Pa.

Garnet Mims and The Enchanters (United Artists Records), Agency: Universal Attractions, 100 West 57th Street New York NY. Agent: Bert Berns United Artists New York, NY.

Ben E. King (ATCO Records), Agent: SRO Artist Inc., 240 Central Park South New York, NY. Agency: Circle Artist Corporation 48 West 48th Street New York NY

Roscoe Shelton (Sound Stage 7 Records), Agency: Phil Walden Artists and Promotions 1019 Walnut Street Macon, Georgia 31201

Joe Hinton (Back Beat Records), Agency: The Buffalo Booking Agency 2807 Erastus Street Houston, Texas.

Little Richard (Specialty Records) Agency: Herald Attractions Inc. 4066 ½ South Central Avenue Suite 3 Los Angeles, California.

Bill Doggett (King Records), Agency: Shaw Artists Corporation 565 Fifth Avenue New York, NY.

Jerry Butler (VeeJay Records), Agency: Shaw Artists Corporation 565 Fifth Avenue New York, NY. Agent: Irv Nelson.

Barbara Mason (Arctic Records). Agency: Penguin Artists Management 1336 Girard Avenue Philadelphia, Pa. 19123.

Jimmy Hughes (VOLT Records), Agency: Phil Walden Artists and Promotions 1019 Walnut Street Macon, Georgia 31201.

Booker T. & The MGs (Stax Music), Agency: Phil Walden Artists and Promotions 1019 Walnut Street Macon, Georgia 31201.

Mel and Tim (Stax Music), Agency: Phil Walden Artists and Promotions 1019 Walnut Street Macon, Georgia 31201. Agent: Rodgers Redding.

Sam and Dave (Stax Music), Agency: Phil Walden Artists and Promotions 1019 Walnut Street Macon, Georgia 31201.

Johnnie Taylor (Stax Music), Agency: Phil Walden Artists and Promotions Artists and Promotions 1019 Walnut Street Macon, Georgia 31201.

Little Johnny Taylor (Galaxy Records) Agent: Nat Margo, Agency: The Dick Boone Agency 200 West 57th Street New York, NY. 212-581-5256.

Gladys Knight & The Pips (Soul/Motown Records), Agency: International Talent Management Inc., 2652 West Grand Boulevard Detroit Michigan.

Otis Redding (VOLT Records), Agency: Phil Walden Artists and Promotions 1019 Walnut Street Macon, Georgia 31201.

Tyrone Davis (DaKar Records) Agency: Queen Booking Corp 1650 Broadway Suite 140 New York, NY. Agent: Carl Davis Sr., 1449 S. Michigan Avenue Chicago, Illinois. 60605.

The Bar Kays (VOLT Records), Agency: Phil Walden Artists and Promotions 1019 Walnut Street Macon, Georgia 31201.

Peggy Scott and Jo Jo Benson (SSS Int'l Records), Agency: Universal Attractions Inc., 200 West 57th Street New York, NY.

The Kelly Brothers (King Records), Agency: Phil Walden Artists and Promotions 1019 Walnut Street Macon, Georgia 31201.

Aretha Franklin (Atlantic Records), Agency: Queen Booking Corporation 1650 Broadway Suite 140 New York, NY. Agent/Manager: Ted White 1721 Field Detroit, Michigan.

Wilson Pickett (Atlantic Records), Agent/Manager: James Evans, Agency: Universal Attractions 200 West 57th Street New York, NY 10019.

Joe Simon (Sound Stage 7 Records), Agency: Phil Walden Artists and Promotions 1019 Walnut Street Macon, Georgia.

Fontella Bass (Prann Records) Agent/Manager: Ike Turner 4263 Olympia Drive Los Angeles, California. (Chess Records) Agent: Galaxy Artist Management 1448 South Michigan Avenue Chicago Illinois.

King Curtis (ATCO Records), Agency: Shaw Artists Corporation 565 Fifth Avenue New York, NY.

Bobby Rush (Galaxy Records), Agency: Sound Alternative Inc. P.O. Box 3471 Gaithersburg, Maryland 30885.

Freddie Scott (Shout Records), Agent/Manager: Carmine DeNoia 1639 Broadway, New York, NY.

Ted Taylor (RONN Records) Agency: Universal Attractions 200 West 57th Street New York, NY. 10019.

Buddy Miles (Columbia Records) TCI Talent Consultants Internationals Ltd. 1560 Broadway New York, NY 10036. 212-730-2701.

The Ohio Players (Mercury Records) Agent: Concept Productions Inc., Dayton, Ohio. Agency: Action Talent 300 West 55th Street Suite 4V New York, NY 212-765-1896.

1960S WELCOME TO SCHOOLBOY'S AND THE ERA OF KELLY'S NITE LIMIT

At the start of the 1960s, it was a special time in Lawtey, as people from across the State of Florida came to Kelly's Nite Limit to watch the performance of many of their favorite blues recording artists, such as Ike and Tina Turner from St. Louis, Missouri. Clifford Kelly promoted the new and very talented husband-and-wife duo to perform their high-powered blues revue in Lawtey, Florida.

In 1961, the musicians arrived in a custom tour bus. The name "Ike and Tina Turner and the Kings of Rhythm" was written in big bold letters on both sides of the coach. Ike and Tina arrived separately in one of their luxury cars—a red and white convertible Cadillac. Besides stage set up and sound check, there was very little to do in Lawtey until it was time for the show. The Kelly children were accustomed to interacting at home with the recording artists their father booked and promoted. Meanwhile, Tina Turner asked where the nearest store was?

That store would be Thompkins Grocery located less than a half mile east of Kelly's Nite Limit. Tina Turner drove Bobby (age 5), Ronnie (age 7) Jean (age 9) and Marylou (age 12) to the store. Everyone referred to the store as "Mr. Arnett's," which was the first name of the owner, Mr. Arnett Thompkins. The store had fresh meat, canned goods, with an array of products for the family, including gasoline and kerosene. There was also a room with a jukebox and dance floor on the back of the store. After Tina got what she needed, she bought ice cream for all of the Kelly children. Just like most small towns, Lawtey had no hotels or motels for indigenous people. Like all recording artists booked to perform at Kelly's Nite Limit, Ike and Tina Turner got dressed at the Kelly home too. Curiosity got the best of Ronnie and Bobby, as they took turns peeping through the keyhole of their parent's bedroom door. The young boys were laughing and playing as they watched the Ikettes get dressed for their show. It was a short walk across the front yard and unpaved parking lot over to the juke joint. The Ike and Tina Turner Revue along with their band The Kings of Rhythm, performed their million-selling hit recordings at Kelly's Nite Limit.

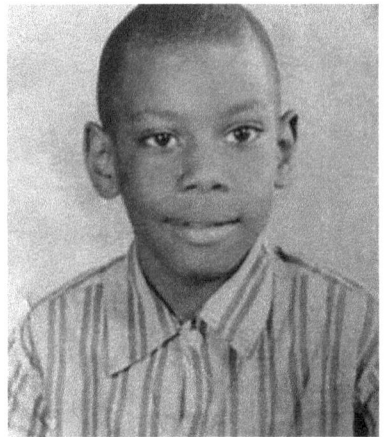

Photographs of Jean and Ronnie Kelly
were provided by Marylou Kelly Williams

Ike Turner was also a talent scout, writer, and musician who was instrumental in the careers of BB King, Bobby Blue Bland and Fontella Bass. The Ike and Tina Turner Revue featured songs by other popular blues artists. Barely out of her teens, Tina Turner's powerful alto falsetto could sing the blues at the level of her predecessors. The song "Fool in Love" reached No. 2 on the Billboard Hot R&B Chart on August 15, 1960. "It's Gonna Work Out Fine" and "Poor Fool" were additional hit records for them during the early days of their career. This would be the first and only performance for the "Ike and Tina Turner Revue" at Kelly's Nite Limit.

Memorabilia: Promotional portraits for Ike and Tina Turner, The Ike and Tina Turner Revue (Sullivan Enterprises), original recordings and company sleeves (Sue Records), provided by Kelly's Nite Limit

The Jordans and the Wage Gap

During segregation, Margurie Kelly's average salary was about a $1,000 per day at her very own Kelly's Nite Limit. The salary of Clifford Kelly's mother, Mrs. Emma Daniel Williams, was about $10 to $15 per week. Emma's husband, Fred Williams, worked multiple jobs, such as Driver, Laborer, or Porter. Emma Daniel Williams was a beautiful soul, but the segregated society she lived in was relentless with unfair treatment. In 1962, the federal minimum wage was one dollar and fifteen cents ($1.15) per hour. Mrs. Emma Williams was employed as a Domestic Housekeeper. She cleaned homes only, no meals were prepared. Emma's employer paid her $2.50 to $3 per day or $10 to $15 per week. That is less than $0.40 per hour in Augusta, Georgia. Emma's granddaughters, Willie Mae and Alwena Jordan, graduated in 1957 from Immaculate Conception Academy in Augusta. Willie Mae Jordan completed three years of study at the prestigious Tuskegee Institute of Technology before graduating from Paine College. She majored in Sociology and Psychology. She earned her master's degree in library science from Clark Atlanta University. Her younger sister Alwena Jordan graduated from Paine College also, with a degree in education. Their mother Mrs. Hazel Turner Jordan graduated from Pearson's School of Cosmetology in Augusta, Georgia. Hazel Jordan is the wife of Robert Willie Jordan, the younger brother of Clifford Kelly Sr. Hazel Jordan registered with the State of Georgia Board of Cosmetology as the owner of Ideal Beauty Shop, 1442 Tutt Avenue, Augusta. She enjoyed her career as a licensed beautician and entrepreneur for over 50 years.

Emma Williams provided care for her granddaughters, Willie Mae and Alwena Jordan, when they were infants. After the birth of her great granddaughter, Andriette Dionne Jordan, Emma Williams became the infant's primary child caregiver while the child's mother, Willie Mae Jordan, was at work.

Willie Mae Jordan, the mother of Andriette Jordan, was employed for the Richmond County School System at A.C. Gregg Elementary School and Clara E. Jenkins Preschool. Willie Mae paid her grandmother, Emma Williams, a salary of $50 per week to provide care for Andriette. That is four times the amount of money Emma was paid to clean houses.

After graduating from Paine College, Alwena Jordan married Walter Allen Sample at the Immaculate Conception Church in Augusta, Georgia. The couple made their home in Inglewood-Hawthorne, California, where they had two sons, Walter A. Sample III and Reginald A. Sample. Emma's youngest son, Robert Willie Jordan—affectionately known as Rob Willie—continued employment with the Continental Can Company (later known as Federal Paper Board) in Augusta. He

Photographs of Hazel Jordan, Willie Mae Jordan, Alewena Jordan, and Andriette Jordan were provided by the Collection of Margurie Williams Kelly)

was employed by the company for well over a decade. Rob Willie and his wife, Hazel, also paid his mother for dry cleaning and ironing their work uniforms. Emma D. Williams lived at 1152 Davison Lane in Augusta. One day, a woman from the community approached Emma, curious to know why she was no longer working as a domestic housekeeper. Emma informed the lady regarding the salary she earned taking care of her great granddaughter. The lady was livid about the amount of money Emma was now earning. The lady was in disbelief over Emma's salary as if Emma did not deserve that money. Emma was smart though, as she did not reveal the additional amount of money she was paid by her son Rob Willie. Emma continued to receive calls for a "day's work" cleaning homes, but she declined all requests. Emma Daniel Williams provided care for her great granddaughter Andriette for a few years. After The Jordans moved from 12th Street over to Albany Avenue, it became too difficult for Emma to take care of the child every day. Willie Mae Jordan placed her daughter Andriette in daycare at Thankful Baptist Church in Augusta. Nevertheless, Emma managed to commute to her family—The Jordans—every weekend to clean and iron their uniforms. The family continued to pay her well enough that she never worked as a Domestic Housekeeper for anyone else ever again. Andriette Jordan started first grade at Conception Christian Academy in Augusta right on schedule.

The Jordans were a successful and prosperous family. However, just like many of the patriarchs of the extended family (Garrer/Blount/Jones), including inlaws and outlaws, Robert Willie Jordan became the father of three more children named Beverly Ponder, Cathy Veronica Jordan, and Bobby Jordan Jr. Their mother's name was Mrs. Jean Ponder. The children were welcomed by their uncle Clifford Kelly Sr. and his family.

Meanwhile, Back in Lawtey, Florida

Photograph of Mrs. Margurie W. Kelly serving customers at Kelly's Nite Limit. Mrs. Aretha Denefield is seated on the right. Photograph provided by Emma Kelly Strong

Largely due to her success, Mrs. Kelly hired a small staff to assist her at the juke joint. Her sister-in-law Haridelle Bright worked at the juke joint as well. Harridelle saw all the great recording artists such as Muddy Waters, James Brown, Ike and Tina Turner, and the blind *the emperor of soul* Ray Charles. Harridelle once implied that even though he was supposed to be completely blind, she saw Ray Charles driving his own car in Lawtey. There were so many customers at times that all Mrs. Kelly did was sit at the cash register to count her money seven nights a week. However, she was a true native of the community born and raised. She was not above serving the customers personally, especially her friends in Lawtey.

Mr. and Mrs. Grady Lee Daniel of Cleveland Ohio, seated on the left at Kelly's Nite Limit

My Eva Jean: Father Knows What's Best

John Wesley Garrer did not hide the fact that he fathered children before, during, and after his marriages. He acknowledged all of his children publicly. Eva Jean Cunningham was his youngest daughter with Geraldine Cunningham of Louisville, Georgia. John Garrer and Geraldine Cunningham were never legally married to each other. John's wife Alavan was well aware of the child along with everyone else in their community. John Garrer continued to have two wives at the time. His wife Ida Belle Garrer lived in Augusta, GA. His wife Alavan Garrer lived in Louisville, GA. Eva Jean was born five years after his marriage to Alavan. As Eva Jean grew up, she had a striking resemblance to her father's sister Mrs. Ina Bell Scott Harris. Eva Jean was accepted by Ina Belle and her father's siblings, Mrs. Agnes Scott-Brown and Harold M. Scott Sr. At some point, young Eva Jean was welcomed in her father's home. On the weekends, she worked at the family clothing store Van's 5 & 10 in Gough, Georgia along with her sister Donna Jean Garrer.

John Garrer, who always kept a $1,000 bill in his money belt, wanted to teach his 13-year-old daughter Eva Jean about saving money. After all, she was a smart young lady who seemed to have inherited her father's keen business instincts. The current federal minimum wage was $1.15 per hour. John Garrer opened a savings account at the local bank in Louisville for his daughter. He deposited $200 into the account in Eva Jean's name. He advised his daughter that regardless of what her older siblings have, she should save money for herself. Eva Jean continued to save her earnings and maintained the same bank account opened by her father for decades to come.

When the true winds of love and romance came her way, Eva Jean Cunningham met and married the love of her life Mr. Isom Evans of Louisville, GA. The couple had two daughters Felicia and Chandrel. They owned two successful businesses Evans & Son Bail Bonds in Louisville as well as Evans Family Diner in Wrens, Georgia.

The Kelly Family. Emma, Clifford Jr., Margurie, Clifford Sr., Marylou, Jean, Ronnie & Bobby. December 1962. Lawtey, Florida

The Extended Kelly Family and the Next Generation

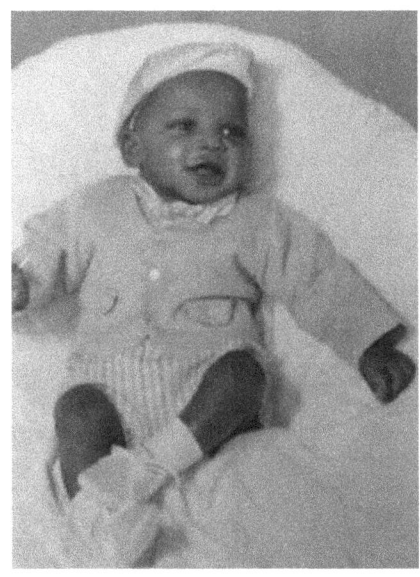

Photograph of Donneil A. Doster Jr., provided by Emma Kelly Strong

On the 4th of July 1963, the first Kelly grandchild was born. Emma Kelly Doster, a Teacher at Sylvester Road Elementary School, gave birth to her son Donneil Anthony Doster Jr. in Albany, Georgia.

Later that same year on November 22, 1963, the news came that a beloved President John F. Kennedy passed away. Marylou Kelly was a tenth grader at RJE High School. It was an emotional day at school to say the very least. After the news

Emma Kelly at Sylvester Road Elementary School Albany, Dougherty County, Georgia

Photograph provided by Emma Kelly Strong

of the President's fate was announced over the school's intercom, the children started crying and screaming. School officials canceled all classes and dismissed students early for the day. After getting off the school bus, Marylou ran home and cried her eyes out for the rest of the afternoon. It was a sad and traumatic era coupled by a media frenzy over the loss of President Kennedy. Total disbelief that a young, handsome beloved President was assassinated in broad daylight while riding in his motorcade in Dallas, Texas. Mrs. Kelly was so moved by the loss that she purchased a portrait of the President and his wife, First Lady Jacqueline Kennedy. The portrait was placed in an electric gold-plated frame with a single shielded light bulb to shine over them. As the nation moved on, so did the Kellys and the indigenous people of East Lawtey.

The following year, there was another special occasion on April 17, 1964, as the Big Spring Ball was held at Kelly's Nite Limit. The venue was decorated with palmettos, extended chains of looped crape paper and multicolored balloons. The girls wore elegant dresses or gowns while the guys wore tailored suits. The Ball started after 9:30 p.m. with music provided by a live band. The young people would somehow get a drink or two, doing what young people do when they're out having a good time. Mr. and Mrs. Kelly sold tickets for the event to raise funds for RJE High School. The funds were donated to the school for the purchase of new uniforms for the cheerleaders and the boys' basketball team.

1960S WELCOME TO SCHOOLBOY'S AND THE ERA OF KELLY'S NITE LIMIT

An Evening at Kelly's Nite Limit from Left to Right: Ora Lee Brown, Johnny Johnson, Martha Johnson-Whitley, and Margurie Kelly. Photograph from the collection of Margurie Williams Kelly

Clifford Kelly Jr.: Brotha' and the Air Force

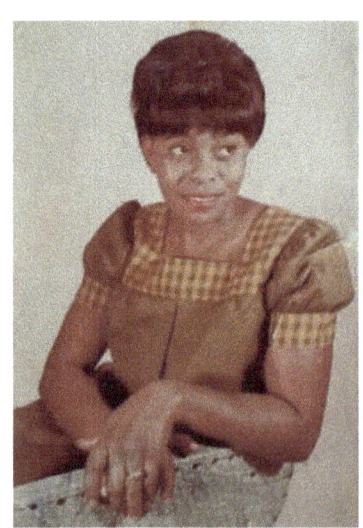

Photograph of Deloris Wynn, provided by Rodney A. Wynn

Also in 1964, Clifford Kelly Jr. also known as "Brotha" to his family and friends, was still residing in Brevard County, where he met a female friend named Deloris Wynn. She was 19, with a son from a previous relationship and lived over in Rockledge. She was the daughter of Chester Wynn and Minnie Lee Hooper of Cocoa, Florida. This family of 12 children is of African American and Muscogee-Yamassee Indian heritage. They are bloodline descendants of Chief Moses Hupue (Hooper) and his principal wife, Laura Starratt Hooper. After the Civil War, the Hooper family resided in their namesake community of Hooperville, Nassau County, Florida.

Deloris Wynn had a sense of humor and loved to tell funny jokes. After Deloris became pregnant with Clifford Jr's child, he proposed marriage. Deloris did not want to get married and said no to the proposal. Clifford Lee Kelley Jr., age 20, was drafted by the U.S. Army but did not want to serve for this branch of the military. He failed to report to the local Army recruiter's office as required. Clifford Jr. was determined that he was not going to serve in the U.S. Army. Instead, he enlisted voluntarily for the United States Air Force.

On April 7, 1964 Clifford became a father as his daughter Sibyl Denise Kelley was born at Wuesthoff Memorial Hospital in Cocoa, Florida. Clifford Jr. went to the hospital, saw the baby, and signed her birth

certificate. On April 19, 1964, two days after the Big Spring Ball in Lawtey, Clifford Kelly Jr. was enlisted with the United States Air Force.

He was assigned for Basic Training at Lackland Air Force Base in San Antonio, Texas. After basic training, he was assigned to Amarillo AFB in Galveston, Texas for six months where he became an Aircraft Mechanic. He would serve the next three years stationed at Spangdahlem Air Force Base in Germany.

Photographs provided by the Collection of Margurie Williams Kelly. Clifford Kelly Jr. standing on the left Amarillo AFB 1964

The Kellys and the East Lawtey Civil Rights Era

The Civil Rights Act of 1964 was initially intended to end discrimination based on race, color, religion, or national origin in the United States. The Act gave federal law enforcement agencies the power to prevent racial discrimination for employment, the use of public facilities, and voting privileges. Millions of Black Americans lived with the ramifications of the Civil Rights Movement. Nonetheless, they were not all directly involved with the organized campaign of events for the era.

Clifford and Margurie Kelly of Lawtey, Florida did not participate in any voter registration drive(s), bus boycotts, sit-ins, freedom rallies, nor the March on Washington. Clifford Kelly Sr. registered to vote eight years prior in Bradford County on February 8, 1956. They never posted signs inside or outside of Kelly's Nite Limit, indicating Black-only or White-only seating for customers nor for the use of bathroom facilities. Clifford and Margurie Kelly never received federal funding for the establishment of Kelly's Nite Limit nor Kelly's Curb Master Construction Company. As a result, they were not mandated to comply with the Equal Employment Opportunity Act: Title VII of the Civil Rights Act of 1964.

During May of 1964, Dr. King traveled to the State of Florida. He planned to be in North Florida for a few weeks. Reportedly, on June 9, 1964, Dr. Martin Luther King, Jr., spoke to five hundred supporters at St. Mary's Missionary Baptist Church in St. Augustine, Florida. Dr. King informed the attendees that he would participate in a sit-in at a local motel restaurant, namely the Monson Motor Lodge. Lawtey is about 52 miles West of St. Augustine. Mr. and Mrs. Clifford Kelly Sr. were not present for the church service nor the protest at any motel restaurant.

The Kellys do not have a family narrative nor folklore that any notoriously iconic civil rights leaders ever campaigned in Bradford County. There's no known history of any civil rights leaders having involvement with any of the five indigenous congregations of churches of East Lawtey.

Notably, the sanctuaries are Macedonia Freewill Baptist Church, est 1928 (Pastor P. Bell), Mt. Nebo Methodist Episcopal Church est 1878 (Pastor Issac Johnson), Mt Zion A.M.E. Church est 1891 (Pastor Rabbi Thompkins,), Philadelphia Baptist Church est 1890 (Pastor C.S. Bullock), and St. John Baptist Church est 1870 (Pastor John Cox).

During Dr. King's visit to North Florida, Democratic U.S. Senator George Armistead Smathers of Florida who was also known as "Gorgeous George" traveled to Lawtey, Florida. The Senator was a fan of Little Richard, who was also performing at Kelly's Nite Limit during Dr. King's visit to St. Augustine. Senator Smathers and his colleague Democratic U.S. Representative Claude Pepper drove down to Kelly's Nite Limit in a government vehicle. The U.S. Government-U.S. Senator tag on the car was all visible for everyone to see. No one bothered or hindered the Congressmen as they entered the venue. There were no security cameras inside nor outside of the building. The predominantly Black American audience at Kelly's were not recording or filming anything. No cameras flashing, no pictures at all.

The Congressmen enjoyed Little Richard's live performance for about an hour. Senator Smathers had to leave early as he was en route to his district in South Florida. Over the course of his political career, Senator Smathers served in the U.S. Senate for sixteen years. Prior to his election as a Senator, he was an attorney who served four years in the U.S. House of Representatives: Florida's Fourth District.

Clifford and Margurie Kelly were not shy or timid. They both loved to talk. Clifford Kelly Sr. loved to be seen, heard, and mingle with people. By now, Kelly's Nite Limit was open for ten years and was known throughout Florida and Georgia. They promoted major recording artists to perform in Lawtey every month. Yet, there is no known documentation, or record that Clifford Kelly Sr. or his wife Margurie Williams Kelly were ever featured, recruited, or applied to participate in any filmed documentaries during the Civil Rights Era. They were not members of the local chapter of the NAACP, nor any other civil liberties organization. There's no known family history, narrative nor folklore that Clifford or Margurie Kelly were ever denied voting privileges nor faced housing discrimination. The Kellys lived in a rural community in which all indigenous residents were primarily homeowners. Of course, they lived with the daily woes of a segregated society whenever they engaged beyond their own indigenous East Lawtey community. Yet, during such a turbulent time in the United States, Bradford County, Florida—located in the Jim Crow South—was still relatively calm.

Clifford and Margurie Kelly were content with the life and lifestyle they achieved. They understood which Bradford County merchants to support and which ones to avoid. To name a few, the Kellys shopped at

Denmark Furniture, Bullington Studio and Gift Shop, Sawyer Gas, Stumps Department Store, Winn Dixie, Pantry Pride, Wishbone's, and Tastee Freeze in Starke, Florida. Their business affairs were conducted with Community State Bank in Starke. In East Lawtey, they had Thompkins Grocery Store. In Uptown (the Lawtey Town square) they purchased supplies at James Waters Grocery Store, Amoco Gas, and paid the fees for the use of Post Office Box 58. Clifford Kelly and his wife Margurie always referred to the city of Lawtey on the other side of the railroad tracks as *"uptown"*. County Rd 200B in East Lawtey was known as Peetsville. Charles C. Anderson Junior High School and St Johns Baptist Church were located along this 1 mile county highway. They purchased cars in Jacksonville, Gainesville and Starke. Mr. and Mrs. Kelly also shopped and dined in the bustling and festive LaVilla/Brooklyn/Mixon Town division of Duval County. During its heyday before integration, the strip from Broad and Forsyth Street to Davis Street was known as the Harlem of the South in Downtown Jacksonville, Florida. Mrs. Kelly loved to shop at the underground or basement department stores downtown, including Sears, Diana's Shop, Woolworths, Montgomery Ward, and Furchgotts. She often bargain shopped at Jim Fields, Pic 'N Save, Atlantic Mills, and various thrift shops. On the other hand, more jobs were now available at Cape Canaveral and needed to be filled. Clifford Kelly hired his own crew of laborers and began subcontracting heavily in Cocoa, Florida and Orlando Florida. His company Kelly's

Curb Master Construction, secured all the subcontracts that it could handle. There were many large families of indigenous people in East Lawtey and Peetsville. Due to the high demand for employees, there was an exodus of people from East Lawtey into East Central Florida. Several of Lawtey's indigenous citizens became permanent residents of Cocoa, Rockledge, and Merritt Island, in Brevard County, Florida. As for Clifford and Margurie Kelly, they were still self-employed and continued to live in Lawtey. Clifford Kelly and his construction workers lived in a boarding house in Central Florida during the work week. Clifford Kelly traveled back home to Lawtey every Friday evening.

By 1964, Kelly's Nite Limit was expanded to accommodate seven hundred to one thousand customers with more tables, chairs, and booths. Mr. Kelly built the stage personally. The final project consisted of a wooden floor over a concrete block foundation. Along the front of the stage, he installed glass blocks within the foundation. Light bulbs were installed underneath the stage floor behind the glass blocks. This design created a bright reflection of light, which cascaded across the dance floor. Mr. Kelly also needed someone to help implement his additional ideas for the interior and exterior. Mr. Oscar Williams of Lawtey was a master painter at Camp Blanding, Florida. He was hired by Clifford Kelly to paint the new extension of the building. He used a dual design of pastel colors for the walls and posts of the interior. Mr. Williams painted the top half of the walls and poles light yellow. The bottom half of the walls were painted light blue. The bottom half of the poles were painted dark blue. An array of psychedelic posters were placed on the walls of the dance hall and stage to reflect the new emergence of soul and blues music as the genres entered the mainstream.

The initial waterfront design for the first section of the building was unchanged. Alternating pink and blue neon lights were installed horizontally on the left side of the building's roof line. The exterior was painted solid pink, which looked very well at night when the neon lights were turned on. A neon light with the name Kelly's Nite Limit along with the moon and three stars was installed under the roof line on the front of the canopy. Mrs. Kelly had a small staff to help her, whenever Mr. Kelly worked full time in Central Florida. All customers placed their order for food and drinks at the front counter only. Due to the expansion of urban and commercial development of Orlando and Cape Canaveral, Kelly's Curb Masters had all the contracts it could handle.

Mary and the Feds

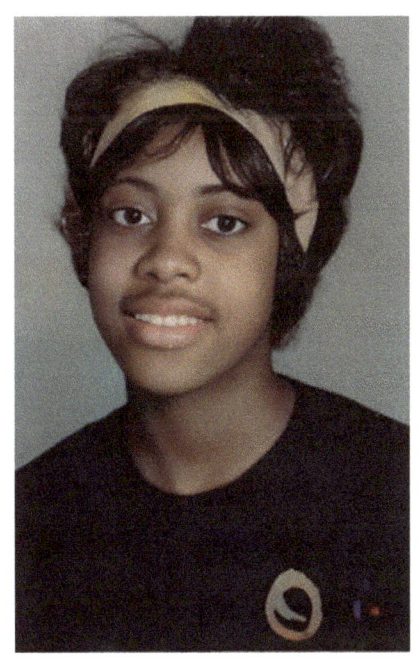

On June 1, 1962, the 9th Grade Commencement Ceremony was held at Charles C. Anderson JHS in Lawtey. All graduating students received a certificate to attend high school. Marylou Kelly received her diploma and started high school at RJE the following school year. During the summer, Marylou often spent a few weeks in Louisville, Georgia with her grandfather John Garrer. As always, he was a well-dressed businessman and to Marylou's surprise, her grandfather was a very good cook. Steak and eggs was one of his specialties. His children Donna and Ray showed Marylou their favorite places around Louisville. Ray would take Marylou into one of his father's funeral homes to look at the clients in the freezer. Ray was a real prankster who thought it was funny to get inside one of the coffins as a joke. Donna and Marylou did everything together like normal teens, hanging out, going to the movies, and shopping. John Garrer always made sure his granddaughter, Marylou, had everything she needed for the upcoming school year. Before her departure on Greyhound back home to Lawtey, Marylou received all of her school clothes from the family store Van's 5 and 10 in Gough, Georgia.

By 1964, 16-year-old Marylou Kelly and her sister, Jean (age 13), would often babysit their younger cousins Deborah Bright, Warren Bright, Judy Bright, Jennifer Jackson, and Jack Jackson. Baby cousin Mischel Bright was not born yet. While babysitting, they would often walk over to Kelly's to get sandwiches and drinks. Richard Allen, the Pitmaster, always cooked some really good BBQ that everyone enjoyed. Marylou, the eldest child still residing at home, was accustomed to seeing police cars on the Kelly property. Her father, Clifford Kelly Sr., was still selling alcohol illegally in Bradford County. As she got a little older, Marylou understood what was really going on at home. One particular night, Marylou saw a fleet of official cars from the Internal Revenue Service pull up to Kelly's Nite Limit to get sandwiches and soft drinks. Her immediate response was to hide all that liquor. Marylou hid the liquor that was in the home in the bushes behind their house. The bushes were thick, and there was no form of light down the pathway where she had to walk. Marylou went into the woods near the home of Miss Louise and Miss Minnie who were sisters. The two older sisters had long braids and resembled Seminole Indians. There was an unpaved side road or trail next to the Kelly property. The home of Louise and her sister Minnie was located at the end of the trail. Marylou walked down the trail with the liquor and hid it in the bushes. Meanwhile, the nightclub was raided by authorities during a live show. Authorities did not find anything incriminating inside the juke joint. When authorities entered the Kelly home, they were looking everywhere. All under the beds, the closets, they went through everything. Authorities could not find anything incriminating. Although Mr. Kelly was taken into custody, authorities had to release him due to a lack of evidence.

The next day, Clifford Kelly Sr. did not know what to think nor understood why the liquor was not found. Clifford Sr. could only laugh after Marylou told him that she hid the liquor in the bushes last night. The officers never knew that while they were raiding Kelly's Nite Limit, a teenager named Marylou Kelly was hiding all that liquor right there in the backyard.

There were people from around the region coming to the Kelly home knocking on the door, looking for a half-pint to purchase. The liquor was not sold at Kelly's Nite Limit. It was sold directly from the Kelly home. For whatever reason, authorities simply could not put two and two together concerning the issue.

Bradford County was a wet county, and it was legal to sell alcohol. The only issue for Clifford Kelly was he had a license to sell beer and wine only. After ten years of business, Clifford Kelly Sr. still did not have a liquor license issued by the Florida Department of Beverages. Margurie Kelly often crossed the county line near Gainesville and legally purchased alcohol. Yet, because her husband Clifford Kelly did not have a liquor license it was illegal for sale at Kellys Nite Limit.

It's rather ironic that Mr. and Mrs. Kelly were both nondrinkers for the most part. Mr. Kelly had a sweet tooth and was addicted to very sugary lemonade. Mrs. Kelly needed a Goody's headache powder and a six-ounce Coca Cola every day. The authorities did not seem to care nor bother Mrs. Kelly for her involvement with the purchase and transport of alcoholic beverages. The authorities would always come after Mr. Kelly for his illegal practice of bootlegging alcoholic beverages.

There was one incident where authorities chased Clifford Kelly and pursued him all the way home. Clifford Sr. would try to outrun police with his car or on foot. Clifford and his cousin Junior Jackson jumped out the car and took off running across the yard from the authorities. Marylou witnessed the entire incident.

Despite his legal woes and ongoing bouts with authorities, Mrs. Kelly made a lot of money at Kelly's Nite Limit. She averaged anywhere from $6,000 to $7,000 per week in cash at the juke joint alone. However, working as a Concrete Finisher with his own company—Kelly's Curb Master Construction—eventually made Mr. Schoolboy a millionaire. Around the same time, Mrs. Kelly went to a three-day work week. Kelly's Nite Limit was open every weekend only (Fri, Sat, and Sun night) while Mr. Kelly worked full time Monday through Friday in Central Florida.

On July 20, 1965, Clifford Kelly and his business partner Richard Allen of Lawtey agreed to book a young singer by the name of Jimmy Hughes. Although he was the pit master at Kelly's Nite Limit, Richard Allen invested with promotions as well. Mr. Kelly contacted Phil Walden Artists and Promotions to schedule the show. The booking was for three nights on August 27th, 28th, and 29th in Cocoa, Florida. Longtime indigenous Lawtey resident James Davis Jr., who was referred to as "Junior Davis," was the owner of Club 520 in Cocoa-Rockledge. The contract listed Richard Allen as the only concert promoter. Mrs. Margurie Kelly signed the Contract Blank in the name of Richard Allen and Clifford Kelly. It was not a real issue for Mrs. Kelly as she often signed contracts in her husband's name. Nonetheless, the contract was voided and the shows were canceled. A new contract would be issued for performances on a later date at Kelly's Nite Limit instead.

Also in 1965, the left-handed genius Jimi Hendrix became the lead guitar player for Little Richard. Jimi was a member of the band for approximately one year. The tour came to Lawtey, Florida as Clifford Kelly booked and promoted Little Richard for another performance at Kelly's Nite Limit. The latest recording for the Architect of Rock 'n Roll was titled "It Ain't Whatcha Do" released by VeeJay Records. Jean Kelly (age 14), Ronnie Kelly (age 12), and Bobby Kelly, the youngest member of the family, was only 10 years old at that time. The Kelly children were growing up, but still too young to attend the live show. All live shows were exclusively for the adult audience. Clifford Kelly was always at the front entrance and he did not tolerate minors on the night of a performance. The young people would often stand afar off to try and catch a glimpse of a featured recording artist. Within a few short years, Jimi Hendrix would become the highest paid entertainer in the world. Yet in 1965, he performed in the tiny town of Lawtey, Florida. Little Richard was one of the first recording artists to appear at Kelly's back in the late 1950s. This show and dance would mark Jimi Hendrix's only appearance at Kelly's Nite Limit and Little Richard's last.

Margaret Jean Kelly age 14

The U.S. Secretary of Labor declared children under the age of 17 may work for their parents in a nonhazardous environment. Jean Kelly (age 14) became the ticket agent at the juke joint. Ronnie Kelly (age 12) simply did whatever his parents instructed him to do. Bobby Kelly, age 10, became "The Runner." Their father Clifford Kelly Sr. built a ticket booth beside the front door of the venue. The one step ticket booth was lit by a single light bulb with a string attached for the on–off switch. Jean Kelly would sit on a bar stool inside the ticket booth for every show. A placard for the live event was placed at the lower half of the ticket booth door. During the winter months, a small heater was placed inside the booth to keep her warm. Bobby Kelly, a fifth grader, simply did as he was instructed. His mother would say to him "go get three." Bobby would go home, get three half pints of either this or that or whatever liquor was available at the house. Little Bobby Kelly would put three half pints in the front of his pants and three half pints in the back of his pants. He would pull his shirt down over all the liquor bottles and "walk-it-back" to the juke joint for his mother. This stratagem of "walk-it-back" would continue for the next few years of Bobby's adolescence.

Jerome "Ronnie" Kelly age 12

Even if the children had school the next day, Mrs. Kelly would wake her children up after 9:00 p.m. and take them with her to Lake Butler in Union County to purchase alcohol. It was hard on them as they witnessed their mother's night time transactions of buying whiskey and gin. Union County was a wet county, and the sale of liquor was completely legal.

Bradford County was now a wet county as well. The customers at Kelly's Nite Limit wanted liquor but Clifford Kelly Sr. did not have a liquor license. The alcohol bought by Mrs. Kelly was always purchased legally in Union County, but was sold illegally in Bradford County. In 1964, 10-year-old Bobby Kelly became "the Runner." Liquor was always stored in the Kelly home hidden underneath the family's laundry in the dirty clothes hamper. Whenever the property was searched or raided by authorities, they never thought to look into the "dirty laundry" inside the home. Growing up in a juke joint environment, life was not easy for the Kelly siblings. The juke joint was so busy that it often took precedence over having a normal or traditional family upbringing. Yet Ronnie and Bobby shared everything, including their room and a cute little white puppy. Besides attending school, having a pet provided a sense of normalcy for them.

During 1965, Bobby Kelly became accustomed to hypocrisy at home and throughout the community. It was commonplace for even elected officials and others of prominence to drive up nightly at the Kelly home to purchase liquor. Bobby Kelly, still age 10, knew the routine all too well. No need to say anything. Just go outside with a half-pint bottle, pass it through the car window, take the money, turn, and just walk away. For some officials, the ritual of Pass, Take, Turn, and Walk Away was ongoing every night. Sometimes, it was twice per night for certain customers.

Out of the abundance of the heart, the mouth speaks. No one really knows what goes on in the heart and mind of the individual.

Regardless of the racial tensions rising in the United States, Bradford County Florida was still rather calm. By now, federal authorities were consulting with local authorities regarding alleged business activities at Kelly's Nite Limit. The Lawtey Police Chief was re-elected time and time again. The indigenous people just seemed to like him for one reason or another. Whenever State authorities consulted with local officials about Kelly's Nite Limit, local authorities would tip-off Mr. Kelly about any pending or upcoming sting operation against his nightclub.

A happier time occurred toward the end of the year. In October 1965, Marylou Kelly and David Jones Jr. were married at the Bradford County Courthouse in Starke. The groom was the son of David Jones Sr. and Gussie Mae Lane Jones of Lincoln City. The following year, the newlyweds welcomed their son David Antonio Jones. The new family lived temporarily in Lawtey before eventually settling in Starke.

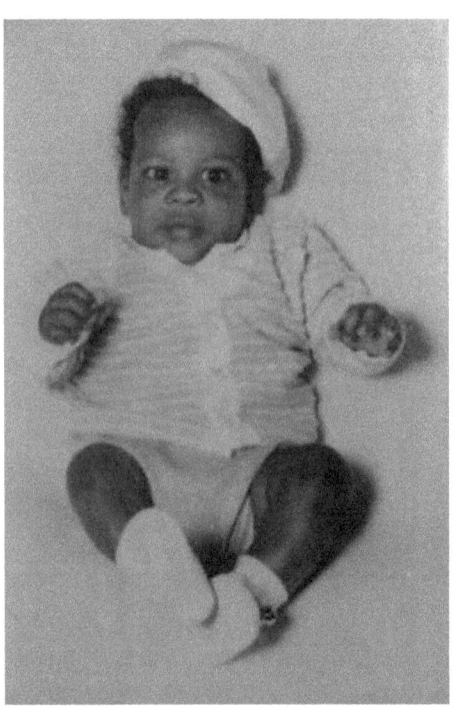

Photograph of David Antonio Jones, provided by Marylou Kelly Williams

Bobby and the King of Soul

The U.S. Federal Minimum Wage in 1966 was $1.25 per hour. It was also the year that Clifford Kelly Sr. promoted a triple threat, a historic delight for Kelly's Nite Limit. Mr. Kelly booked Otis Redding (The King) of Macon, Georgia; Carla Thomas (The Queen) of Memphis, Tennessee; and Booker T & the MG's for one special night. Carla Thomas is the daughter of legendary WDIA Disc Jockey & Soul recording artist Rufus Thomas. He performed his Billboard R&B hit recordings: "Bear Cat" (#3), "Do the Funky Chicken" (#5), "Do The Funky Penguin" (#11), The Push & Pull" (#1), Walking the Dog (#5), and The Breakdown (#2) at Kelly's a few years later. All artists were represented by Phil Walden Artist & Promotions of Macon, Georgia.

After twelve years of business, the Kellys' school-age children were still too young to attend a live show. They feasted their eyes and ears during the sound check and rehearsal as the artists arrived early that day. Otis Redding and the musicians traveled to Lawtey with a caravan of four Station Wagons. One of the cars was used to transport musical instruments and equipment only. Bobby, age 11, recalled Otis and Carla's hit song titled "Tramp," which became an iconic Billboard R&B record.

Memorabilia: Promotional portrait and original recording of B.A.B.Y. by Carla Thomas (Stax Records) was released on July 18, 1966. The song went to #3 on Billboard's R&B Chart and #14 on Billboard's Pop Chart provided by Kelly's Nite Limit

Memorabilia: Original recording of TRAMP with company sleeve by Otis Redding and Carla Thomas for (Stax Records) was a Billboard R&B #2 hit record and #26 on Billboard's Hot 100 chart in 1967 provided by Kelly's Nite Limit

1960S WELCOME TO SCHOOLBOY'S AND THE ERA OF KELLY'S NITE LIMIT

Portrait Author: Stax Records Company

Memorabilia: Promotional portrait, original recording of Green Onions with company sleeve (Stax Music) by Booker T & The MGs provided by Kelly's Nite Limit. The song was a Billboard R&B #1 hit & #3 hit on Billboard's Hot 100 chart in 1962.

The album titled "Otis Blue"

"Otis Redding Sings Soul" debuted at #1 on Billboard's R&B Chart on October 2, 1965.

His discography includes fourteen Billboard R&B Top 10 hit singles and eleven R&B Top 10 albums.

Memorabilia: Promotional portrait (Stax Records) and original recordings (Stax-VOLT Records) for Otis Redding provided by Kelly's Nite Limit

THE BAR-KAYS

As Otis Redding stepped on the stage to rehearse, he was wearing a short sleeve, black, turtleneck shirt, tight-fitting pants, and hard bottom leather shoes. Bobby immediately recognized just how large of a man Otis Redding really was.

The Bar Kays are the actual touring band of musicians for Otis Redding. Their hit single "Soul Finger" reached #3 on Billboard's R&B singles chart and #17 on the Hot 100 Chart. Although Booker T and The MGs were headliners for the show, during rehearsal, they were on stage at Kelly's performing backup for Otis Redding instead of the Bar Kays. During the sound check, Bobby Kelly listened to Otis Redding perform four of his hit songs titled "Respect" (#4), "These Arms Of Mine" (#20), "Fa-Fa-Fa-Fa" (#12), and "I Can't Turn You A Loose" (#11). Carla Thomas was not on stage while Bobby watched and listened to these soul legends in the making rehearse for their show. Whenever a major artist like Otis Redding performed at Kelly's Nite Limit, it was common for the cars to be parked from the venue all the way up to the railroad at highway 301. For those who walked the full length of Kingsley Road to see the show, the venue was just under a mile away. It would be a historic night in Lawtey, Florida for Kelly's Nite Limit. A magnificent showcase for the admission price of $3 at the door.

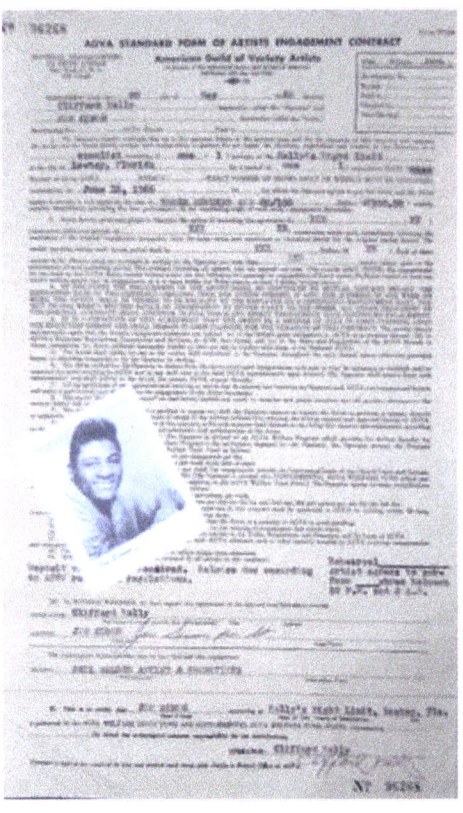

As the blues evolved and progressed into what became known as soul music, Clifford Kelly booked and promoted more newcomers in the music industry. On June 18, 1966, a young singer by the name Joe Simon from Richmond, Contra Costa, California, performed at Kelly's. Released on Sound Stage 7, Joe Simon's song "Teenager's Prayer" peaked at #11 on Billboard's R&B Chart. The young singer gained wider exposure after he performed his hit on American Bandstand.

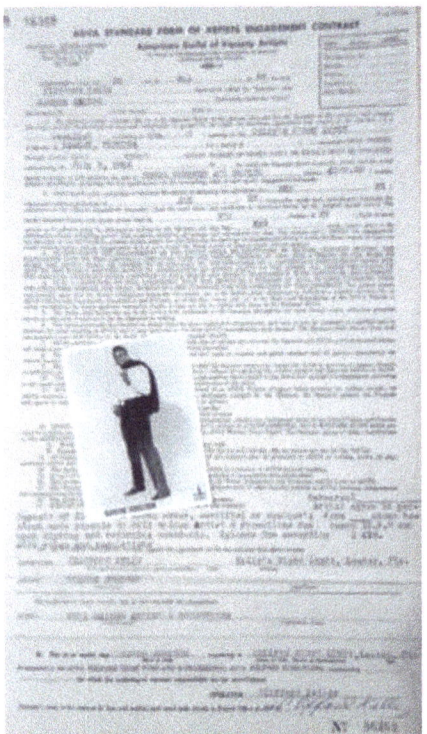

On July 9, 1966, Clifford Kelly booked a double-header show starring a young singer known as Roscoe Shelton from Nashville, Tennessee and the Kelly Brothers from Chicago, Illinois. The Kelly Brothers and Roscoe Shelton both achieved Billboard Top 40 success and made TV appearances while touring the United States. Shelton, also a Sound Stage 7 Recording artist, saw his single "Strain on My Heart" reach #25. His recording titled "Easy Going Fellow" peaked at #32.

Memorabilia: Agency Contract(s) (Phil Walden Artists & Promotion and promotional portrait(s) The Bar Kays (Volt), Joe Simon, Roscoe Shelton (Sound Stage 7) and The Kelly Brothers (Prescsent Records Limited) provided by Kelly's Nite Limit.

The Kelly Brothers, also known as The King Pins, recorded "It Won't Be This Way Always" reached #12 on Billboard's R&B Chart. The group reached #39 on the R&B Chart with their single "Falling in Love Again." This was an era when teenagers and adults did not attend events together at nightclubs. Jean Kelly (age 15) and Bobby Kelly (age 11) were still too young to see a live performance at Kelly's Nite Limit. The children were always somewhere nearby whenever recording artists arrived early in Lawtey for a performance. Otis Redding, Carla Thomas, Booker T & the MGs, Joe Simon, Roscoe Shelton, and the Kelly Brothers were all represented by Walden Artists and Promotions. The publishing company, RedWal Publishing, was founded in partnership with Otis Redding. At just 26, Otis Redding was a gifted soul-singer whose stardom was skyrocketing. Yet fate would have it that only Joe Simon would enjoy continued success well into the next decade. Carla Thomas continued to record and tour for a few more years. She also completed her education at Tennessee State University and Howard University.

A New Home for the Kellys

In October 1967, after twenty-three years of residing in a wood frame house, the Kelly family finally moved into their new three bedroom and two bathroom cinder block home. Only Jean, Ronnie, and Bobby lived with their parents. Emma was married and resided in Albany, Georgia. Clifford Jr., was stationed in Germany. Marylou resided in Starke with her family. The new Kelly home was built right next door to the old one. It was hard for Mrs. Kelly to part ways with the past. So much so that she left all of the furniture, books, and food she canned over the years in the old house. Brand new furniture for every room, including a corner section bookcase, was purchased for the new home. Over the years, Mrs. Kelly acquired a nice collection of science books. She enjoyed practicing the home health-care information she learned from reading her books. In her new home, Mrs. Kelly proudly showcased her full set of champagne-colored, leather-bound encyclopedias with gold-glinted pages. Yet, there were times she would go into the ole' house and retrieve a few dusty quart size jars of canned pears for a snack or some gumbo to prepare a side dish.

In the Spring of 1968, Margaret Jean Kelly graduated from RJE High School. Her younger brother Jerome Kelly completed his sophomore year at the school as well.

Photograph of Margaret Jean Kelly was provided by Ernest Copeland Sr.

Jerome Kelly was a 10th grader in 1968 at RJE High School. Photograph provided by Marylou Kelly

Photograph of John Wesley Garrer 1895–1968, provided by Donna J. Garrer Miller

In addition, during the summer, the Kelly family had to say goodbye to their patriarch. On July 17, 1968, Clifford Kelly received the sad news that his father, John Wesley Garrer, had passed away at home in Louisville, Georgia. His daughter, Donna Garrer, was at her father's bedside as he smiled and peacefully passed away. His memorial service was held on July 22, 1968, at Jones Chapel AME Zion Church in Blythe, Georgia. His wife, Alavan Garrer, had passed away four years prior. His second wife, Ida Belle Garrer, attended his memorial service. John Wesley Garrer was laid to rest at Jones Chapel Cemetery in Blythe. All of his tangible assets were distributed by the guardians of his estate, his sister Mrs. Ina Belle Scott Harris and his brother Mr. Abbie "Buddy" Scott. John Garrer's youngest son, Ray Garrer, along with his wife, Jean Garrer, continued the legacy of mortuary services in Louisville, Georgia.

Mrs. Emma Daniel Williams 1904–1968. Photograph provided by the Collection of Margurie Williams Kelly

On August 14, 1968, Clifford Kelly Sr. received more sad news. His mother, Mrs. Emma Daniel Williams, died after a brief illness. Memorial Services for her were held on August 30, 1968, at Liberty Baptist Church in Augusta, Georgia. She was laid to rest at Walker Memorial Park Cemetery in Richmond County, Georgia.

Civil unrest was rampant in the United States during the late 1960s. The indigenous citizens of Lawtey/Peetsville were concerned about the quality of their school and the education of their children. In addition, the loss of several civil rights leaders had an emotional impact on the community. Despite civil unrest, the loss of his parents, and distribution of his father's estate, Clifford Kelly Sr. was a man of resilience who moved forward.

The Two Spot in Jacksonville, Florida was more than twice the size of Kelly's Nite Limit. The two story night club founded in 1940 had 1,000 seats on the second floor. The dance floor accommodated 2,000 people with ease. The Two Spot had private dining rooms, a cafeteria, a bar, and several cabins for overnight guests and recording artists. B.B. King, Sam Cooke, James Brown, Charlie Singleton, Jackie Wilson, Lionel Hampton, Ray Charles, Diana Washington, Tiny York, and Nat Small all performed live at the establishment. After integration, Black-owned businesses experience a nationwide commercial decline. In 1967, the famed Two Spot was sold and redeveloped into an apartment complex.

Kelly's Nite Limit, on the other hand, continued to thrive into the next generation. In the Fall of 1968, Clifford Kelly booked a 15-year-old singer named Betty Wright to perform her first hit record at Kelly's Nite Limit. Betty Wright was a minor; therefore, her mother Mrs. Rosa Wright Norris traveled with her. Betty's hit record at that time was titled "Girls Can't Do What the Guys Do."

Indigenous Lawtey resident Bobby Austin Jr. (who was 17 at the time) attended the show with a friend and recalled that night: "There weren't many teens there due to the fact that although Betty Wright was a teen herself, the club dances were mainly for adults. However, Mr. Kelly permitted us to attend that show. If I had to guess, I would say less than twenty [teenagers] under the age of 18. Yes, the place was packed! Mr. Kelly, also known as "Boss," only charged us teens a few dollars. Oh yes, I had lots of fun! My first time at a show. When they escorted Betty into the club, me and my friend tried to get close up and speak. Her bodyguards kept us at bay. I do remember her attire was a tiger printed outfit."

On Billboard, the recording reached #33 Pop and #15 R&B. It was only the beginning for this talented young singer. As her stardom continued to rise, she was booked for repeat performances at Kelly's. The next time Betty Wright performed at Kelly's Nite Limit, she did not require a chaperone.

Memorabilia: The original print advertisement for Betty Wright appeared in Billboard Magazine on July 27, 1968. The print Ad and original recording (Alston Records) provided by Kelly's Nite Limit.

In Lawtey, Kelly's Nite Limit continued to grow in popularity. In the late Fall of 1968, Clifford Kelly once again booked Etta James to perform her new bestselling hit titled "Tell Mama." The song was written by a new young musician named Clarence Carter from Montgomery, Alabama. The record was released by Cadet Records and debuted on Billboard's R&B Chart earlier in November the previous year. The recording reached #10 on Billboard's R&B Chart and #23 on Billboard's Hot 100.

At Kelly's Nite Limit, the crowd went wild during Etta's performance of the song "Tell Mama"! Next, Etta hit it and burst into "I'd Rather Go Blind" and the juke joint capacity crowd of over one thousand people exploded!!! Bobby Kelly was 14 years old during Etta James's 1968 show in Lawtey. It was also the year that changed everything at the juke joint. Bobby Kelly was working behind the counter as he did occasionally to help his mother. Although he was under age 21, it was lawful for a child under age 17 to work for their parents in a nonhazardous environment. On this night, during the live performance of Etta James, two gentlemen came into Kelly's Nite Limit and ordered a couple of beers. Bobby sold the alcoholic beverages to one of the men. Unknown to Bobby, that gentleman was an undercover agent. Bobby Kelly and his father Clifford Kelly Sr. were arrested and charged with beverage law infringement and contributing to the delinquency of a minor. Clifford Kelly was fined an assessment fee of $20,000.

The beverage license of Kelly's Nite Limit was suspended. Clifford Kelly maintained his State of Florida business license for hotels and restaurants only. For the next five years, the beverage license for the sale of beer and wine at Kelly's Nite Limit was purchased in the name of Marylou Kelly Jones.

It was not an easy decision for Marylou because she was married and had her own family to consider. Yet she loved her parents too and agreed to have the licenses issued in her name to help maintain the family business.

After the 1968 incident, Mrs. Margurie Kelly refused to sell beer in a can every Sunday. After a local baseball game on Sunday evening, Mrs. Kelly poured beer in a cup and served it to her customers. Even though she owned a nightclub, Mrs. Kelly always confessed to being a Christian. It was her personal way of showing respect to the Lord.

Kelly's Nite Limit remained open, but as always, Clifford Kelly discarded law enforcement and operated on his own terms. It was difficult moving forward as Mrs. Kelly faced opposition while attempting to purchase the alcoholic beverages for Kelly's Nite Limit. With the help of her close friend, Mrs. Hermia Thompkins Sherman (the owner of Thompkins Grocery Store in Lawtey), Mrs. Kelly was able to obtain the inventory of beverages she needed. Mrs. Sherman would order everything Mrs. Kelly requested and had it delivered to Thompkins Grocery Store. Mrs. Kelly would simply pay Mrs. Sherman for the shipment. Although it would be a few years, eventually Mrs. Margurie Williams Kelly applied for a beverage license in her name only.

Clifford Lee Kelley: Why Did I Return to Cocoa, Florida?

After three years of service at Spangdahlem AFB in Germany, Sergeant Clifford Lee Kelley served the last six months (November 1967–April 1968) at Shaw Air Force Base in Sumter, South Carolina. It was in South Carolina where Sgt. Kelley met the very elegant Ms. Maggie Spann. She was the daughter of Eugene and Kathryn J. Spann of Sumter County. After an honorable discharge on April 18, 1968, Sgt. Kelley returned to Florida. He enrolled at Brevard Junior College in Cocoa, where he majored in COBOL (Common Business Oriented Language), which is a computer programming language used in business administration by corporations and government entities. After graduation, Clifford Kelly Jr. was offered a job as a Computer Operator by RCA in Cocoa Beach Florida. Eventually, his new love Maggie Spann moved to Cocoa as well.

Photograph: Sergeant Clifford Kelly, Shaw AFB 1968

Just as a leaf never falls far from the tree, history truly repeats itself. Following in the footsteps of his great grandfather (Joshua Daniel), his grandfather (John W. Garrer), and his father (Clifford Kelly Sr.)—all admired by ladies—Sergeant Clifford Kelly Jr. proved to have a similar charm. Sergeant Kelley was a ladies' man by nature—and by blood.

He was a tall, good-looking young man, well dressed, with money to spend. Clifford Jr. was primarily successful with his business endeavors just like the men of his bloodline.

During this time, Clifford Jr. was reunited with his first love, Ester Marie Allen. She was known in Lawtey by her nickname, Midge Allen. Clifford Jr. and Midge were literally childhood sweethearts since the day they met in first grade at Charles C. Anderson JHS in Lawtey. They grew up together and became high school sweethearts at RJE High School. After graduation, Midge went away to attend Florida Memorial College in St. Augustine, Florida.

Upon his return to Cocoa, Florida, Clifford Jr. and Midge reunited but only dated temporarily. Midge soon left Cocoa and never returned, as Clifford Jr. was romantically involved with Maggie Spann. It was not long afterward that Midge Allen wrote to Clifford Jr. informing him that she was expecting. Although Midge was carrying his child, Clifford Jr. did not break up his relationship with Maggie Spann, who later became his fiancée. As the couple moved forward with their wedding plans, Clifford Jr. asked his cousin Counselman Herman Johnson to be his Best Man. Cousin Herman was the son of Deacon Cephus Johnson and Mrs. Minnie L. Hendreith Johnson of Lawtey. Clifford Lee Kelley Jr. and Maggie Ophelia Spann were married in November of 1968. Not long afterward, Clifford Jr. was offered employment by Lockheed Aircraft. In 1969, Clifford Jr. accepted the job offer and relocated to Marietta, Georgia with his new wife.

Midge Allen was the daughter of John and Marie Allen of Lawtey. The Allens were a family of eleven children. Their daughter Midge Allen gave birth to Clifford Kelly Jr's second child, a daughter named

Tess Laquell Allen. Midge Allen was also employed as a Teacher at Anderson Jr. High School in Lawtey. However, due to desegregation laws, the school was eventually closed. Midge Allen, a graduate of Florida Memorial College, relocated to Miami, Florida and made a new life for herself there.

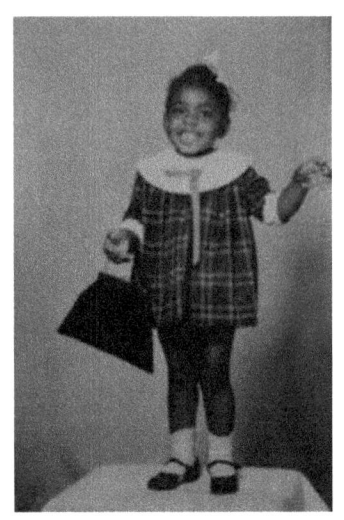

Clifford Jr's firstborn daughter Sibyl (age 3) was living in Cocoa with her mother Deloris Wynn (age 23), her brother Rodney Wynn (age 6) and stepfather Richard Drayton. Deloris Wynn and Richard Drayton were married earlier in April of 1968. The family resided at the Lincoln Apartments 640 Poinsette #44, Cocoa, Florida. Unfortunately, the home environment of Mr. and Mrs. Drayton was unsafe for Deloris and her children. The home was filled with ongoing domestic violence. For years, Deloris was physically abused by her husband. Sibyl's maternal grandparents, Mr. and Mrs. Chester Wynn, were concerned because the child spent a great portion of her infancy living between the Kelly family and the Wynn family while the child's father, Clifford Kelly Jr., was stationed in Germany. The child's grandfather, Chester Wynn, noticed the toddler was becoming emotionally confused.

Clifford Kelly Jr., along with the child's paternal and maternal grandparents, made the decision to place his daughter Sibyl in the home of his parents Clifford and Margurie Kelly in Lawtey. The child never returned to the care nor custody of her mother. Mrs. Kelly also wanted custody of Sibyl's elder brother Rodney Wynn. Mrs. Kelly wanted to keep the children together. The child Rodney Wynn was never placed in the care of Clifford and Margurie Kelly.

Moving forward, Deloris Wynn became a seamstress. She also enjoyed helping individuals diagnosed with Autism at the local New York State Hospital. Years later, she married Walter Papin, a native of the Caribbean Island nation of St. Lucia, where French was his first language. After their marriage in Polk County, Florida, Walter and Deloris Papin lived the remainder of their lives in Sodus-Lyons, Wayne County, New York.

In 1969, as the decade came to a close, it was the end of Charles C. Anderson Jr. High School (Anderson Elementary School) in Lawtey. In order to comply with Title VI of the Civil Rights Act of 1964, Bradford County officials closed all schools for colored students in the county's municipalities of East Lawtey-Peetsville, Brooker-New River, Hampton, and Starke: (Lincoln City-Thurston, Pleasant Grove, and Water Oak). The following academic year, all Black American students in Lawtey were enrolled and bused to Lawtey Elementary School, or Bradford Middle School and Bradford County High School in Starke, Florida.

Photograph: The Class of 1969-1970. A few indigenous students of the final kindergarten class at Anderson Elementary (Charles C. Anderson Junior High School) in Lawtey, Florida. Pictured left to right are: Keith Harmon, Sibyl Kelley, Charles Brown, Salatheia Jenkins, Harriette Davis, and Lois Moore. (Photograph provided by Harriett Davis Tyson

Classmates Not Pictured: Yallah Slocum, Bernadette Bright, Brenda Mack, Sylvia Hollis, Carla Lee, Tony Bell, Jimmy Diggs, and Willie Strong

Charles C. Anderson JHS Faculty: Principal Jessie J. Moore Jr. Teachers: Alice Anderson, Annie B. Anderson, Alphonso Franklin, Zeporah Jennings, Dorothy S. Moore, Doreatha Richardson, Minot L. Standby, Mildred W. Turner, and Willie Mae Randolph. Clerical Staff: Edna Allen and Odessa Hamilton

BONUS TRIBUTE

A Photo Parade

Memorabilia: Promotional portraits for recording artists booked and promoted by Clifford Kelly Sr. to perform at Kelly's Nite Limit 1950s and 1960s

Author of Photography:

ABC Booking Corporation
General Artists Corporation
International Management Company
Phil Walden Artists and Promotions
Queen Booking Corporation
Shaw Artists Corporation
The Gale Agency
Universal Attractions Inc.

Invented in 1873, silver gelatin printing of promotional portraits elevated in prominence during the 20th Century. All major studios and agencies utilized this process of imagery to promote their clients.

"Money Honey"

1953

Author of Photography: General Artists Corporation

"My Babe"

1955

Author of Photography: Shaw Artist Corporation

"Let The Good Times Roll"

1955

Author of Photography: The Gale Agency

Forty Days and Forty Nights"

1956

Author of Photography: Shaw Artist Corporation

"Since I Met You Baby"

1956

Author of Photography: Bettye Berger

"Candy"

1956

Author of Photography: The Gale Agency

"Please, Please, Please"

1956

Author of Photography: Universal Attractions Inc.

"Honky Tonk"

1956

Author of Photography: Shaw Artists Corporation

"Lucille"

1957

Author of Photography: Herald Attractions Inc.

1960S WELCOME TO SCHOOLBOY'S AND THE ERA OF KELLY'S NITE LIMIT

"I'm Walkin"

1957

Author of Photography: ABC Paramount

"Paying The Cost To Be The Boss"

1957

Author of Photography: Shaw Artist Corporation

"Hey Bo Diddley"

1957

Author of Photography: Shaw Artist Corporation

"So Long"

1957

Author of Photography: Shaw Artist Corporation

"Fever"

1958

Author of Photography: Universal Attractions Inc.

"Try Me"

1958

Author of Photography: Universal Attractions Inc.

"Tears On My Pillow"

1958

Author of Photography: General Artists Corporation

"What'd I Say"

1959

Author of Photography: Shaw Artist Corporation

1960S WELCOME TO SCHOOLBOY'S AND THE ERA OF KELLY'S NITE LIMIT

"Money"

("That's What I Want")

1959

Author of Photography: Berry Gordy Jr.

"The Twist"

1960

Author of Photography: General Artist Corporation

"Please Come Home For Xmas"

1960

Author of Photography: Shaw Artist Corporation

"Let Go, Lets Go, Lets Go"

1960

Author of Photography: Universal Attractions Inc.

1960S WELCOME TO SCHOOLBOY'S AND THE ERA OF KELLY'S NITE LIMIT

"Fool In Love"

1960

Author of Photography: Sullivan Enterprises

1960S WELCOME TO SCHOOLBOY'S AND THE ERA OF KELLY'S NITE LIMIT

BOBBY BLAND
Duke Record Artist

Personal Management
Evelyn Johnson
Houston, Texas

"Turn On Your Lovelight"

1961

Author of Photography: Associated Booking Corporation

"Cry To Me"

1961

Author of Photography: Universal Attractions Inc.

"Stand By Me"

1961

Author of Photography: Circle Artists Corporation

1960S WELCOME TO SCHOOLBOY'S AND THE ERA OF KELLY'S NITE LIMIT

"Gee Whiz"

(Look at His Eyes)

1961

Author of Photography: Circle Artists Corporation

1960S WELCOME TO SCHOOLBOY'S AND THE ERA OF KELLY'S NITE LIMIT

"Bring It On Home To Me"

1962

Author of Photography: RCA Victor

"Don't Make Me Over"

1962

Author of Photography: Russ Carter

"Make It Easy on Yourself"

1962

Author of Photography: Shaw Artist Corporation

1960S WELCOME TO SCHOOLBOY'S AND THE ERA OF KELLY'S NITE LIMIT

"Soul Twist"

1962

Author of Photography: Queen Booking Corporation

1960S WELCOME TO SCHOOLBOY'S AND THE ERA OF KELLY'S NITE LIMIT

"Mashed Potato Time"

1962

Author of Photography: Paramount Artists Corporation

"Walking The Dog"

1963

Author of Photography: Universal Attractions Inc.

Little Johnny Taylor

"Part Time Love"

1963

Author of Photography: Universal Attractions Inc.

"Cry Baby"

1963

Author of Photography: Universal Attractions Inc.

OTIS REDDING   Personal Management: PHIL WALDEN   

"I Can't Turn You a Loose"

1965

Author of Photography: Phil Walden Artists and Promotions

"Rescue Me"

1965

Author of Photography: Ike Turner (PRANN)

"Stay In My Corner"

1965

Author of Photography: Queen Booking Corporation

1960S WELCOME TO SCHOOLBOY'S AND THE ERA OF KELLY'S NITE LIMIT

"Yes, I'm Ready"

1965

Author of Photography: Penguin Artists Management

1960S WELCOME TO SCHOOLBOY'S AND THE ERA OF KELLY'S NITE LIMIT

"Stay Away from My Baby"

1965

Author of Photography: Buffalo Booking Agency

"Mustang Sally"

1966

Author of Photography: Universal Attractions Inc.

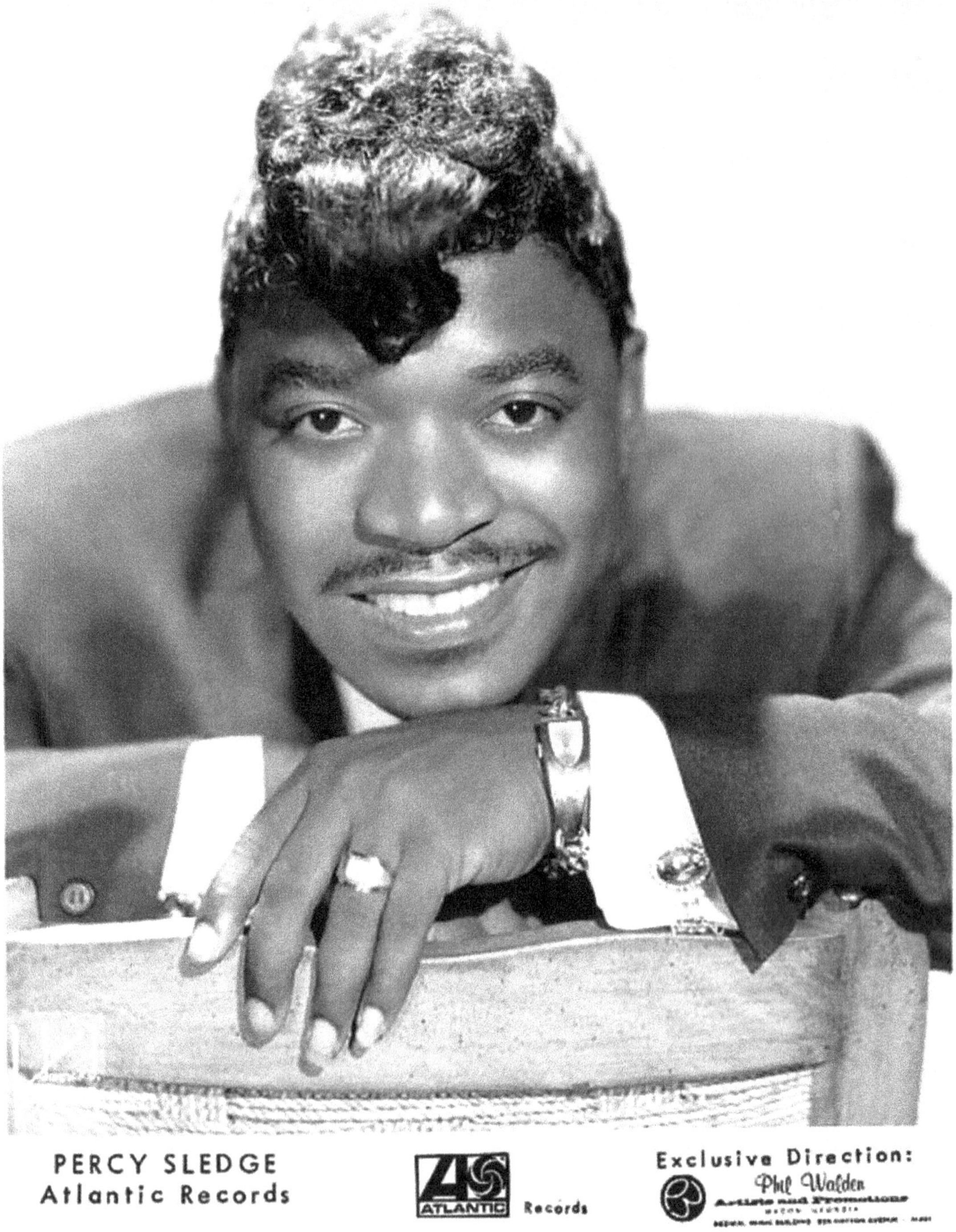

PERCY SLEDGE
Atlantic Records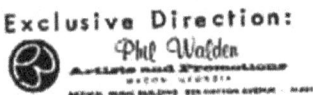

"When A Man Loves A Woman"

1966

Author of Photography: Phil Walden Artists and Promotions

Patti Labelle and the Blue Belles

"Over the Rainbow"

1966

Author of Photography: The William Morris Agency

"Knock on Wood"

1966

Author of Photography: Phil Walden Artists and Promotions

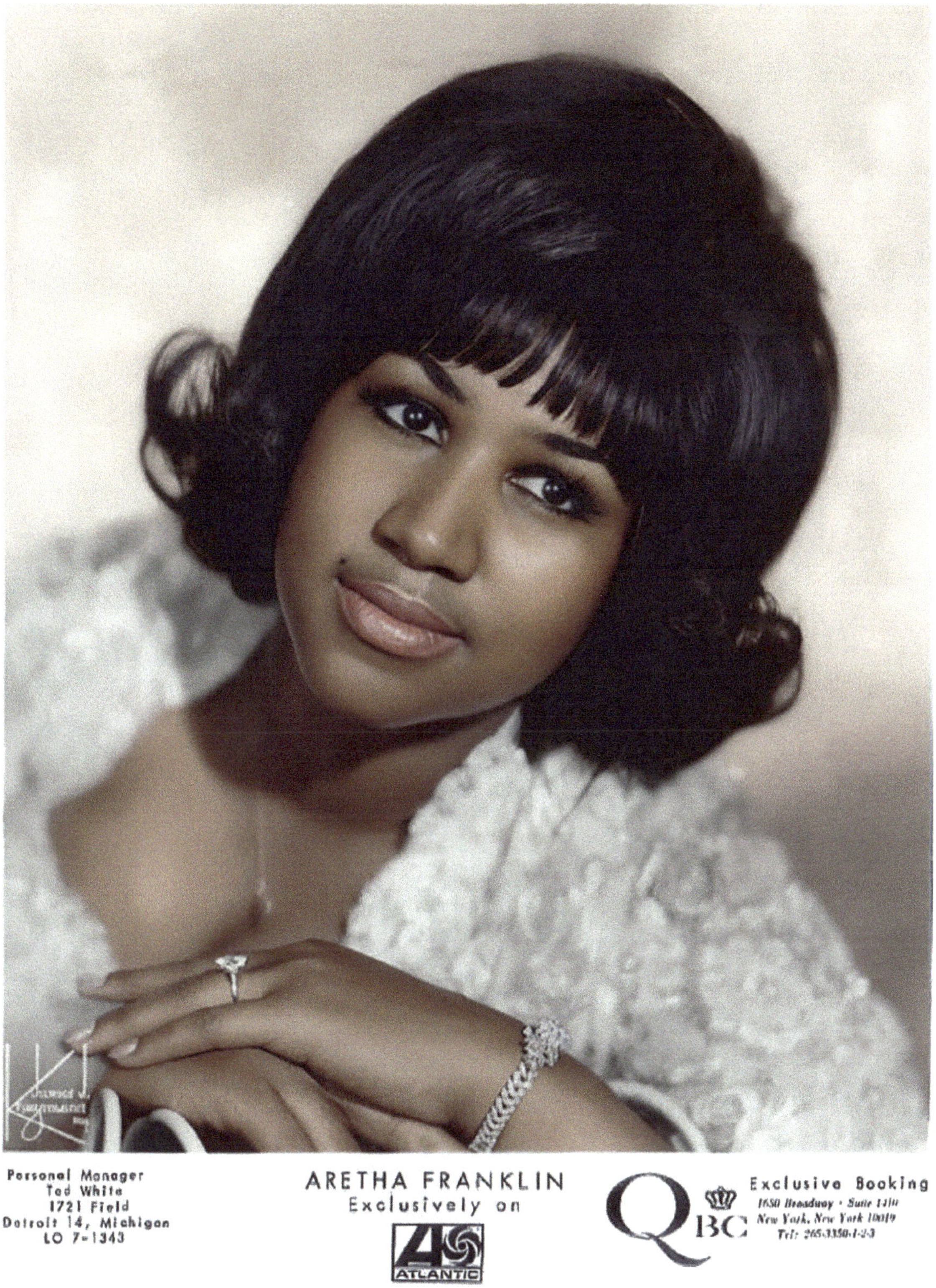
Personal Manager
Ted White
1721 Field
Detroit 14, Michigan
LO 7-1343
ARETHA FRANKLIN
Exclusively on
ATLANTIC
QBC
Exclusive Booking
1650 Broadway • Suite 1410
New York, New York 10019
Tel: 265-3350-1-2-3

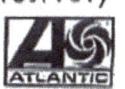

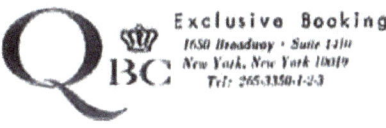

"Chain of Fools"

1967

Author of Photography: Queen Booking Corporation

"Everyday Will Be Like a Holiday"

1967

Author of Photography: Universal Attractions Inc.

1960S WELCOME TO SCHOOLBOY'S AND THE ERA OF KELLY'S NITE LIMIT

"I Heard It Through the Grapevine"

1967

Author of Photography: Berry Gordy Jr., International Management Company

"Soul Man"

1967

Author of Photography: Phil Walden Artists and Promotions

"Close Your Eyes"

1967

Author of Photography: Associated Booking Corporation

"Are You Lonely for Me"

1967

Author of Photography: Carmine De Noia

"Sweet Soul Music"

1967

Author of Photography: Phil Walden Artists and Promotions

"Slip Away"

1967

Author of Photography: Phil Walden Artists and Promotions

"Who's Making Love"

1968

Author of Photography: Phil Walden Artists and Promotions

1960S WELCOME TO SCHOOLBOY'S AND THE ERA OF KELLY'S NITE LIMIT

"Turn Back the Hands of Time"

1969

Author of Photography: DAKAR-Cotillion

"Soul Shake"

1969

Author of Photography: Universal Attractions Inc.

1960S WELCOME TO SCHOOLBOY'S AND THE ERA OF KELLY'S NITE LIMIT

"The Chokin Kind"

1969

Author of Photography: Phil Walden Artists and Promotions

CHAPTER 8

The 1970s: Margurie W. Kelly vs The Florida Division of Beverage

On April 20, 1970, Mrs. Margurie Williams Kelly submitted an application for a new beverage license in her name only, which was denied by the State of Florida. She filed an appeal to the Department of Business Regulations for reconsideration of licensing. The matter came on for hearing after due notice before D. J. Bauer, Hearing Examiner, at the Jacksonville District Office on October 9, 1970; by order of the Honorable R. E. Beary, Director, Division of Beverage, Department of Business Regulation, State of Florida. Appearing for the State was Mr. J.F. Warren, Jr. The applicant [Margurie Williams Kelly] appeared without Counsel. The subject matter of the hearing involved reconsideration of the prior disapproval of the applicant for a new license. As the case opened, it was made known by State's Counsel that the basis for the disapproval of the applicant were the past convictions of the husband [Clifford Kelly] dating from 1956 through 1968, which included, among other things, beverage law infractions. In this connection, exhibit #4 was later introduced into evidence. It consisted of approximately forty pages detailing the past charges and the disposition of each administrative case involved. Other exhibits allowed into evidence without objection were #1, a letter dated October 6, 1970 from Attorney G.H. Pierce; #2, a letter dated October 2, 1970 from Representative E. Shaw of District 16; and #3, a composite exhibit consisting of the licenses from 1956 to 1968 contained the name of Clifford Kelly, husband of the applicant who was the former licensee. The testimony and prior history disclose no convictions of the wife, Margurie Kelly, the applicant herein. The wife offered testimony as to her good character, including exhibits 1 & 2, and made a voluntary statement that she alone will do all the work on the premises, which is located in a rural area in Lawtey, Florida. The husband will not be present, nor will he engage or participate in the business operation if she is approved for a license. It has long been the policy of the Department to deny a license where the spouse of an applicant has violated the beverage law during the last five years immediately preceding the application. The husband's convictions are well established by the testimony, witnesses, and the evidence of record all of which were confirmed and corroborated by the District Supervisor, E. Ashley. Included also is the fact that there is no record of any violation against the wife. It is persuasive that the contents of exhibit #1 contains the strong personal recommendation of Pierce and disclose the fact that all the charges against the husband had been dismissed except one. In addition, exhibit #2 presents evidence of the good character of Mrs. Kelly and is quite impressive considering its source and the fact that the writer, Representative Shaw, makes his disclosure and recommendation as a

Marylou behind the counter at Kelly's Nite Limit in 1972. Photograph provided by Marylou Kelly Williams

former prosecuting attorney in Bradford County, where the cases were heard. He further assures no participation by the husband Clifford Kelly Sr. In view of the foregoing, it is recommended that the license application be approved for processing in due course, with a provision prohibiting any activity by the husband on the licensed premises. Provided further that any breach of the provision prohibiting activities of the husband Clifford Kelly on or about the premises shall effect an invalidation of the Order of approval as the date of this Order and shall effect an automatic revocation pursuant to Florida Statute 561.15(3). The recommendation for new licensure for Margurie Kelly was submitted on November 23, 1970 at Tallahassee, Florida.

State of Florida Department of Business Regulation License for Clifford Kelly/Kelly's Nite Limit, May 1, 1974 (14000244)

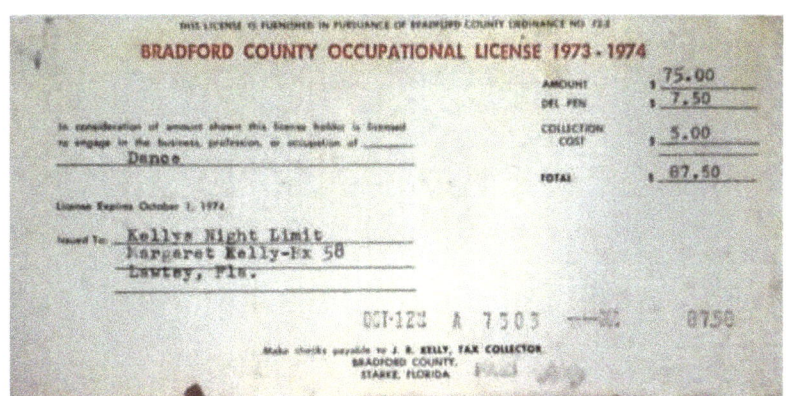

Bradford County Occupational License for Kellys Nite Limit/Margurie Kelly October 12, 1973. (A7303)

Although 1970 was a trying and eventful year, Clifford and Margurie Kelly ended it on a more positive note. They surprised their youngest son Bobby Kelly with a sweet 16 birthday party at Kelly's Nite Limit. David Jones, his brother-in-law, preoccupied Bobby all day with cat 'n mouse switch 'n bait activities while family and friends decorated the juke joint for the party. The venue was filled with teenagers from Lawtey. Everything inside the building was glowing in the dark, including the green leather jacket Bobby Kelly wore to the party.

Bobby Kelly's Sweet 16 Birthday Party at Kelly's Nite Limit in November 1970. Photograph provided by the Collection of Margurie Williams Kelly

Clifford "Schoolboy" Kelly
"You Run Your Mouth, I'll Run My Business"

Clifford Kelly, age 52, was now living under court order not to step foot on his own property. The dressing room at Kelly's Nite Limit was less than 20 feet away from the carport of his home. Mrs. Kelly did the best she could to comply with the Order. She worked a lot of weekends at Kelly's without her husband. However, he was still Clifford "Schoolboy" Kelly. He still went inside his juke joint to mingle with the local patrons every Sunday after a baseball game. He continued to book and promote recording artists to perform at Kelly's Nite Limit with blatant disregard of the Order and Recommendations by the Florida Division of Beverage. When it was showtime, Clifford "Schoolboy" Kelly was at the front door of his establishment. For every show in the 1970s, he continued to post placards in the Florida counties of Alachua, Baker, Bradford, Brevard, Broward, Clay, Columbia, Duval, Marion, Putman, Orange, Swannee, St. John, Union, and Volusia. He continued to purchase radio airtime to broadcast the announcement of his upcoming show(s) on WOBS, WERD, WPDQ, WZAZ, and WGGG.

The General Manager for WOBS, WERD, and WZAZ was Mr. Willie Martin of Jacksonville, Florida. Prior to becoming a broadcasting executive, he was known as DJ "Captain Groovy" at all radio stations. Other extremely popular disc jockeys were Don Smith—known as "The Pressure Cooker" on WERD and WZAZ—and Nat Johnson—known as "Soul Finger," who was featured on WOBS, WERD, and WZAZ as well. For years, radio personality "Soul Finger" was the preferred DJ of Clifford Kelly to entertain the crowd at Kelly's Nite Limit before a live show and during intermission.

To promote his upcoming show, Clifford Kelly Sr. would post placards throughout Florida anywhere he could in Lawtey, Starke, Raiford, Hampton, Waldo, Mcclenny, Sanderson, Penny Farms, Gainesville, Jacksonville, Baldwin, Lake Butler, Lake City, Live Oak, St. Augustine, Palatka, Middleburg, Keystone, Green Cove Springs, Daytona Beach, Orlando, Altamonte Springs, Eatonville, Cocoa/Rockledge, Sandford, Deland, Ocala, Coleman, Ft Lauderdale, Pompano Beach, and West Palm Beach.

Emma Kelly posing at "The Wall" inside Kelly's Nite Limit in 1973 for the featured recording artist Joe Simon

Photograph provided by the collection of Margurie Williams Kelly

THE 1970S: MARGURIE W. KELLY VS THE FLORIDA DIVISION OF BEVERAGE

The 1970's saw an influx of more recording artists booked to perform live at Kelly's Nite Limit. Three of Mr. Kelly's favorite recording artists were Joe Simon, Clarence Carter, and Betty Wright. All three artists were booked multiple times to perform in Lawtey, Florida.

Mr. Joe Simon was the recipient of the 1970 Grammy Award for Best Rhythm & Blues Vocal Performance-Male for his hit recording "The Chokin' Kind" on Spring Records. Overall, Mr. Simon received four Grammy Nominations during the 1970s.

Memorabilia: "Thanks for the Grammy:" The Original Print Advertisement for Joe Simon appeared in Billboard Magazine on March 28, 1970. The Ad was provided by Kelly's Nite Limit

THE 1970S: MARGURIE W. KELLY VS THE FLORIDA DIVISION OF BEVERAGE

Clarence Carter's recording titled "Patches" on Atlantic Records won the 1971 Grammy Award for Best R & B Song. He scored a total of seven Billboard R&B Top Ten hits. Patches #2, Slip Away #2 and Too Weak To Fight #3. All three recordings sold over a million copies each.

Memorabilia: Promotional portrait (Paragon Agency) provided from the collection of Margurie W. Kelly. All original recordings, and company sleeves (Atlantic Records) provided by Kelly's Nite Limit. The original print advertisement "Another Million Seller" appeared in Billboard Magazine on November 2, 1968 for Clarence Carter provided by Mrs. Tracy Faulkner Wynn

THE 1970S: MARGURIE W. KELLY VS THE FLORIDA DIVISION OF BEVERAGE

Betty Wright won the 1976 Grammy Award for Best Rhythm and Blues Song: "Where Is the Love" on Alston (RCA) Records Ms. Wright received six Grammy Nominations over the course of her career. She was booked to perform at Kelly's after the release of her mega hit single "Clean Up Woman" in 1972 on Alston Records. The song reached #2 on Billboard's R&B Chart and #6 on Billboard's Pop Chart. The recording sold six million copies worldwide.

Memorabilia: Promotional portrait and recordings, (Alston Records), recording & company picture sleeve (RCA Records) for Betty Wright provided by Kelly's Nite Limit

During the early 1970s, Clifford Kelly continued to utilize the services of booking agencies such as ABC Booking Corporation and Universal Attractions. Nevertheless, he booked the majority of his shows with The Paragon Agency (formerly Phil Walden Artists and Promotions). The primary booking agent for Mr. Kelly was Rodgers Redding, who's also the brother of Soul Music legend Otis Redding. Clifford and Margurie Kelly, along with their granddaughter Sibyl, age 6, traveled to 1019 Walnut Street in Macon, Georgia to meet with Rodgers Redding personally at The Paragon Agency.

Throughout the decade, Clifford Kelly Sr. continued to book and promote recording artists of the 1960s as well as new recording artists of the 1970s. Clifford Kelly Sr. promoted popular fan favorite artists of blues and soul music to perform live at Kelly's Nite Limit and other nightclubs throughout the State of Florida. Listed with their respective record labels, managers and booking agents, the recording artists are:

Archie Bell and The Drells (Atlantic Records), Agent/Manager: Skipper Lee Frazier, 1831 Southmore Street, Houston, Texas 77004. Agency: Associated Booking Corporation, 445 Park Avenue, New York, NY 20022.

Arthur Conely (ATCO Records), The Paragon Agency, 1019 Walnut Street, Macon, Georgia 31208. Agent: Rodgers Redding.

Betty Swann (Money Records), The Paragon Agency, 1019 Walnut Street, Macon, Georgia 31208. Agent: Rogers Redding.

Clarence Carter (Atlantic Records), The Paragon Agency, 1019 Walnut Street, Macon, Georgia 31208. Agent: Rodgers Redding.

Eddie Floyd (Stax Records), The Paragon Agency, 1019 Walnut Street, Macon, Georgia 31208. Agent: Rodgers Redding.

Jackie Moore (Atlantic Records), Agent: Dave Crawford, Atlantic Recording Corporation 75 Rockefeller Plaza New York NY 10019.

Betty Wright (Alston Records), Agency: The Paragon Agency 1019 Walnut Street Macon, Georgia 31208. Agent: Rodgers Redding.

King Floyd (Chimneyville Records), The Paragon Agency 1019 Walnut Street Macon, Georgia 31208. Agent: Rodgers Redding.

Percy Sledge (Atlantic Records), Agent: Rodgers Redding. The Paragon Agency 1019 Walnut Street Macon, Georgia 31208

Bobby Williams & The MarKings (REW Records), Agent/Management: TQC 367 West Church Street Orlando, Florida. 305-849-9071.

Joe Tex (DIAL Records), Agency: Universal Attractions 200 West 57th Street New York, NY.

Rufus Thomas (Stax Records) Agency: Continental Artists Inc. 305 South Bellevue Suite 105 Memphis, Tennessee 38104. Personal Manager: Irv Nathan.

The Impressions (Curtom Records), Agency: Lee Taylor Productions 157 Peachtree Street NE Suite 6223 Atlanta, Georgia 30303, (404) 524-8992.

Jr. Walker & The All Stars (SOL/Motown Records), Agency: International Talent Management Inc., 2652 West Grand Boulevard Detroit Michigan.

O.V. Wright (Back Beat Records), Agency: Buffalo Booking Agency 2807 Erastus Street Houston, Texas 77028.

McKinley Mitchell (OneDerful Records), Agent: George Leaner 1827 South Michigan Ave Chicago, Illinois.

ZZ Hill (United Artists Records), Agent: Velma Redding. The Paragon Agency 1019 Walnut Street Macon, Georgia 31208

Ted Taylor (ATCO Records), Agent/Manager: Nat Margo, Agency: Universal Attractions INC., 200 West 57th Street New York NY. 10019.

Luther Ingram (KOKO/Stax Records), Personal Manager: Johnny Baylor 98 North Avalon Memphis, Tennessee.

Joe Simon (Spring Records), Agency: Universal Attractions 200 West 57th Street New York NY.

Chuck Roberson (Albradella Records) Agent/Management: Jessie Boone 319 Highland Avenue Albany, Georgia 31701

The Devastations (GIMP Records) Agent: Lonnie Bobo P.O. Box 1086 Ruskin, Florida 33570.

Little Milton (Checker Records) Agent: CAMIL Productions, Jacki Sutton 320 East 21st Street Chicago, Illinois 60616.

Jean Knight (Stax Records), Agency: Universal Attractions 200 West 57th Street New York NY

Denise LaSalle (Westbound Records), Agent: The Paragon Agency 1019 Walnut Street Macon, Georgia 31208 Agent: Rodgers Redding.

The ChiLites (Brunswick Records), Agent: Tommy Vastola, Agency: QBC Queen Booking Corporation 1650 Broadway Suite # 1410 New York, NY. 10019.

Candi Staton (FAME Records), Agent: Rodgers Redding. Agency: The Paragon Agency 1019 Walnut Street Macon, Georgia 31208

Pattie Hendrix (Hilltak Records) Agent: C. & S. Productions 1918 Kay Avenue Brunswick, Georgia 31520.

Bobby Thomas (Boblo Records) Agent: Charlie Cross Jr., 1918 Kay Avenue Brunswick, Georgia 31520, (912) 265-1995.

B.E.E. The Black Exotics (Funk 45 Records) Agent: The Black Exotics Enterprises Agent: Albert Wright 1309 S.W. 55th Street Ocala, Florida.

TRAMA (CAT Records) Agent: T&K Productions 495 S.E. 10th Court Hialeah, Florida 33010.

Millie Jackson (Spring Records), Agency: The Paragon Agency 1019 Walnut Street Macon, Georgia 31208. Agent: Rodgers Redding.

Tyrone Davis (DaKar Records), Agent: Rodgers Redding. Agency: The Paragon Agency 1019 Walnut Street Macon, Georgia 31208

Dorothy Moore (Malaco Records), Agent/Manager: Tom Couch and James Stroud, (Malaco 3023 West Northside Drive Jackson, Mississippi).

Shirley Brown (Truth Records), Agency: The Paragon Agency 1019 Walnut Street Macon, Georgia 31208. Agent: Rodgers Redding.

BT Express (Roadshow Records), Agent: King Davis New York, NY. Direction: Dock Productions Inc., New York, NY.

George McCrae (T&K Records), Agent: Sherry Smith Agency: T&K Productions Direction and Management Division 495 South East 10th Court Hialeah, Florida 33010. (305) 888-1685 (305) 887-4052.

Gwen McCrae (CAT Records), Agency: The Paragon Agency 1019 Walnut Street Macon, Georgia. Agent: Rodgers Redding

Bobby Womack (United Artists Records), Agency: Marshall Brevetz and Associates 1720 North La Brea Avenue Los Angeles, California 90046

Betty Wright (Alston Records) Agent: The Paragon Agency 1019 Walnut Street Macon, Georgia. Agent: Rodgers Redding

Syl Johnson (HI Records), Agent: Rodgers Redding. The Paragon Agency 1019 Walnut Street Macon, Georgia 31208

Benny Latimore (Glades Records), Agent: Rodgers Redding and Associates POB 4603 Macon, Georgia 31208.

William Bell (Mercury Records), Agent: The Paragon Agency 1019 Walnut Street Macon, Georgia 31208. Agent: Rodgers Redding.

Bobby Blue Bland (ABC Dunhill Records), Agency: ABC Booking Corporation 445 Park Avenue New York NY 10023. Manager: T.B. Skarning.

James Brown (Polydor Records), Agent: James Brown Enterprises 850 Seventh Avenue Suite 703-706 New York NY. 10019.

The JBs w/bass guitarist **Bootsy Collins** (People Records), Agent: James Brown Enterprises 850 Seventh Avenue Suite 703-706 New York NY. 10019.

Southside Movement (20th CenturyRecords) Agent/Management: J.R. Vanleer 8255 Sunset Blvd Los Angeles, California.

Mark IV (Mercury Records) Agent: Rodgers Redding. Agency: The Paragon Agency 1019 Walnut Street Macon, Georgia 31208

Brass Construction (United Artists Records) Agent/Manager: Jeff Lane 1700 Broadway New York, NY 10019. 212-757-4534. Moondock Productions Chicago, Illinois.

CANDI STATON

As a result of all the bookings and promotions, the display of PR photographs on the walls at Kelly's continued to expand. The roll out for recording artists in 1971 was well underway for Kelly's Nite Limit. On July 19, 1971, Clifford Kelly contacted The Paragon Agency in Macon to book Arthur Conley, Candi Staton, Eddie Floyd, Percy Sledge, Clarence Carter, and Tyrone Davis.

On July 25, 1971, Clifford Kelly received the first contract for Clarence Carter. The deposit and signed contract from Mr. Kelly was received by Paragon on August 4, 1971. However, there was conflict with the scheduled dates for the other five artists. All of the artists were scheduled back to back at Kelly's Nite Limit every other week: Tyrone Davis on July 31, 1971, Arthur Conley on August 21, 1971, Candie Staton on August 25, 1971, Eddie Floyd on September 3, 1971, and Percy Sledge on September 5, 1971.

There were issues with the Rider's list of accommodations between Clifford Kelly and Clarence Carter. As a result, the contract for Clarence Carter was canceled along with all proposed bookings for the five other artists. Nevertheless, the contracts were eventually reissued as all artists were rescheduled and booked to perform at Kelly's Nite Limit over the next two years. All artists had previous and ongoing hits on Billboard's R&B Chart and the Hot 100 Chart.

1. Arthur Conley: Sweet Soul Music #2 R&B, #2 Pop (ATCO Records) 1967
2. Candi Staton: Stand By Your Man: #4 R&B, #24 Pop (Fame Records) 1970
3. Eddie Floyd: Knock On Wood: No #1 R&B (Stax Records) 1966
4. Percy Sledge: When A Man Loves A Woman #1 R&B #1 Pop (Atlantic Records) 1966
5. Clarence Carter: PATCHES #2 RB #4 Pop (Atlantic Records) 1970
6. Tyrone Davis: Turn Back the Hands of Time #1 R&B, #3 Pop (DaKar Records) 1970

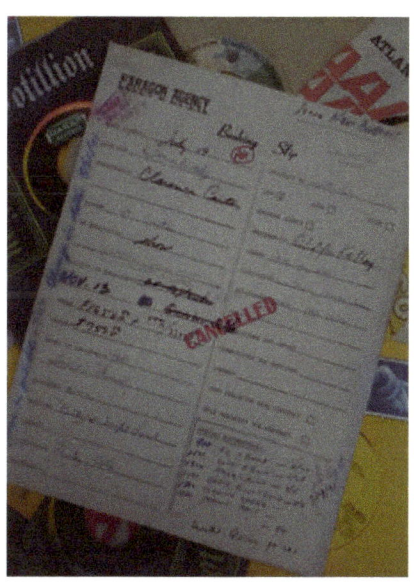

Memorabilia: *Booking Slip (Paragon Agency 1971), Promotional portraits (QBC, Warner Bros, Stax, American Best Artist, Walden Artist and Promotions) original recordings with company sleeves (ATCO, Stax, Warner, Atlantic, Cotillion, and Dakar) (Provided by Kelly's Nite Limit)*

Clifford Kelly: The Curb Master

By 1971, Clifford Kelly Sr. completed approximately a decade of subcontracting in Central Florida, primarily in Brevard and Orange Counties. The commercial and suburban development of Cape Canaveral, Merritt Island, Walt Disney World, and NASA proved to be financially beneficial for his very own Kelly's Curb Master Construction Company. The construction of Walt Disney World occurred from May 1967 to September 1971. As only one of numerous subcontractors, Clifford Kelly Sr. and his laborers specialized in the formation of curbs, flats, foundations, driveways, and sidewalks only for these Central Florida developments. On October 1, 1971, Clifford Sr. and his wife Margurie Kelly took their grandchildren Tony Doster, Sibyl Kelley, and Antonio Jones to the "Opening Day" ceremony at Walt Disney World in Orlando, Florida. Thousands of families attended Day One for the grand opening of the brand new theme park. Clifford Kelly always treated his extended family to a day at Disney whenever they visited him in Lawtey. Walt Disney World was his go to vacation destination for his family.

THE 1970S: MARGURIE W. KELLY VS THE FLORIDA DIVISION OF BEVERAGE

Clifford Kelly Jr.: Hooray for West Hollywood!

After an honorable discharge from the U.S. Air Force three years prior, it was always the dream of Sergeant Clifford Kelly Jr. to live and work on the west coast. Fate intervened as Sgt Kelley was offered another job with Lockheed Aircraft in Los Angeles, California. His wife Maggie chose to remain in Georgia. Clifford Jr. accepted the position as an Aircraft Mechanic with all expenses paid as he transitioned into his new life. Due to his dashing good looks and slender physique, Clifford Jr. also worked as a model in Hollywood. Clifford Kelly Jr. and Maggie Spann parted ways as friends. She resided in Decatur, Georgia, where she worked for Southern Bell/AT&T for the next fifty-three years.

AGE: 28
HEIGHT: 5' 11"
WEIGHT: 150 Lbs.
HAIR: Black
EYES: Brown

Military Services For Bobby and Ronnie Kelly

In June 1972, at age 17, Bobby King Kelly graduated from Bradford County High School. He was eager to leave his hometown of Lawtey, Florida, for a new life. He wanted to forget about the difficulty of transitioning into an integrated school district. A system in which his older brother Jerome Kelly was suspended after a school riot two years prior. Anxious and impatient he submitted a parental consent form to enlist with the U.S. Navy six weeks before his 18th birthday. On October 10, 1972, Bobby Kelly was entrained at NSGL: Naval Station Great Lakes, at Lake, Illinois. It's the Navy's largest training installation and the home of its Boot Camp. Six weeks later, in November, he celebrated his 18th birthday. He became an Hm3 Hospital Corpsman 3rd Class, at Naval Station Norfolk in Virginia.

The Navy Hospital Corps service members are deployed as combat medics for the Marines. He served aboard the USS America (CV66) in Athens, Greece. He received an honorable discharge three years later. Upon returning to Florida, Bobby Kelly made his home in Jacksonville. He became the father of three sons and a daughter: Bobby Jr., Justin, Justice, and Corey.

Bobby K. Kelly

Photograph provided by Marylou Kelly Williams

Private Jerome S. Kelly

Photograph provided by Marylou Kelly Williams

Jerome Sims Kelly, nicknamed "Ronnie Kelly," enlisted with the U.S. Army on July 20, 1972. He was stationed at Fort Jackson, South Carolina; Fort Bragg, North Carolina; and Kimpo Air Base in Seoul, Korea. While stationed in Korea, Jerome Kelly commissioned an artist to create an oil-on-canvas portrait of his mother, Margurie Kelly. The painting was inspired by a photograph of her taken in 1962.

THE 1970S: MARGURIE W. KELLY VS THE FLORIDA DIVISION OF BEVERAGE

Photograph of Mrs. Margurie Kelly (left) was provided by Emma Kelly Strong

The oil-on-canvas photograph (right was) provided by Clifford Kelly Jr. The original picture of Mrs. Kelly was photographed at Bullington Studio and Gift Shop in Starke, Florida

Once completed, the oil-on-canvas portrait was shipped to his mother in Lawtey, where it was displayed as the centerpiece of her home. Due to medical issues, Jerome Kelly served only two years of his enlistment. He obtained the National Defense Medal and received an Honorable Discharge on September 11, 1974. Upon return to the United States, Jerome Kelly settled in Albany, Georgia, where he met and married the love of his life, Laura Alexander. She's the daughter of Eunice and Ernestine Carroll of Dougherty County, Georgia. Jerome and Laura Kelly had two children: a son named Jerome Anthony Kelly and a daughter named Vakela Lynette Kelly. The family made their home in Albany, Georgia.

Photographs provided by the collection of Mrs. Margurie Williams Kelly

Seasons Change with King Floyd

Memorabilia: Signed contract, rider and original recording of "Grove Me" on Chimneyville Records was provided by Kelly's Nite Limit

For years, Mr. and Mrs. Kelly had black berries, raspberries, and three large fruit trees of oranges, dates, and grapes on their property. There were also trees of Palm and Magnolias, which blossomed every summer. Immaculate hedges of Boxwood Evergreen lined the front of their home and driveway. Every Spring, the yard blossomed with sweet grass and thick, lush wild clover. In 1972, their granddaughter, 8-year-old Sibyl Kelly, and her cousins, Tony Doster (age 9), Antonio Jones (age 6), and Mischel Bright (age 6), would often eat the fruit and berries. The magnolias had a fresh sweet aroma like ginger and cotton candy. The children learned from their 11-year-old cousin, Judy Bright, how to pull the inner stem from the magnolias and eat the nectar without losing a single petal. It was midsummer in East Lawtey, and Clifford Kelly remained steadfast in his commitment to providing live entertainment at his café, Kelly's Nite Limit.

On July 11, 1972, Clifford Kelly contacted The Paragon Agency to book a young singer, named King Floyd, from New Orleans, Louisiana. The deposit was paid, and the show was scheduled for August 4, 1972.

The artist's biggest hit single "Groove Me" ranked #1 on Billboard's R&B Chart and sold a million copies two years before. The RIAA awarded him a gold record in December that same year. His follow-up hit "Baby Let Me Kiss You" climbed to #5 on Billboard's R&B Chart.

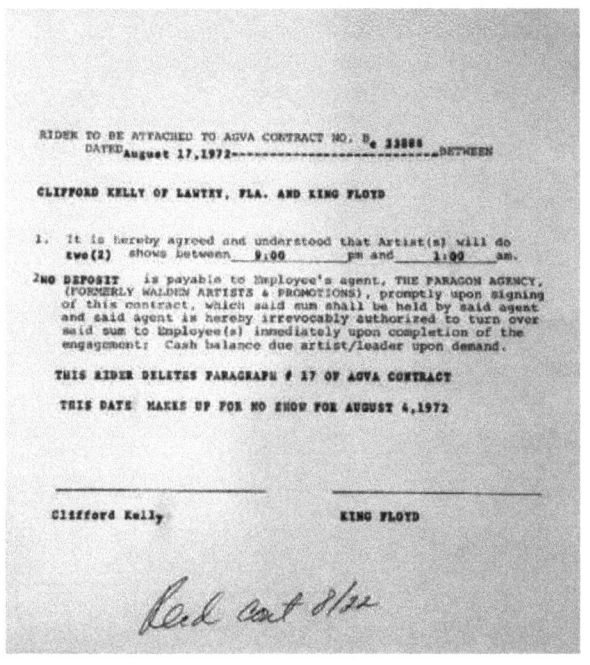

It is unknown as to what truly happened, but King Floyd was a no show for his performance. On August 17, 1972, a new contract was issued to make up for the "no show" on August 4th.

Under the new contract, King Floyd was scheduled to perform at Kelly's Nite Limit on September 30, 1972. Mr. Floyd and his musicians arrived early that Saturday morning. So early that Mr. Kelly's grandchildren along with their cousins were inside the venue running around and playing during the sound check. During rehearsal, King Floyd appeared bare-chested, wearing a gold chain and tan pants. His afro was neatly shaped as he sat on the stage guard rail facing the musicians. Suddenly, he stood up and started singing to the children as if he were performing to a live audience. Later that evening, it would be another historic night as King Floyd performed live in Lawtey, Florida.

In 1973, Clifford Kelly promoted Archie Bell and the Drells to perform at Kelly's Nite Limit. They were an R&B vocal group of musicians from Houston, Texas. They were known primarily for their hit soul single titled "Tighten Up," five years prior. The song topped #1 on Billboard's R&B and Pop Chart. The recording also received an RIAA gold certification for selling one million copies. Additional hit records followed, including "Let's Groove" and "It's Gonna Be a Showdown." It was on a Saturday morning in the Spring of 1973 when the musical group arrived in Lawtey. The band set up their equipment and completed the sound check. Yet, it was still several hours before the time of their show at Kelly's. The musicians were outside while the Kelly grandchildren were playing in the front yard. The band members came over and played a friendly game of flag football right there in the parking lot with the Kelly grandchildren: Sibyl Kelley (age 8), Tony Doster (age 9) and Antonio Jones (age 6). Since there were no actual flags for anyone to use, they played a game of touch football instead. The musicians could not believe how well Sibyl understood the game because after all she was just a little girl. History truly repeats itself. For a pastime, Etta James and her musicians went fishing with Clifford Jr. before her show at Kelly's in 1958. Tina Turner took the Kelly children to get ice cream before her show at Kelly's in 1960. Fast forward to 1973, and you'll find Archie Bell and the Drells playing a fun game of touch football with the Kelly grandchildren in the parking lot of Kelly's Nite Limit.

Memorabilia: Promotional portrait of Archie Bell and The Drells (Atlantic Records) and Emma Kelly standing at the Wall inside Kelly's Nite Limit. Promotions for the group were underway.

Kelly, Parker and West
A Friendship and Partnership

Lee Parker, a graduate of Jackson State University, was a professional Record Agent and Blues Music Promoter. He worked under contract for T&K Records, Malaco Records, Capitol Records, and JIVE Records. As an Independent Consultant, his primary objective was to ensure that an artist's latest recording(s) were played on numerous radio stations in the United States. He was also the General Manager of Club 295 on Lem Turner Road in Jacksonville, Florida. The night club was founded by Mr. Emory Robinson. By 1973, Lee Parker began attending shows at Kelly's Nite Limit with his entourage of friends. Clifford Kelly would always have a special table for Mr. Parker and his guests. Clifford Kelly and Lee Parker became friends over their shared interest in soulful blues music recording artists and concert promotions. For the next couple of years, they collaborated and invested together in several shows. Their partnership featured the following recording artists at Kelly's Nite Limit: Denise LaSalle, Little Milton, Tyrone Davis, Benny Latimore, Joe Simon, ZZ Hill, and Bobby Blue Bland.

Denise LaSalle was from Jackson, Madison County, Tennessee. Her hit record "Trapped by A Thing Called Love" was originally released in 1971 by Westbound Records. The song ascended to #1 spot on Billboard's R&B Chart and #13 on Billboard's Pop Chart. The recording sold over a million copies and was certified gold by the Recording Industry Association of America (RIAA) on November 30, 1971. In 1972, she followed up with two Billboard R&B hits "Now Run Tell That" at #3 and "A Man Sized Job" reached #4.

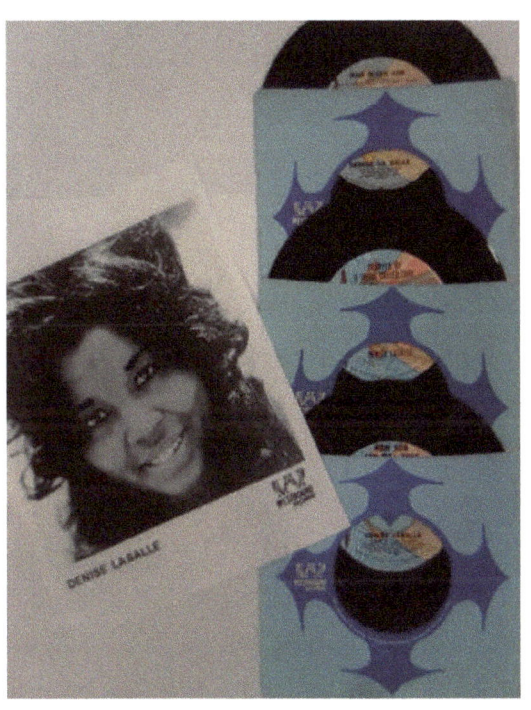

Memorabilia: Original recordings, company sleeves, promotional portrait (Westbound Records), and print music (Screen Gems) for Denise Lasalle, provided by Kelly's Nite Limit

Z.Z. Hill from Dallas, Texas performed at Kelly's Nite Limit on Sept 9, 1972. The following year, he was booked for a repeat performance for two nights. The first show was on April 21, 1973, at Kelly's. The next performance was promoted for the Eldorado Club in Live Oak, Florida on April 22nd. Z.Z. Hill released sixteen albums and scored 10 Billboard R&B Top 40 hits over the course of his career. His bestselling album titled "Down Home" on Malaco Records remained on Billboard's Soul Music Albums Chart for two years.

Memorabilia: *Original signed contract (The Paragon Agency) promotional image, original recording, and picture sleeve (United Artists) for Z.Z. Hill, provided by Kelly's Nite Limit*

Joe Simon was from the Bay of Richmond, California. His biggest hits included three songs (ranked #1 on Billboard's R&B Chart) for Spring Records: "Power of Love" (1972), "Drowning in The Sea of Love" (1972), and "Get Down, Get Down (Get on the Floor)" (1975). The songs were produced by Kenny Gamble and Leon Huff. Known as Gamble & Huff, they were a prolific songwriting duo who created the music genre of Philadelphia Soul or The Sound of Philadelphia. All three recordings on the Spring Records label sold over one million copies and were certified gold by the RIAA. Mr. Simon had fifty-one Billboard R&B/Pop hit records over the course of his career.

*Memorabilia by Spring/Event Records for Joe Simon
provided by Kelly's Nite Limit*

Benny Latimore, professionally known as "LATIMORE," was from Charleston, Bradley County, Tennessee. His hit single "Let's Straighten It Out" reached #1 on Billboard's R&B Chart and #31 on Billboard's Hot 100 Chart in November 1974. He followed up with more hits, including "Keep The Home Fire Burnin'" (#5 R&B, 1975) and "Somethin' 'Bout' Cha" (#7 R&B, 1976). He recorded for the Glades Records label, which was distributed by RCA Records.

Memorabilia: Promotional portrait and original recording with company picture sleeve (RCA Records) for Benny Latimore, provided by Kelly's Nite Limit

Tyrone Davis, from Chicago, Illinois, scored three #1 hits on Billboard's R & B chart for Dakar Records, beginning with "Can I Change My Mind" in 1968, which was certified Gold on February 24, 1969. "Turn Back the Hands of Time" (1970) was certified gold by the RIAA on May 4, 1970. "Turning Point" (1975) reached #1 on February 7, 1976. "Give It Up (Turn It Loose)," released by Columbia Records, peaked at #2 on Billboard's R&B Chart on October 2, 1976. Starting in 1968, fourteen of his recordings reached the Top 10 on Billboard's R&B Chart over the next fifteen years. Mr. Davis scored a total of forty-three hits on Billboard's R&B Chart over the course of his career.

Memorabilia: Original print advertisement for "Can I Change My Mind" appeared in Cash Box Magazine on November 30, 1968, with original recordings on Dakar Records. All collectables for Tyrone Davis were provided by Kelly's Nite Limit

THE 1970S: MARGURIE W. KELLY VS THE FLORIDA DIVISION OF BEVERAGE

In the summer of 1975, Clifford Kelly booked and promoted Soul legend Tyrone Davis for three consecutive shows. On June 27th the performance was at The Silver Lock Club in Coleman, Florida. June 28th at Kelly's Nite Limit in Lawtey. June 29th, the performance was at the historic and iconic Club Eaton of Eatonville, Florida.

Club Eaton was founded in 1946 by prominent businessman Condor Merritt. All three shows were booked by Phil Walden Artists and Promotions of Macon, Georgia.

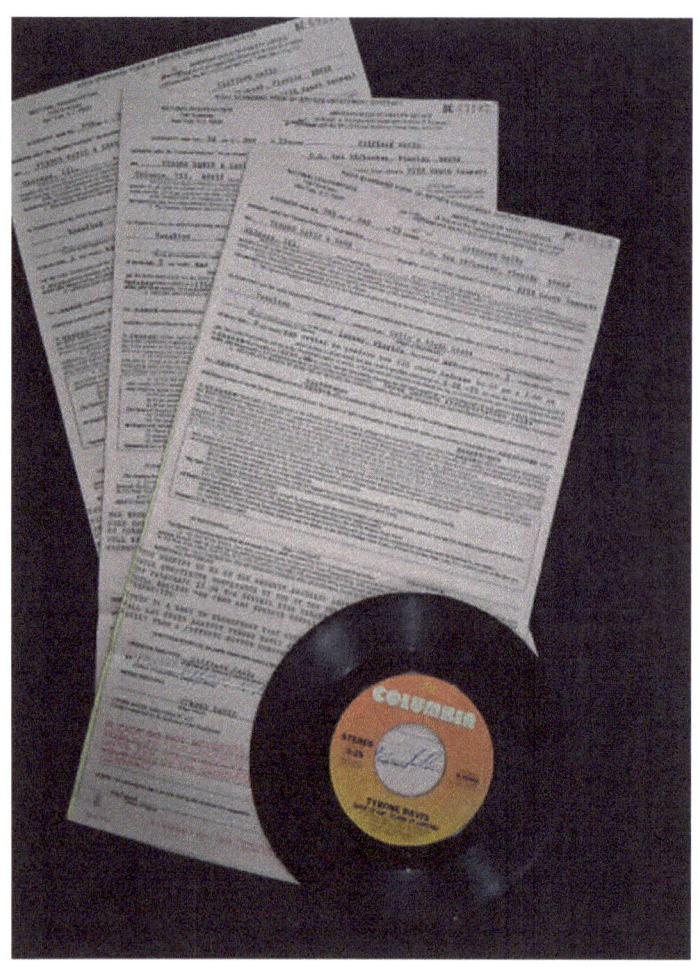

Memorabilia: *Original booking contracts for Tyrone Davis with an original recording of "Give It Up, Turn It Loose" on Columbia Records were provided by Kelly's Nite Limit*

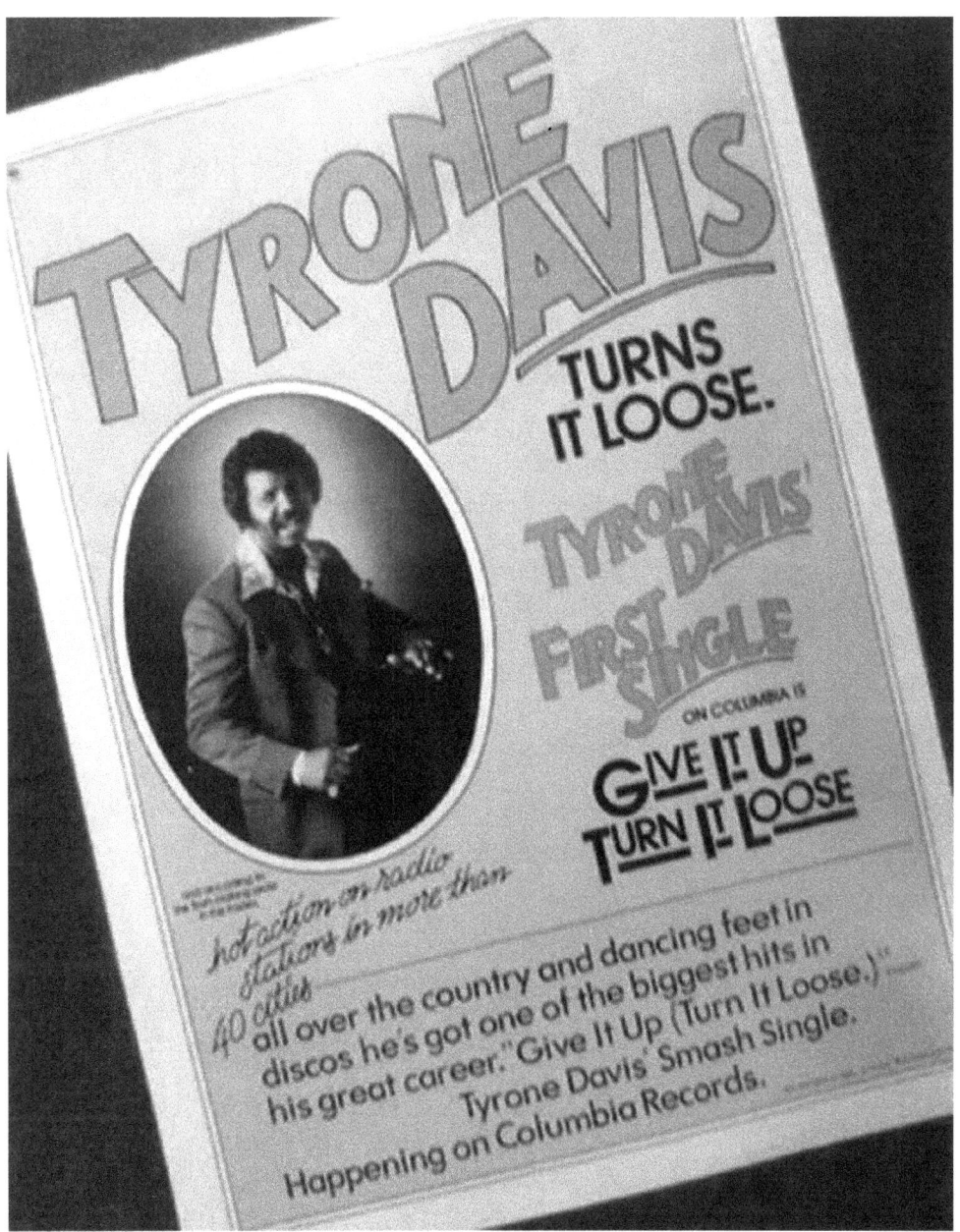

Memorabilia: "Hot action on radio stations in more than 40 cities." The original print advertisement of "Give It Up, Turn It Loose" for Tyrone Davis appeared in Cashbox Magazine on August 21, 1976 and was provided by Mrs. Tracy Faulkner Wynn

THE 1970S: MARGURIE W. KELLY VS THE FLORIDA DIVISION OF BEVERAGE

Memorabilia: Original advertisement "Stax Has Got the Blues" for Little Milton appeared in Rolling Stone Magazine on August 30, 1973. Provided by Kelly's Nite Limit

Mr. James Milton Campbell, known professionally as "Little Milton" was from Memphis, Tennessee. In 1965, he scored a #1 hit for three weeks on Billboard's R&B Chart for his recording: "Were Gonna Make It" on Checker Records. He released additional R&B hits such as "Who's Cheating Who?" #4 (1965), "Feel So Bad" #7 (1966), "Baby I Love You" #6 (1970), and "That's What Love Will Make You Do" #9 (1971). Over the course of his career, Little Milton had seventeen Billboard R&B Top 40 hits. He received two Grammy Award Nominations for Best Blues Contemporary Album and Best Traditional Blues Recording.

Memorabilia: Promotional portrait (Camil Productions) provided by the Collection of Margurie W. Kelly. Original recording (Checker Records) provided by Kelly's Nite Limit

It was during their heyday as each recording artist had successful shows in Lawtey under the partnership of Clifford Kelly & Lee Parker. Artists: Hill, Simon, Lasalle, Latimore, and Davis were all booked for repeat performances at Kelly's Nite Limit later in the decade and beyond. Lee Parker and Clifford Kelly were also friends with Jerry "DJ" West, entrepreneur of DJ's Record Shop in Jacksonville, Florida. The business was formerly known as DJs Records & Tapes. The iconic music store has been a pillar on Jacksonville's Westside for fifty-five years and counting. A place where music fans could literally spend the day looking through the massive collection of old school "still-in-the-shrink-wrap" albums/LPs, cassettes, cds, DVDs, 45 rpm singles, vhs movies, posters, videos and conveniently purchase concert tickets. Jerry West was also an agent who rated music for Billboard Magazine, Jet Magazine, and The Urban Network.

Clifford Kelly Sr. met Jerry West in 1968, the same year the store opened for business. Jerry West began selling show tickets at his store for TicketMasters a few years later. Clifford Kelly passed by DJs Records & Tapes each time he went to purchase airtime at WERD/WZAZ on King Street for one of his shows. Well, fate would have it that Clifford Kelly stopped by the record store one day and met with Jerry West. Clifford wanted Jerry to sell tickets for Kelly's Nite Limit at the record store too. Jerry agreed and a new friendship was born. In the early days, Clifford would stop by the record store every Sunday afternoon to simply hang out and tell a few jokes. Jerry West remembers Clifford Kelly as being what he refers to as a "sportsman" who was always a lot of fun to be around. Clifford Kelly was sharply dressed on the night of a show at Kelly's Nite Limit. However, Jerry West remembered how Clifford Kelly would come to the record store dressed in Overalls: one side buckle or button attached over his

Lee Parker

Founder of the Downhome Blues Festival and Brimstone Music Group was inducted into the Blues Music Hall of Fame as a Master Blues Promoter in Memphis, Tennessee May 10, 2023. Photograph provided by Mr. Lee Parker shoulder, with the other one dropped down over his chest. They would just talk about life and how Clifford made it to Lawtey from Georgia on a freight train and decided to stay. Jerry was more than just one of the ticket agents associated with Clifford Kelly. He was a friend who used to travel from time to time with Mr. Kelly, promoting an upcoming show or ride to the local barber shop. They were two men raised in small towns in Georgia who found a way to start a successful business to earn a living for themselves. Clifford Kelly always bartered with his ticket agents as compensation. If the agent were a business owner, Mr. Kelly would provide free tickets and a reserved table for them at the nightclub. Jerry West sold show tickets for Kelly's Nite Limit for years but never attended a single show at the venue nor any other nightclub. Jerry West was surrounded with music all the time at his record store. Since he was an agent for Billboard Magazine, many recording artists would come to the record store to see Jerry in person. In retrospect, Jerry West and Lee Parker understood just how much Clifford Kelly Sr. loved his own cultural music and had a special spirit for helping blues artists and musicians.

Jerry West received six Platinum Sale Awards presented to him by the Recording Industry Association of America (RIAA). He also received special recognition awards from Billboard Hot 100, Billboard Hot Black 100, and The RAL (RUSH Associated Labels). All photographs provided by Kelly's Nite Limit. (Pictured on August 8, 2023)

THE 1970S: MARGURIE W. KELLY VS THE FLORIDA DIVISION OF BEVERAGE

Awards line the walls for Jerry West at his historic music store on Jacksonville Florida's Westside (August 8, 2023)

Clifford Kelly: More ROAD TRIPs!
"Let's Go!"

When the Kelly family prepared for a road trip one thing was for certain. If you were riding in the car with Clifford Kelly Sr, you better be ready to go well before he headed towards the door. On the day of the road trip, he would remain in bed while everyone else got showered and dressed. Once everyone was done and waiting in the living room or Florida room, he'd get up to get dressed. He would shave, shower, put on one of his dress casual shirts and pants, a pair of Stacy Adams and a fedora. He'd exit his bedroom, then walk through his son's bedroom. You could hear his footsteps shake the dishes in the china closet as he walked across the hard wood floor through the dining room. That's when you heard him say Let's Go!

If you were riding with Clifford Kelly Sr. on a road trip, you had no choice but to listen to his music only. In the early 1970s, the recording artists he enjoyed were played on an eight-track cassette tape in his car. You had to listen to Joe Simon traveling to Orlando and Tyrone Davis back to Lawtey. You had to listen to Joe Simon going to Cocoa-Rockledge, and Tyrone Davis back to Lawtey. You had to listen to Joe Simon riding along to Sarasota and Tyrone Davis back to Lawtey… on repeat. From Lawtey, these frequent road trips were 150 plus miles one way. When riding with Clifford Kelly Sr., you had the option(s) of 1. Ride! 2. Listen! 3. Hush! 4. Walk! That's just the way it was, and you had no say in the matter. Mr. Clifford "Schoolboy" Kelly fanatically loved his own cultural music. He booked and promoted Joe Simon, Tyrone Davis, Clarence Carter, and Bobby Blue Bland, repeatedly to perform at his nightclub Kelly's Nite Limit, time and time and time again…and you had NO SAY in the matter period.

Kelly Family Weddings 1973 and 1974

In 1973, the campus of the former Charles C. Anderson JHS became a faith based community vocational center housing work release inmates. The facility was renamed the Lawtey Correctional Institution a few years later. On Mar 29, 1973, after nearly a decade, involvement of the United States in the Vietnam War officially ended as the last military combat unit left South Vietnam. Jean Kelly's future husband, Ernest Copeland Sr., served in Vietnam for four years. Upon his return to Florida, Ernest Copeland proposed marriage to Jean, and she accepted his ring.

It was also during this time that Clifford Kelly was informed about a new movie titled "Cleopatra Jones." For unknown reasons, he was convinced that one of his favorite singers, Mr. Joe Simon, was starring in the film. His son Clifford Jr., who was employed with Lockheed Aircraft, was a bachelor again and lived in Hollywood, California. It was Clifford Jr.'s dream to live on the West Coast.

Mr. and Mrs. Kelly planned for their vacation to Los Angeles to see their son. They planned to attend the new movie and visit other family members residing in Inglewood. The film was released on July 13, 1973. Mr. and Mrs. Kelly could not attend the movie during premiere week because their daughter Jean Kelly was getting married on July 16, 1973, to Mr. Ernest Copeland of Raiford, Florida. His parents are Willie and Florine Copeland, also of Raiford. Ernest Copeland was the founder of Copeland Construction Company in Jacksonville. Ernest Copeland and Margaret Jean Kelly were married at the Bradford County Courthouse in Starke, Florida.

Their wedding reception was held at Kelly's Nite Limit hosted by Emma Kelly, a fourth grade teacher at Starke Elementary School and Jean's elder sister. Emma's new boyfriend Benjamin Strong was "In the Back" enjoying some refreshments but provided Emma with assistance as needed during the reception.

There was no live music nor DJ. It was an elegant midsummer dress casual reception with light refreshments and lots of gifts. Ernest Copeland Sr was the founder of Copeland Construction Company in Jacksonville, Florida. Their sons Brian Copeland and Kenny Copeland were born a few years later.

Like many indigenous men of Lawtey, Benjamin Strong, the son of Enoch Strong Jr. and Maxie Belle Ford-Strong of Lawtey, was employed by EI Dupont Nemours off County Rd 230, located about 5 miles east of Kelly's Nite Limit in the Kingsley Lake region. Emma Louise Kelly and Benjamin Franklin Strong were married the following year at the Kelly home with a reception afterward at Kelly's Nite Limit. Emma's younger sister Margaret Jean Copeland was the Matron of Honor.

Mrs. Emma Kelly Strong (on the left) and Mrs. Margaret Jean Kelly Copeland (on the right) were photographed at the Kelly home in Lawtey, Florida December 23, 1974

Kelly Family Vacation

Just a few short weeks after the wedding reception for Jean and Ernest Copeland, Clifford and Margurie Kelly went on vacation. For some reason, Clifford went to see his sister Harridelle Bright at her home. They took a few pictures together and said their goodbyes. Then, it was time as Mr. and Mrs. Kelly along with their granddaughter Sibyl, age 9, departed from Lawtey on August 10, 1973. It was their first cross-country journey to Los Angeles, California. The drive across Interstate 10 West was smooth from coast to coast. The family arrived in Los Angeles on August 13, 1973 on a Monday night around 7:00 p.m. Mr. Kelly was so overwhelmed by the Los Angeles infrastructure that he stopped at a Mobil gas station to call his son Clifford Jr. for directions. Clifford Jr. arrived at the gas station and the family followed along to his apartment in Hollywood. The next morning the Kellys toured NBC Studios in Burbank, California. They were on the set of Adam 12, the pool setting for McMillan & Wife and other shows on the network.

Mr. and Mrs. Clifford Kelly Sr. and their granddaughter, Sibyl, at NBC Studios in Burbank, California on August 14, 1973

Next the family traveled down to Tijuana, Baja, Mexico. The marketplace was super crowded with locals and tourists. For souvenirs, Mrs. Kelly purchased a huge 3.5-ft tan and orange clay flowerpot with a catch plate and brass holding rack. Next Mr. Kelly picked up a 3-foot gray-silver colored stone-pottery lion with a pedestal. Their granddaughter, Sibyl, selected a set of multicolored outdoor hanging lamps.

Clifford Kelly Sr. was amused with the high level foot traffic of panhandlers selling any and everything on the street. He gave one lady dollars 5 for a pack of Doublemint chewing gum. When she realized he gave her cash money instead of a few coins like most people did, she came back over to him asking for more money. He gave the lady another dollar and said, "that's it." Clifford Kelly Sr. walked off laughing picking his teeth with a half torn matchbook. He grinned and chuckled as he impersonated the lady's accent, body language, and mannerism right there on the street in front of his wife and granddaughter.

The Kellys shopping at the marketplace in Tijuana, Baja, Mexico. August 1973. Photograph provided from the collection of Margurie Williams Kelly

THE 1970S: MARGURIE W. KELLY VS THE FLORIDA DIVISION OF BEVERAGE

Then, Friday evening arrived for the family to attend the new hit movie "Cleopatra Jones." Mr. Kelly was a loyal music fan who was ready for some Joe Simon action on film. As the movie began, Mr. Kelly heard the vocals and music of the artist. He paid close attention waiting for Joe Simon to appear. Mr. Simon however, was not in the movie at all. As it turned out, Joe Simon wrote, produced, and performed the theme song for the movie soundtrack only. The song was titled "Theme from Cleopatra Jones." On Billboard the song ascended to #3 R&B, #18 Pop. It was a letdown of disappointment for Clifford Kelly of sorts. After the movie, the family ventured out for dinner and attended an outdoor concert featuring the music group WAR. It was a long night, and everyone was over it.

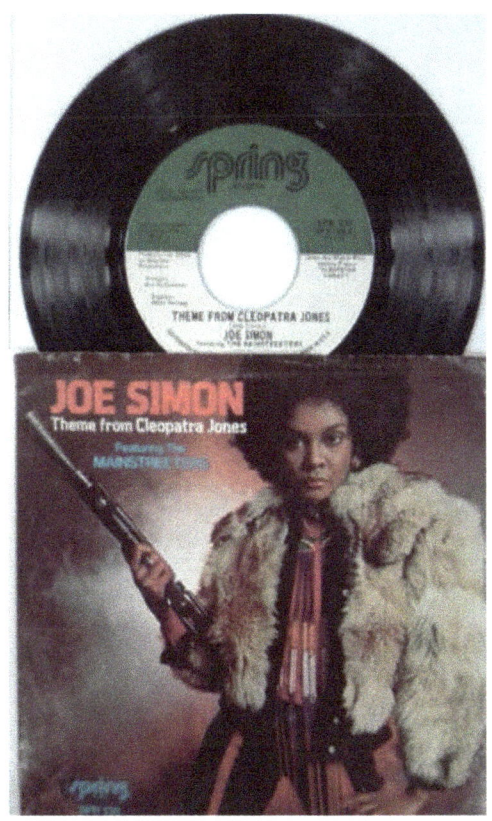 

Memorabilia: Promotional portrait, original Spring Event recording, and company picture sleeve (Theme from Cleopatra Jones) for Joe Simon provided by Kelly's Nite Limit

The Kellys photographed after the movie and concert in Los Angeles: (Clifford Sr., Sibyl age 9 and Clifford Jr.) August 1973

Next, there was a nice family dinner with Walter and Alwena Sample in Inglewood. The Samples lived across the street from the LA Forum, where the Lakers played their home games. Alwena is Clifford Kelly's niece and daughter of Robert Willie Jordan, Clifford's younger brother. Walter and Alwena Sample had two children named Al Sample (age 7), and Reginald Sample (aka Reggie; aged 10 months). Walter Sample was an RTD City Driver. Alwena Sample was an elementary school teacher of Spanish-speaking children in Los Angeles County. Alwena Jordan Sample worked for the Los Angeles Unified School District for thirty-five years. All good things come to an end. After seventy-two hours of driving on I-10 East, the Kellys returned to Lawtey and back to their lives.

Kelly's Nite Limit
The Show and Dance

Photograph of Clifford Kelly Sr. provided by Bobby Kelly Sr.

On March 25, 1974, Clifford Kelly booked one of his all-time favorite artists Mr. Bobby Blue Bland from Barretville, Shelby County, Tennessee. It would be approximately five months later until Mr. Bland's actual performance in Lawtey.

A true blues legend, Mr. Bland released a new record titled "I Wouldn't Treat a Dog the Way You Treated Me." It was also good business to promote the artist's latest record at the nightclub on the jukebox. Mrs. Kelly liked the song so much that she purchased a copy and wrote a jukebox strip for it herself. She had no way of knowing which new records Mr. Carter would provide next for the Piccolo. Just in case he did not bring Bobby Bland's latest record, she wanted to be prepared with a copy of her own.

THE 1970S: MARGURIE W. KELLY VS THE FLORIDA DIVISION OF BEVERAGE

Memorabilia: Original recording "I Wouldn't Treat a Dog" with company sleeve (ABC Dunhill Records) and promotional portrait for Bobby Blue Bland (ABC Booking Corp) provided by Kelly's Nite Limit

Clifford Kelly Sr., Owner & Founder of Kelly's Nite Limit

THE 1970S: MARGURIE W. KELLY VS THE FLORIDA DIVISION OF BEVERAGE

Memorabilia: Original print Ad of Bobby Blue Bland appeared in Billboard Magazine on October 20, 1973. Original recording (ABC Dunhill Records) provided by Kelly's Nite Limit

Memorabilia image for Bobby Williams and The MarKings, provided by Forced Exposure Arlington, MA

Monday through Friday, Clifford Kelly Sr. continued his rigorous work schedule as a subcontractor in Central Florida. The weekend, as always, was all about Kelly's Nite Limit or promotions at other venues throughout the State of Florida. It was also customary for Clifford Kelly and his business partners to book recording artists to perform at the following venues:

*Club 295 (Jacksonville, Florida)

*Club 436 (Altamonte Springs, Florida)

*Club 520 (Cocoa-Rockledge, Florida)

*Club 747 (Jacksonville, Florida)

*Club Casino (Lake City, Florida)

*Club Eaton (Eatonville, Florida)

*The Cedar Hills Armory (Jacksonville, Florida)

*The Eldorado Club (Live Oak, Florida)

*The High Hat Club (Deland, Florida)

*The Jai Alai Fronton (Daytona Beach, Florida)

*The Quarterback Club (Orlando, Florida)

*The Rainbow Club (Eatonville, Florida)

*The Silver Lock Club (Coleman, Florida)

*Vicks Supper Club (Palatka, Florida)

THE 1970S: MARGURIE W. KELLY VS THE FLORIDA DIVISION OF BEVERAGE

There was a heavy rotation of promotions going into the mid-1970s. Margurie Kelly signed contracts and corresponded with the agencies for all live shows. Clifford Kelly preferred to speak with the agent by phone or in person. Mrs. Kelly wrote all of her checks, notes, and letters in shorthand. She wrote a note on the back of the contract rider for blues recording artist Z.Z. Hill, dated April 5, 1973. Mrs. Kelly wrote the following message to Velma Redding, the widow of Otis Redding. Mrs. Velma Redding was a Booking Agent at The Paragon Agency.

"Dear Mrs. Redding: Here's $1,500 on ZZ. I will mail you the balance of deposit Saturday the 14th. Look for it by Monday the 16th and thank you kindly Mrs. Clifford Kelly P.O. Box 58 Lawtey, Florida."

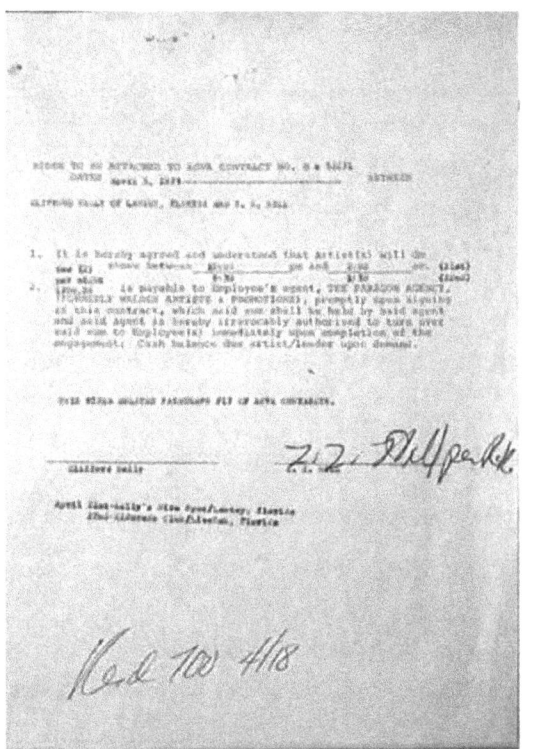 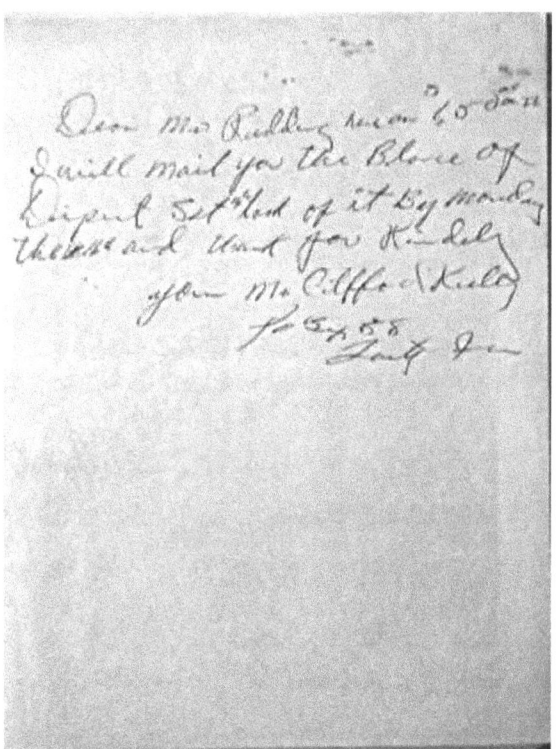

Memorabilia letters provided by Kelly's Nite Limit

THE 1970S: MARGURIE W. KELLY VS THE FLORIDA DIVISION OF BEVERAGE

Clifford Kelly received a letter dated April 9, 1974, from Rodgers Redding of the Paragon Agency. Mr. Redding wrote to inform Mr. Kelly of a schedule change for Millie Jackson due to a price increase for her concerts. In addition, he wrote to declare the status and availability of more recording artists for his area in Florida.

The artists were King Floyd, Bettye Swann, Syl Johnson, Tyrone Davis, Mel & Tim, William Bell, Otis Clay, Betty Wright, Willie & Anthony, Mark IV, Don Convay, The Manhattans, and Leon Haywood. Clifford Kelly was encouraged by Mr. Redding's letter to contact the agency to schedule more recording artists for the month of June.

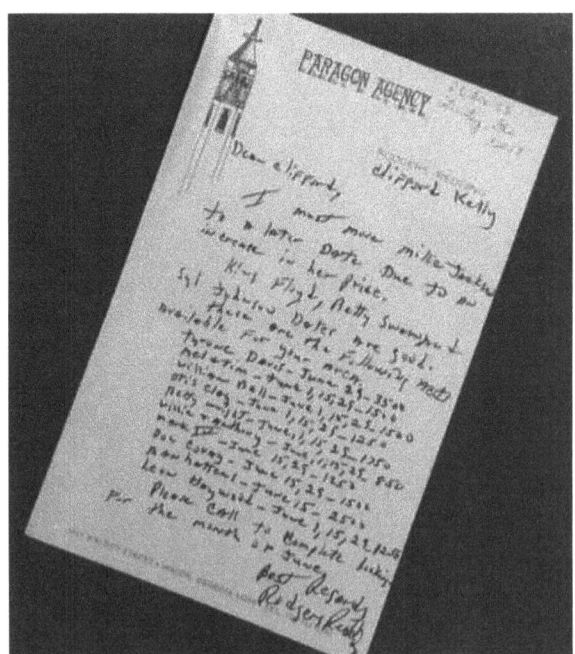 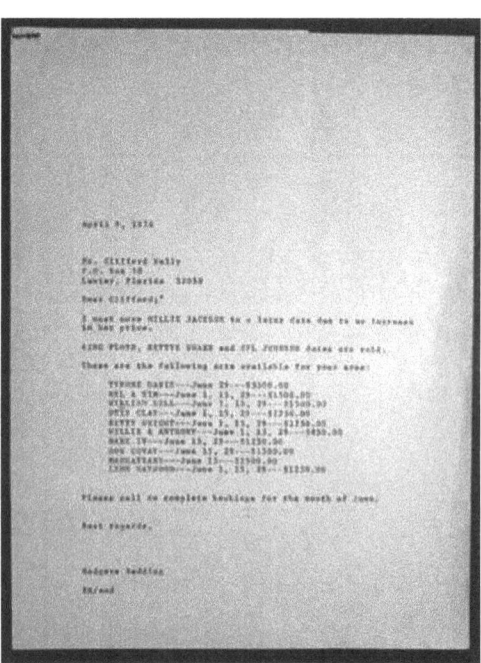

Memorabilia: Status Letters from Rodgers Redding to Clifford Kelly Sr., provided by Kelly's Nite Limit

Clifford Kelly also received a letter dated June 3, 1974, from Associated Booking Corporation (ABC) in regard to the upcoming shows for Melvin Jackson featuring Bobby Blue Bland. The shows were scheduled for the month of August. The status letter was sent as confirmation of a previous phone call between Clifford Kelly and TB Sharning, a Manager at ABC. Three contracts were included with the letter. Finally, after five months, it was show time for three nights at three venues. Clifford Kelly Sr. promoted legendary blues guitarist Melvin Jackson from Houston Texas, featuring Bobby Blue Bland to perform on Friday August 16th at Club Casino in Lake City, Florida. Saturday August 17th at Kelly's Nite Limit along with a Sunday night August 18th performance in Orlando. Bobby Blue Bland's latest recording was released nationally on July 25, 1974 titled "I Wouldn't Treat a Dog the Way You Treated Me." The recording was his 25th Billboard R&B Top 10 hit.

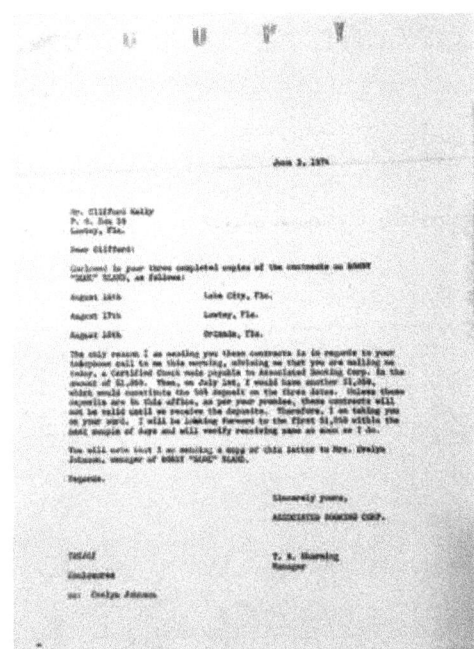 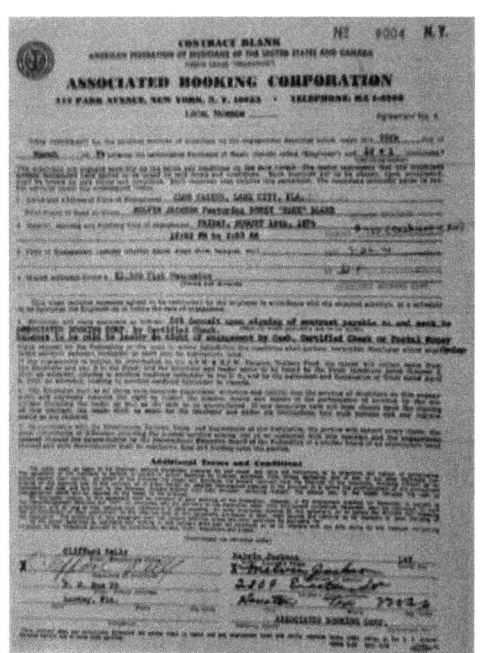

Memorabilia: A Letter & signed contract for Melvin Jackson featuring Bobby Blue Bland (ABC Booking Corp) provided from the collection of Margurie Williams Kelly

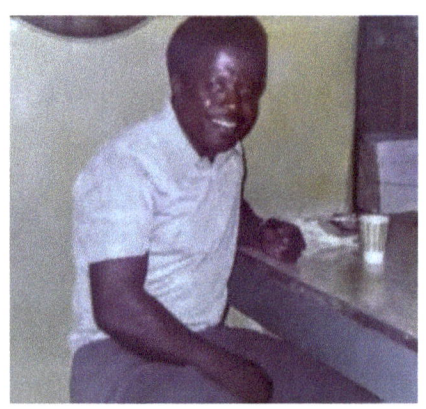

Photograph: Emmet Bright Jr. at Kelly's Nite Limit on March 30, 1975 provided by the Collection of Ernest Copeland Sr.

Emmett Bright Jr., is the brother-in-law of Clifford and Margurie Kelly. He and his wife Harridelle Taylor Bright celebrated their wedding reception at Kelly's Nite Limit nearly twenty years prior. He was a regular at Kelly's from the very beginning and saw many of the great artists perform there over the decades. However, not every artist booked to perform at Kelly's Nite Limit had a major record deal. Regional music groups and solo artists such as KUDU, Kracked Mirror, The One Man Band, The Four Counts, The Devastations, The Black Exotics, and Lawtey's very own Milton Floyd had their own following. KUDU from Jacksonville, Florida, were excellent musicians and extremely popular in North Florida. Due to their ability to sound almost identical to any R&B music artist on the charts, they normally drew a sizable audience for their show in Lawtey. Whenever requested under contract, Clifford Kelly booked KUDU as the backing band for recording artists who performed at Kelly's Nite Limit.

The year of 1975 was a benchmark for Soul Music as it transitioned into the Sound of Philadelphia also known as Disco Music. George McCrae from West Palm Beach, Florida was a gifted soul-singer with a first tenor falsetto that was heard around the world. He was booked and promoted by Clifford Kelly Sr. to perform his Billboard #1 R&B and Pop hit record titled "Rock Your Baby" on T&K Records. Mr. Kelly's business partner Lee Parker was an Independent Consultant for T&K Records. The recording sold over 10 million copies in over 50 countries. George McCrae also received a Grammy Award nomination for Best

THE 1970S: MARGURIE W. KELLY VS THE FLORIDA DIVISION OF BEVERAGE

R&B Vocal Performance-Male at the 17th Annual Grammy Awards in 1975. That was the year George McCrae performed in Lawtey at Kelly's Nite Limit.

The nightclub capacity of 1,000 people was overstuffed with music lovers. All seats and booths were sold; therefore, the huge dance floor at Kelly's became a general admission area. All of Mrs. Kelly's food was sold out. All drinks—beer, wine, juice, and sodas—were sold out all the way down to the rust and condensation at the bottom of the cooler. It was an epic night at Kelly's Nite Limit as George McCrae performed his multi-platinum selling hit record live on stage in Lawtey, Florida.

The night club and parking lot were a total wreck after the show. There was a sea of debris all over the property when the night ended. The next day, as he stared through the side door of his Florida Room, Clifford Kelly could not believe the condition of his property.

Memorabilia: Promotional portrait, recording (RCA Records, T&K Records) company sleeve (RCA, T&K), for George McCrae & Promotional portrait & recording (CAT/T&K Records) for Gwen McCrae provided by Kelly's Nite Limit

The show was so successful that after the cleanup, Clifford Kelly booked and promoted recording artist Gwen McCrae to perform next at Kelly's Nite Limit. Gwen McCrae from Pensacola, Florida, is the wife of George McCrae. She had a Billboard #1 R&B hit titled "Rockin Chair." The song reached #9 on Billboard's Hot 100 chart. The record was released in the Spring of 1975 on CAT Records, which was also a division of T&K Records. The recording is credited with vocals by her husband George as he dubbed a call and response overture from his hit recording "Rock Your Baby" with her hit record "Rockin Chair." Once again about two months after her husband George McCrae performed at Kelly's, the fans came back faithfully in support of her 1975 show.

On Saturday May 3, 1975, Clifford Kelly promoted William Bell from Memphis, Tennessee, to perform live at his place Kelly's Nite Limit. Mr. Bell was a bona fide soul music legend who recorded for Stax Records early in his career. William Bell was booked multiple times during the mid to late 1960s, usually for a Christmas show at Kelly's. "Everyday Will Be Like a Holiday" (1967), "Private Number" (1968), and "You Don't Miss Your Water" (1961) were among his most memorable recordings. Mr. Bell, who now recorded for Mercury Records, scored a mega hit on Billboard with a song titled "Tryin' to Love Two." The song reached #1 on Billboard's R&B Chart, #10 on the Hot 100, and sold over one million copies. Mr. Kelly was so pleased to see such a huge heyday size crowd at his place again. "Grown Folks," dressed to the nines, came out in droves to Kelly's that night. The show and attendance was a huge success with a shoulder-to-shoulder, standing-room-only audience. Every seat at Kelly's Nite Limit was filled to see and hear the smooth, soulful, golden, melodic vocals of Mr. William Bell.

THE 1970S: MARGURIE W. KELLY VS THE FLORIDA DIVISION OF BEVERAGE

Memorabilia: Recordings (Mercury Records and Stax Music) Promotional images (Stax/Universal Attractions) for William Bell provided by Kelly's Nite Limit

Jerome Kelly pictured at "The Wall" in front of the placard for William Bell's performance at Kelly's in 1975. Photograph provided by Marylou Kelly

Dorothy Moore was a fan favorite in East Lawtey. Even with the youth who would sing her version of Misty Blue as they walked down Kingsley Lake Road to the Lawtey Recreation Center also known as "The Rec" for program activities and lunch. The summer youth program was spearheaded by lifetime East Lawtey resident Mrs. Edna Belle Allen. The acoustics inside Kelly's Nite Limit riveted off the walls whenever the jukebox was playing. One could literally hear the music blasting from Kelly's down the road of Highway 225. Soul-singer Joe Simon recorded Misty Blue in 1972 for Spring Records. Dorothy Moore recorded the song in 1973. The recording was a jukebox and local radio sensation in the South for Ms. Moore in 1974. Clifford Kelly promoted Dorothy Moore from Jackson, Mississippi to perform her hit recording at Kelly's Nite Limit. Dorothy Moore performed before a standing-room-only audience during the early summer of 1975.

Every seat, booth, and every inch of the dance floor from the stage to the back wall of the side barroom was covered. Total gridlock inside and outside of the venue. Fans parked their cars 1/4 to ½ mile along both sides of highway 225 and walked back to the nightclub for Dorothy Moore's live performance.

Misty Blue by Dorothy Moore was released nationally in 1975 on Malaco Records. The song went to #2 on Billboard's R&B Chart and #3 on Billboard's Hot 100 selling millions of records around the world. At the 19th Annual Grammy Awards (Recording Academy), she was nominated for Best R&B Vocal Performance, Female for Misty Blue. The following year the Recording Academy nominated her hit single "I Believe You" in the same category as the previous year.

Memorabilia: Promotional portrait, original recording of Misty Blue (Malaco Records), and print music (Talmont Music Co.) for Dorothy Moore was provided by Kelly's Nite Limit

Shirley Brown performed her mega hit record at Kelly's Nite Limit in 1975 to a standing-room-only audience. After selling a million copies in eight weeks, the hit record titled "Woman to Woman" on the Truth/Stax label spent two weeks at #1 on Billboard's Hot Soul Singles chart in November 1974. From her album "Woman to Woman," the hit single crossed-over to Billboard's Hot 100 chart at #22. The song was also nominated for Best R&B Vocal Performance Female at the 17th Annual Grammy Awards in 1975.

Promotional portrait of Shirley Brown by Rodgers Redding and Associates, provided by Kelly's Nite Limit

A Blues Artist Encounter at Kelly's Nite Limit

MILLIE JACKSON

Also in 1975, Clifford Kelly promoted model-turned-soul-singer diva Ms. Millie Jackson—"The Queen of Extreme"—for a live performance at Kelly's Nite Limit. Born Mildred Virginia Jackson, she was a comedic, wild, and risque blues singer from New York City.

Three of her albums were certified gold by the RIAA. She also scored nineteen Billboard R&B Top 40 hits. Millie Jackson toured the world as a singer and actress. She was nominated for Best R&B Performance Female at the 17th Annual Grammy Awards. Jackson also hosted her radio show on KKDA of Dallas Texas for well over a decade.

ECKO Recording Star Chuck Roberson

It was also a landmark year for an upcoming recording artist named Chuck Roberson. He was a soul-singer from Madison, Florida, who just released his first single titled "Love Affair" in July 1975 on Albradella Records. An independent label where he enjoyed regional success in the Southern United States. Music promoter Johnny Terry worked for Soul music pioneer James Brown. Mr. Terry was a former member of The Famous Flames and The Drifters. After Johnny Terry heard the new song recorded by Chuck Roberson, he wanted to meet with the artist. "She was hot back then," as Roberson remembered Millie Jackson. Concert promoter Lee Parker remembered Ms. Jackson as well, he recalled, "She was hot as a firecracker, her records were selling."

On the night of the show at Kelly's Nite Limit, Johnny Terry brought Chuck Roberson to Lawtey to meet with Millie Jackson at the venue. The juke joint was packed out, and there was a lot of commotion but Millie and Chuck finally met. Millie Jackson agreed to tour with Chuck Roberson as her opening act. This tour led to a five-year contract with additional blues tours for Chuck Roberson. He became the opening act for B.B. King, Ray Charles, Johnny Taylor, Clarence Carter, Tyrone Davis, Denise LaSalle, Benny Latimore, and Bobby Blue Bland. Eventually Chuck Roberson had the pleasure of touring overseas as a solo artist. He performed at very elegant upscale clubs in Barcelona, Madrid, London, and Paris. Chuck Roberson was a very popular artist among blues fans, as he toured throughout the United States performing at clubs and blues festivals. Chuck Roberson performed twice at Kelly's Nite Limit. He recorded twenty-five albums over the course of his forty-five-year career. He was the founder of Cruise On Records and Desert Sound Records. In 2020, Chuck Roberson was honored with the Living Legend Award presented by Simply Entertainment Southern Soul Music Production Network.

Memorabilia: Placard for Chuck Roberson provided by Mrs. Patricia "Bonnie" Brown. Promotional portraits of Millie Jackson (Spring/Polydor) and Chuck Roberson (Ecko Records) provided by Kelly's Nite Limit

Clifford Kelly Sr. and Robert Austin Sr.: My Best Friend

Mr. & Mrs. Kelly with Mrs. Aretha Austin in Nassau, Bahamas (1975). Mr. Robert Austin is behind the camera. Photograph provided by Emma Kelly Strong

In August of 1975, the Kelly's planned their next much needed vacation. Mr. and Mrs. Kelly traveled to the Bahamas along with their good family friends Robert and Aretha Austin Sr. of Lawtey. Clifford Kelly Sr. and Robert Austin Sr. were the best of friends. They met early in life as they were employed by the railroad (Seaboard Air Line Railroad-SAL) back in the late 1940s. During their tenure at SAL, Clifford Sr. was a Laborer while Robert Sr. became a legendary Forman. Robert Austin Sr. was well known in the community for his efforts with helping others obtain employment for the company. Both men raised their families in Lawtey, and ironically, both men had sons named Ronnie and Bobby.

Anderson Jr. High School Lawtey, Florida, 1956

Previously in 1958, Clifford Sr. and Robert Sr. participated in an all-male mock wedding as a fundraiser at Charles C. Anderson Junior High School. Lifelong resident of East Lawtey, Robert Austin Jr. also known as Bobby Austin, a retired Educator, Entrepreneur, and graduate of Florida Memorial University recalled when and where the event took place: "There was a building there we called the old building. It was the original wooden school building before the present brick and mortar building was constructed. That is where the mock wedding program was presented. By 1969, it was no longer in use, but it was still there. Probably used for storage. When I started at Anderson in 1956, it was used as the homeroom for the 9th graders. In addition to a classroom, it also housed the library and a shop room." For the "mock wedding ceremony," Bobby Austin vividly remembers his father Robert Austin Sr. as the Minister, Clifford Kelly Sr. as the Best Man, and Joseph Britt Sr. as the groom. They were all dressed in men's attire.

Margurie Kelly in Nassau Bahamas, August 1975

The male bride, however, was dressed in a white gown and wore white gloves and a veil. The all-male bridesmaids wore spaghetti strap white gowns and carried a bouquet. The entire skit was hilarious from start to finish.

On the other hand, whenever Clifford Sr. and Robert Sr. got dressed up with a hat, suit and tie, one might think they were siblings, or twins. They were two big and tall men who understood each other and viewed the world virtually through the same lens. As like-minded buddies, they had a lifelong friendship. Their wives, Margurie and Aretha, were close like siblings. Marguie Kelly always referred to her friend, Mrs. Aretha Austin, simply as "Retha." From the early days at Seaboard Airline Railway, to a mock wedding at Anderson JHS, and beyond, these two fifty-something couples were so close that they decided to vacation together. In the summer of 1975, the Kellys and Austins had fun and sun on the beautiful Caribbean island city of Nassau, Bahamas.

The Kelly's Return to Lawtey

Memorabilia: Promotional portrait and original recording (United Artists) for Bobby Womack, provided by Kelly's Nite Limit

On September 15, 1975, Bobby Kelly received an honorable discharge from the U.S. Navy. His parents were happy that he returned safely to the USA after three years of service in Greece.

After his vacation in the Bahamas, Clifford Kelly returned to promoting more live entertainment. It was at this time that soul music legend Bobby Womack returned to the Kelly's Nite Limit Stage. As the former guitar player on Sam Cooke's Live at The Copa, Bobby Womack developed a well-established repertoire as a blues singer, songwriter, and musician. He was a member of The Valentinos, which was a family group along with his four brothers. They recorded a song titled "Looking for a Love," which became a Billboard R&B hit at #8. He composed a song titled "It's All Over Now" in 1964. The group recorded on Sam Cooke's SAR Records label. The record went to #8 on Billboard's R&B Chart.

As a soloist for the United Artist record label, his Billboard R&B Chart hit recordings include "That's the Way I Feel About Cha" (#2 R&B) (#27 Hot 100 in 1972) "Woman's Gotta Have It" (#1 R&B in 1972), Harry Hippie (#8 in 1972) certified Gold on February 14,

1973 and a remake of "Looking For A Love" went to #1 (#1 R&B &, number #10 Pop) in 1974. The song was certified Gold on April 8, 1974. He released twenty-three albums over the course of his career.

In 1975, Clifford Kelly promoted Bobby Womack for an unusual Wednesday night performance at Kelly's Nite Limit. Although the artist was popular with blues enthusiasts, Kelly's was open on the weekends only. Saturday night was always the preference for a show and dance at Kelly's. Shockingly, an unbelievable size audience showed up in Lawtey, Florida during the middle of the week. Fans crowded into Kelly's Nite Limit to hear the soulful sound of blues artist Mr. Bobby Womack. The Place was PACKED!!! The following day, Clifford and Margurie Kelly both were speechless over their success that night.

Even though this live event was profitable, it was for one night only. The turnaround time after this show was too brief for them. Normally Kelly's Nite Limit was open for the weekend only. They had less than 48 hours to prepare, rest, and recover after this Wednesday night show. Clifford Kelly (age 57) and his wife Margurie Kelly (age 54) never booked another weeknight show for Kelly's Nite Limit ever again.

Meanwhile, in the mid-1970s, the extended Kelly family was growing with the birth of more grandchildren. Born throughout the decade were: Anthony Kelly, Toika Strong, Brandon Kelley, Brian Copeland, Bobby Kelly Jr., Vakela Kelly, and the first great grandchild for Clifford and Margurie Kelly was Marie Jenkins Clark.

The Return of the Godfather of Soul to East Lawtey

The year of 1976 was America's 200th birthday. On April 22, 1976, Soul music legend Johnnie Taylor became the first recording artist ever to receive the RIAA Platinum Award for his hit single titled "Disco Lady." For selling two million copies, the hit record spent four weeks at #1 on Billboard's R&B & Hot 100 Charts. In addition, former Georgia Governor, Jimmy Carter became the nation's 39th President. Clifford Kelly was a registered Democrat, so he was pleased with the election of President Carter later that year. While the preparation for patriotic celebrations throughout the nation were underway, Clifford "Schoolboy" Kelly had a plan of his own. Mr. Schoolboy booked and promoted the Godfather of Soul, Mr. James Brown, from Augusta, Georgia for a live performance in Lawtey, Florida.

"Please, Please, Please," "Try Me," "This Is a Man's World," "I Feel Good (I Got You)," "Night Train," "Papa's Got A Brand New Bag," "Get Up," "On the Good Foot," "Papa Don't Take No Mess," "Superbad," "Live at the Apollo," "Get Up Offa That Thang" and many more.

James Brown scored 96 hit records on Billboard's Hot 100 chart and 110 hit records on Billboard's R&B Chart. Seventeen of Mr. Brown's single recordings, along with five songs with "The Famous Flames," were #1 on Billboard's R&B Chart. James Brown was one of the very first recording artists to perform at Kelly's in the late 1950s. Clifford Kelly booked and promoted James Brown multiple times during the early days of Brown's career. James Brown performed so often in Lawtey that he practically became a staple there. Clifford Kelly and

James Brown were both natives with roots tied to Augusta, Richmond County Georgia. During the 1950s, some of the local indigenous people of East Lawtey would almost swear that James Brown performed at Kelly's Nite Limit on a weekly basis during the early days of his career. Just like most recording artists promoted by Clifford Kelly during the early years, James Brown got dressed at the Kelly home prior to his performances at the night club. While at the home, James Brown once said to a very young Marylou Kelly "little girl, don't let nobody steal my shoes". He then patted her on the head and went on his way.

Memorabilia: A Kelly's Nite Limit flyer for James Brown's performance on June 6, 1976 in Lawtey

It was now a new day, and the date was set for June 5, 1976 for Mr. James Brown and the JBs to perform live at Kelly's Nite Limit.

After the show was announced publicly, North Florida was in disbelief. No way would a super star with the caliber of James Brown ever step foot back into a small town like Lawtey, Florida. The media called the Kelly home to inquire about the show. When the reporter asked how many people could fit inside the nightclub, Bobby Kelly stated "about a thousand." The reporter was surprised at the size of the venue located in such a tiny town like Lawtey. Well, the day arrived, and the James Brown Tour pulled into the Kelly's Nite Limit parking lot. The driver parked the tour bus right next to the carport of the Kelly home. The Kelly grandchildren Tony Doster, age 13, Sibyl Kelley, age 12 and Antonio Jones, age 10 went outside to meet the Godfather of Soul in person. Mr. James Brown was very personable, cordial, and polite. He was soft spoken with a sparkle in his eyes along with his iconic smile. He was engaged in a conversation with another gentleman but stopped long enough to speak with the Kelly grandchildren for a few moments. The children obtained his autograph later that evening. Tony did not have a piece of paper for Mr. Brown to use. So, Tony went back into the house and got the Bradford Middle School Yearbook instead. Mr. Brown was cooperative and pleased to sign the yearbook for Tony. Of course the children were too young to attend the show, so they stayed outside in the parking lot near the tour bus during the live performance. Sibyl was always observant and noticed there were hardly any cars parked along highway 225. The parking lot at Kelly's was almost half full but that was it.

Memorabilia: Promotional Portrait (Universal Attractions) and original recording (Polydor Records) for James Brown provided by Kelly's Nite Limit

Also in 1976, "Get Up Offa That Thing" was the title of his 43rd studio album. The song was released as a single in May or about a month before his performance at Kelly's Nite Limit. As the show began, the announcer came to the microphone to warm up the audience. Instead of repeating the words "I'm Back" "I'm back" "Im back," as recorded in the intro of the song, the announcer started chanting "James Brown" "James Brown," "James Brown." The JBs horn section would hit a note or beat between the chanting. Crisp, Clean, Tight, Professional, and Perfection are the words to describe the talented musicians for James Brown.

Everything with the show musically was superb. After his performance, James Brown left the stage and walked down to the kitchen to speak with Mrs. Kelly. While in the kitchen, he autographed a promotional photograph for her with the following message:

To: Mr. and Mrs. Kelly,

Thanks always, I'll never forget you and if you want me to come back regardless of what my cost per night, I'll give you a cheaper price. James

Memorabilia: An autographed promotional portrait of James Brown (Polydor Records) (June 5, 1976), provided from the Collection of Margurie Williams Kelly

The following day, 12-year-old Sibyl asked her grandmother about the show and how many people were there. Margurie Kelly showed her granddaughter Sibyl the photograph James Brown signed for her and stated "about a hundred." About 100??? Kelly's Nite Limit could accommodate up to one thousand (1000+) people. The child was in disbelief that only one hundred people came to see the James Brown Show last night. The parking lot was about over half full. As for the highway, only two cars facing each other were parked under the streetlight near the flashing neon arrow shaped marquee.

The fans and general public simply did not believe James Brown, an international superstar, would dare return to perform in Lawtey, Florida. So, just like that, the heyday of Kelly's Nite Limit was over. No more back to back month to month bookings & promotions for recording artists. After 1976, Clifford Kelly promoted an average of 1 or 2 recording artists per year for performances in Lawtey. Moving forward for the next few years, Clifford Kelly and his business partners invested in tour packages in major cities and venues throughout Florida.

Clifford Kelly Sr.: I'm Back!

In 1977, Clifford Kelly booked and promoted Joe Tex along with a new R&B group named "BRICK" for a music double feature at Kelly's Nite Limit. Joe Tex from Rogers, Bell County Texas, was a well-established veteran on the Blues/R&B music scene. Mr. Tex had four of his twelve Billboard Top 10 R&B hits to sell a million copies. His RIAA Gold Record Certifications are: "Skinny Legs and All" (January 26, 1968), "I Got'cha!" (March 22, 1972), and "Ain't Gonna Bump No More with No Big Fat Woman" (June 9, 1977).

THE 1970S: MARGURIE W. KELLY VS THE FLORIDA DIVISION OF BEVERAGE

Memorabilia: Promotional image, original recordings (Dial Records) Original recording & company sleeve (EPIC Records) for Joe Tex, provided by Kelly's Nite Limit

BRICK, however, was a new musical group from Atlanta, Georgia. They had the #1 single on Billboard's R&B Chart titled "Disco Dazz." The record went to #3 on Billboard's Hot 100. The song was released on July 16, 1976 on the Bang Record Label. Their Billboard Chart hit recordings titled "Dusic" peaked at #2 R&B and #18 Pop, and "Ain't Gonna Hurt Nobody" went to #7 R&B, #92 Pop. Both records were released nationally in 1977.

Joe Tex was promoted for the first show and BRICK was promoted for the second show. Kelly's Nite Limit was at capacity. The Kelly family's backyard, the parking lot and both sides of HWY 225 were packed with vehicles. Mr. Tex performed all of his hit songs and comedy with fans laughing and cheering. BRICK on the other hand was a NO Show! Fans started beating on the tables and chairs chanting "We Want Brick," "We Want Brick"!!! Clifford Kelly had to go on stage to announce the bad news and refunded everyone half the ticket price for the show.

As time and technology moved forward, Mrs. Kelly became more stalwart of the past. Even though Bradford County was a "wet county," Mrs. Kelly would not agree with her husband to acquire a liquor license. They continued to maintain their beverage license for beer and wine only. It was still 1977, and East Lawtey had local DJs on the horizon. Alvaughn Golden, Erol Brown, Mickey Slocum, and Nathan Mack all wanted to showcase their skills. Mr. and Mrs. Kelly welcomed the new local talent to the stage.

The young people would come out to dance but they were not spending a lot of money on food and drinks. Not even on snack food. Even if there was no cover charge, the young people were not spending money at all. Kelly's Nite Limit was just a packed out place of teenagers or "young-folk" as Mr. Kelly viewed them. Mr. Kelly would suck his teeth and grin as he referred to the new young crowd as "jitterbugs" or "teenage stuff." Clifford Kelly wanted "Grown Folks" at his juke joint. People who bought show tickets, beer, ice, wine, cigarettes, cigars, BBQ, deep fried: (fish, shrimp, pork chops, chicken, livers, & gizzards), hamburgers, french fries, potato salad, garden salad, Bone-In sandwiches, with an assortment of pickled products. Customers who would shake hot sauce on everything, including their spicy potato chips, pork rinds, or french fries and wash it down with a malt liquor or Pepsi Cola or even a grape soda. If there was not a live show, Clifford Kelly wanted customers to put money in the jukebox, play pinball, 8 ball, and buy bone-in sandwiches to eat and drink beverages for hours. On the night of a live show, Clifford Kelly wanted his juke joint filled with mature paying customers who drove nice cars, dressed up and came out to have a good time. Men and women who jammed packed every inch of the dance floor while movin' to some live Soul music. The ladies in high heels and the men wearing hard bottom Stacy Adams. No one sitting in parked cars watching the building nor standing outside drinking in the parking lot. Everyone was inside the nightclub during a live show. Ticket buyers looking good and having fun on the dance floor was paramount. This was always the central theme at Kelly's Nite Limit among the average mature adult patron.

As soul music moved forward, proven and widely popular hit makers such as Brass Construction and ConFunkShun were also promoted to perform at Kelly's Nite Limit. Yet, somehow DJ shows became most prevalent for the next couple of years at Kelly's.

Billboard Hit Albums for Brass Construction on the United Artists record label are:

1975 Brass Construction #10 Pop/#1 R&B
RIAA Platinum: Certification

1976 Brass Construction II #26 Pop/#3 R&B
RIAA: Gold Certification.

1977 Brass Construction III #66 Pop/#16 R&B
RIAA: Gold Certification

ConFunkShun scored a string of Top 10 hits for Mercury Records on Billboard's R&B Singles chart.

"Fun" (No. #1-1978)
"Shake and Dance with Me" (No. #5-1978)
"Chase Me" (No. #4-1979)
"Got to Be Enough" (No. #8-1980)
"Too Tight" (No. #8-1981)
"Baby I'm Hooked" (No. #5-1983)
"Electric Lady" (No. #4-1985)

Memorabilia: Promotional portraits for Brass Construction and ConFunkShun are provided by Kellys Nite Limit

Kelly's Nite Limit and Kelly Home Improvement

By the late 1970s, business for Kelly's Nite Limit was in a real slump. Business for Kelly's Curb Masters Construction was still very productive. It was during this time in 1978 that Clifford Kelly completed additional construction and landscaping on his property. The Kelly home was extended with a new private den, home office, second floor master bedroom suite, master bathroom, and garage. Mr. Kelly wanted a special place for his business partners to meet with him privately at his home. He built a black-and-white block fence with a sidewalk for his wife Margurie Kelly. She had a green thumb and loved working in her yard and garden. The idea left enough space to exclude her yard from the paved parking lot. One sidewalk was for customers to use. The other sidewalk landscaped her front yard for personal use. As a Concrete Finisher, Clifford Kelly Sr. constructed all the curbs, sidewalks, and driveways of his home personally. As for Kelly's Nite Limit, he hired a subcontractor to pave the 18,000 sq. ft parking lot in 1975, *(OB/XF Code 1603-Asphalt-pa 18,050 sq. ft)*. It was an established tradition for recording artists to utilize the Kelly home as needed for the past two decades. Lawtey was still a tiny town with only one motel. If a performer requested hotel accommodations in their contract, Mr. and Mrs. Kelly would offer the use of the upstairs master bedroom of their home instead. Mr. Kelly was satisfied and well pleased with all of the additions and renovations for his property.

As for upgrades at Kelly's Nite Limit the lobby/foyer or "The Front" received a facelift. Mr. Kelly lowered the ceiling, and installed a new yellow floral pattern countertop for the bar. He added multicolored light blue and teal paneling on the outer walls of the kitchen. He painted the interior walls pastel blue, added an indoor BBQ pit, game room, a separate full size bar room, and a new women's bathroom with a vanity.

Clifford Kelly Sr.: For the Love of Ebony Jones

Little Ebony lived in Jacksonville with her owner Marylou Jones, who was of course Clifford Kelly's second daughter. Pets, however, were not allowed at the apartment complex where they lived. Therefore, Marylou brought Ebony to live with her parents Clifford and Margurie Kelly in Lawtey. The little dog Ebony loved her new owners and the Kelly grandchildren. Mrs. Kelly purchased a brass bed for the family's spoiled and lovable Pekingese poodle Ebony Jones. Clifford Sr. referred to the little dog as "Gal." Ebony would light up when she saw Clifford Sr. and he would say "Hey Gal." "this daddy Gal." Eventually, every weekend that Clifford Kelly sat down for lunch, Ebony sat with him in the kitchen.

Margurie Kelly seemed to enjoy preparing all her husband's down home favorite meals and entrees. She always peeled a bowl of fresh cucumbers, cantaloupe, and honeydew on Saturday morning. Otherwise, when seasonal, she would serve fresh strawberries 'n cream or canned peaches 'n cream, as her husband loved to drink the sweet and syrupy milk right from the bowl. Just like his Kemetic ancestors, Clifford Kelly loved watermelon. His wife would often shake some extra sugar on the melons to satisfy her husband's sweet tooth. Her sweet potato pies were always a melt in your mouth delight. Baked in a flaky, smooth, crispy, buttery pie crust, her sweet potato pies were given as gifts during the holidays. She always used fresh peeled potatoes. The pies were so delicious, rich with flavor and spice that her husband, Clifford would often devour an entire pie by himself. Margurie Kelly knew how to make any cut of fish, beef, pork, meat organs, various assorted meat parts, or wild game tasty and scrumptious. The meat was seasoned with her own unique combinations of salt, black pepper, cayenne pepper, paprika, onions, sage, poultry seasoning, brown sugar, hot sauce, allspice, Worcestershire, apples, oranges, pineapples, fat drippings or some of that leftover fish grease as needed. Her fish grease was conveniently preserved in a little silver canister on the stove. A stack of hot corn cakes, a platter of fried Bream with some seasoned collards, peas, or beans became a Friday night favorite for Clifford Kelly. The aroma of seasonings would fill the kitchen over into the Florida Room where their family pet Ebony knew it was time for a treat.

Clifford Kelly Sr. would sit down on his favorite bar stool next to the refrigerator. With his elbows on and off the table, he would start feasting on one of his favorites. Like some succulent oxtails, or crispy fried pork chops, a pig ear sandwich, fried sirloin with gravy and onions, fried liver and onions or one of his all-time favorites, the smoked neckbone-finger-sandwich. Clifford Kelly Sr. would wrap one or two slices of white bread around a meaty savory cut of seasoned pork neck bones dripping with a tidbit of broth. While munching down and around the flavorful tender meat, bones, and gristles, Clifford Kelly Sr. would extend his right arm out with the bones in his hand. Ebony would leap 2 or 3 feet into the air to get the bones from her owner's hand. Then, he would go right back to eating his food. After brunch, Ebony returned to the Florida Room to sit on her little brass bed or her favorite pillow. This mealtime endeavor for Clifford Kelly Sr. and the family dog Ebony continued for sixteen years.

Margurie Williams Kelly:
"Prepare for War in a Time of Peace."

Margurie Kelly believed you cannot get ready after the battle starts because it is too late. You have to get prepared while things are going great. In the late 1970s, Lockheed Aircraft was under a U.S. Government contract for The Peacelog Protect to upgrade the inventory and logistics systems of the Iranian Government. Clifford Kelly Jr. accepted an offer of employment by the company to work overseas as an Auditor. He was one of the six employees from a pool of 112 applicants trained by Lockheed's Computer Processing Financial Department for international commercial logistics. His employment assignment for the Peacelog Project in partnership with the U.S. Air Force was in the Middle East. In the Spring of 1978, Clifford Kelly Jr. requested for his young teenage daughter, Sibyl Kelley, to join him and his wife, the former Jane Marie Halling, in the city of Tehran, Iran. Jane Marie is the daughter of Mr. and Mrs. Richard Earl Halling of Boone, Iowa. It was also the first time the teen was on an airplane. In June 1978, Sibyl flew from Jacksonville, Florida to New York City, where she changed flights. The teen remembered her father's instructions as it was a long walk outside John F. Kennedy International Airport over to Iranian Airlines. Fourteen-year-old Sibyl Kelly flew all the way to Tehran, Iran without a chaperone nor a layover. Sibyl spent nearly two months in the Middle East with her family. She made some new friends and joined an American girls softball team whose mascot was known as The Undertakers (1,2,3 Bury Em!). Although the weekend in Iran was during the week, Sibyl would meet with other teens on Friday or Saturday night at a compound for the Americans. There was a DJ who played the records as the teens danced to R&B, Funk, and Disco Music.

While in Iran, the Kellys were excited as they were expecting their first child. To ensure the child's United States citizenship, the couple made the decision for their child to be born in the United States. In early August, Sibyl and her stepmother Jane returned to America together. Sibyl's father, Clifford Kelly Jr., remained in Iran to complete his employment assignment. A few weeks later, Brandon Lee Kelley was born in Boone County, Iowa. It's the community where his mother grew up and his maternal grandparents, Richard and Dorothy Halling, resided. Weeks afterward, arrangements were made for the child, and his mother to travel back to Iran. Later that year, during the Fall season of 1978, due to an uprising over the Iranian Government, all Americans were ordered to leave the country. The dependents (women and children) of all Lockheed Aircraft employees were ordered to leave the nation of Iran first. Jane and Brandon returned to America, while Clifford Jr. remained in the capital city of Tehran. Mrs. Kelly was deeply grieved, watching the news every night and worrying about her son. She just could not take it. Mrs. Margurie Kelly contacted the Hallings family and traveled to Boone, Iowa to see her infant grandson. The visit with her new grandchild provided a sense of relief and calm for her. Eventually, Mrs. Kelly received a letter from her son, Clifford Jr. He wrote to his parents that he was okay and that no one was bothering him. He walked around freely in the capital city of Tehran, Iran during all the commotion as seen on TV. By July 1979, the remainder of Lockheed Aircraft employees were evacuated out of Iran by the United States Air Force. Clifford Kelly Jr., returned safely to America. For the next couple of years, he worked as an Independent Consultant/Auditor for EGNG in Idaho Falls, Idaho and the Environmental Protection Agency (EPA) in Springfield, Illinois.

As the 1970s were ending, on October 25, 1979, Mrs. Kelly purchased airtime at WGGG-1230 Radio in Gainesville, Florida. Her sales agent at the station was Walter Bickmeyer. A repeat performance starring one of Clifford Kelly's all-time favorite entertainers Mr. Clarence Carter was announced over the airwaves. The show was booked and scheduled for October 27th. Having sold millions of records, Mr. Carter had a steady flow of Billboard Chart hits. Nonetheless, attendance for this show at Kelly's Nite Limit was mediocre as Carter did not have any current chart hits. Nevertheless, Clarence Carter did not disappoint his most loyal fans and performed all of past hits of brash and humorous R&B country blues.

CHAPTER 9

The 1980s
The Kellys Standing Together

After forty years of marriage, Clifford Kelly Sr. still wore 3 or 4 gold caps on his teeth. Mrs. Margurie Kelly wore a round diamond solitaire on her top-right central incisor along with two gold crowns on her teeth. Their son Ronnie Kelly gave his mother the diamond as a gift. Since she already wore a diamond ring, Mrs. Kelly had the diamond from her son implanted in her tooth.

The extended Kelly family grew as more and more grandchildren and great grandchildren were born: Frank Green, Kenny Copeland, Justin Kelly, Christopher Kelley, Vakela Kelly, Tia Jones, Jacquline Kelley and Britany Highland. Their grandfather and great grandfather started the new decade off by contacting Associated Booking Corporation in New York to inquire about the availability of more recording artists.

On March 19, 1980, once again, Clifford Kelly Sr. booked and promoted Bobby Blue Bland to perform live at Kelly's Nite Limit for May 3, 1980. Mr. Kelly was so happy like a kid in the candy shop so to speak. He worked very hard during the week leading up the show. He obtained the

sound system and microphones requested in Mr. Bland's contract. Rather than use rented lights, Clifford Kelly installed new stage lights to meet the specifications of the contract as well. He rented additional tables and chairs to accommodate the overflow of ticket buyers. Nevertheless, Clifford Kelly was also very frugal.

His wife Margurie Kelly would cut old placards from a previous show in half to make placement cards for customers who reserved a table and chairs. The reservation cards were cut into different-sized squares. No two cards were alike. With a black magic marker, the customer's name along with the city and state they were from was written in shorthand on each card. Each reservation card was folded in half and placed on the table with an ashtray. Clifford Kelly would laugh afterward. The customers thought it was flat out hilarious and ingenious. To use the placard of a blues legend to create handwritten reservation cards was insightful coupled with down home thoughtfulness plain and simple. Impressive and totally unexpected, Mr. Bland arrived in Lawtey via a custom blue and silver coach with his full stage name painted in big, bold, block, and cursive blue letters. As always, the driver parked the tour bus next to the carport of the Kelly home. Every seat in the nightclub and the dance floor overflow was sold out. Mr. Kelly only used half of the dance floor for the overflow ticket buyers. The other half was left clear so the fans could get up and dance. For the show in Lawtey, fans who paid for reserved tables traveled from Jacksonville, Gainesville, Cocoa, Daytona, Orlando, and Fort Lauderdale. Bobby Blue Bland, age 50, wore a tan-colored suit as he stepped onto the stage. He performed many of his hits and fan favorite tunes to a full house in Lawtey.

Cleosie Daniel, Cleo Kelley, and Clifford Kelly Have Their Day in Court (1982)

Clifford Kelly's birth name is Cleosie Daniel. His adoptive parents John Kelley Jr. and his wife Nellie Kelley named him Cleo Kelley as entered on April 25, 1930 of the U.S. Federal Census for Tarvers, Burke County Georgia. He was 12 years old at the time. In March 1939, he obtained his social security number under the name of Clifford Kelly. For more than sixty years, his name was never changed legally in a court of law. The circumstances were now causing issues for him with the Social Security Administration. Clifford Kelly hired Attorney R.E. Welty who filed a petition on Mr. Kelly's behalf. This cause came on to be heard upon the Petition to Change Name filed by Petitioner Cleosie Daniel. In the Circuit Court for Bradford County, Florida, Civil Action Case, comes now Cleosie Daniel, petitions this Court to change his name and for grounds would show: The Petitioner is a resident of Bradford County Florida. He was born to Emma Kate Daniel in Blythe, Richmond County, Georgia. Since birth, he has resided in Georgia and Florida. The Petitioner is married to the former Margurie Williams and they have six children. Their names are Emma Louise Kelly Strong, Lawtey, Florida; Clifford Lee Kelley, London, England; Mary Lou Kelly Green, Jacksonville, Florida; Margaret Jean Kelly Copeland, Jacksonville, Florida; Jerome S. Kelly, Albany, Georgia; Bobby K. Kelly, Jacksonville, Florida. They had one other child [Vernon Lee Kelly] who died in infancy. The Petitioner desires to change his name to Clifford Kelly. At a young age, he was given and raised by a family named Kelley and they named him. He has used the name in all matters, including Social Security, marriage, children's birth records, and all of his employment records. His name has never been legally changed and this is now causing him problems with Social Security. He feels it would be simpler to change his name instead of every other record. The Petitioner is a Construction Contractor, and has been self-employed in that occupation for approximately fifteen years. The name of his business is Curb Master Construction, and he operates out of his home in Lawtey, Florida. The Petitioner has been known as Clifford Kelly and has not gone by any other name. The Petitioner has never been adjudicated bankrupt, nor has he been convicted of a felony. This petition is filed for no ulterior or illegal purpose and the granting of this Petition will in no way invade the property rights of others. Wherefore, the Petitioner prays that this Court enter an Order changing his name to Clifford Kelly. Having examined the verified petition and having an opportunity to inquire of the Petitioner, the Court finds that allegations of the petition are true and the Petitioner is entitled to the relief sought. Therefore, it is Ordered and Adjudged that the Petitioner's name is hereby changed and he shall be known as Clifford Kelly from this day forward. Done and Ordered in Starke, Bradford County Florida this day, March 29, 1982.

THE 1980S: THE KELLYS STANDING TOGETHER

Sibyl D. Kelley

On June 4, 1982, two and half months after the hearing, Clifford Kelly's first granddaughter Sibyl Kelley graduated from Bradford County High School. Her father, Clifford Kelly Jr., returned from England to Lawtey as a bachelor and spent a week with the family before the graduation ceremony.

Sibyl D. Kelley graduation night at BHS Stadium Starke, Florida. Photograph provided by Clifford Kelly Jr.

Clifford Kelly Sr. was proud of all the home improvement and new landscaping on his property. He had a ball being photographed throughout the entire week

Photograph of Clifford Kelly Sr., provided by Clifford Kelly Jr. June 4, 1982

Clifford Kelly under the balcony of his home in Lawtey

Clifford Kelly " On the Fence" in Lawtey Photographs provided by Clifford Kelly Jr.

THE 1980S: THE KELLYS STANDING TOGETHER

The Kelly home in Lawtey 1982

Clifford "Schoolboy" Kelly on the front porch of his home in Lawtey, Florida (June 1982)

Photographs provided by Clifford Kelly Jr.

Kelly's Nite Limit 1982: A smaller version of the Soul Music venue was initially built during 1954 in the adjacent lot to the Kelly home. This present structure was completed after 1960

The Kelly home on Lake Street (Hwy 225) in Lawtey

Photographs provided by Clifford Kelly Jr.

THE 1980S: THE KELLYS STANDING TOGETHER

Clifford Kelly Jr. and Clifford Kelly Sr. 1982

Photograph provided by Clifford Kelly Jr.

THE 1980S: THE KELLYS STANDING TOGETHER

Mr. and Mrs. Clifford Kelly Sr. June 4, 1982 Lawtey, Florida

The Kellys: Clifford Kelly Sr., Margurie Williams Kelly, and Clifford Kelly Jr. at home in Lawtey, Florida June 4, 1982

Photographs provided by Clifford Kelly Jr.

THE 1980S: THE KELLYS STANDING TOGETHER

Clifford Kelly Sr. and his cousin Mrs. Margaret Johnson Newton were photographed at Kelly's Nite Limit in 1982. She's the mother of Nate Newton (Dallas Cowboys) and Tim Newton (Minnesota Vikings). Photograph provided by the Collection of Mrs. Margurie Williams Kelly

Mrs. Margurie Kelly
My Kind of Music

In the early 1980s, the sound of Soul/R&B music changed again and was marketed to an even wider audience. Mr. and Mrs. Kelly, both aged over 60, remained faithful to their love for soulful gospel-infused blues/R&B. One such artist who fit the bill for them was a singer named Tony Troutman. He was a guitarist and singer/songwriter from Atlanta, Georgia. On May 17, 1975, he received regional attention in the Southern United States for his recording "What's The Use" (Jerri Records) and "I Truly Love You" (Gram-o-phon Records). The song peaked at #82 on Billboard's R&B Chart. His album titled "Your Man Is Home Tonight" on (T. Main Records) was released as a single on May 6, 1982. The song peaked at #57 on Billboard's R&B Chart the following month. The song was a jukebox favorite of Mrs. Kelly. She obtained a copy of the recording and created her own handwritten juke box title strip for it.

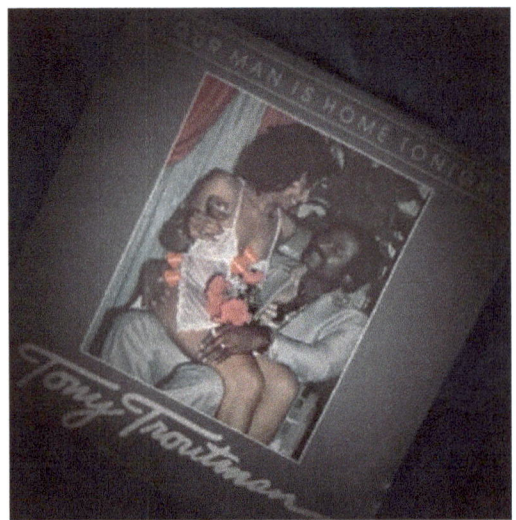

Mrs. Kelly wrote the title of the song as "I'm On the Way," which is in fact the first lyrical line of the song. The next time Maxie Carter Jr. came out to rotate the records on the jukebox, she asked him to include this recording. The record was a catchy sing along jukebox hit with the customers at Kelly's. The popularity of the record grew as local DJ Alvaugh Golden featured it with his lineup every weekend. Mis'-Margurie liked the song so much that Tony Troutman was booked to perform live at Kelly's Nite Limit. Surprisingly, hundreds of people came out to the show! The dance floor at Kelly's was completely full. The next generation of indigenous adults (under the age of 30) came out in droves to dance at Kelly's Nite Limit. In the Fall of 1982, Mr. and Mrs. Kelly were all smiles that evening as they watched the next generation sing and dance to live soulful blues music. Mr. Troutman did two shows of extended play for "Your Man Is Home Tonight." The crowd was pleased, appreciative, and very receptive to the song. The show was so successful, to the extent that Tony Troutman was booked for a repeat performance later that same year.

This next performance was booked during the Christmas holiday week. Unfortunately two days before Christmas, the weather in Florida changed. The temperature was so tremendously cold that less than ten people were inside the venue, including Mrs. Kelly. As a professional under contract Mr. Troutman went on stage and performed one or two songs and spoke of the cold weather that kept the crowd away this time. He reflected on the huge turnout in Lawtey for his previous appearance. Nevertheless, the handwriting was on the wall; Mr. Troutman and his entourage discontinued the set and left. Live shows at Kelly's Nite Limit normally started at 9 o'clock or 10 o'clock at night. Nevertheless, it was so bitterly cold on this night that Mrs. Kelly turned off the lights early and vacated the building before 9:30 p.m.

Ironically, a few years later, Clifford Kelly booked soul-singer Millie Jackson to perform again at Kelly's Nite Limit for another Christmas weekend show. Ms. Jackson called him about two weeks prior to cancel her performance, citing she could not do the show. The weekend of her scheduled appearance in Lawtey was two days before Christmas.

A blizzard far worse than the 1982 storm hit Florida with temperatures below 10 degrees Fahrenheit.

Mr. and Mrs. Kelly were all smiles during the holidays because they knew this time there would be no financial dart to the heart. As business was slowing down at Kelly's Nite Limit, Mr. Kelly used caution moving forward prior to booking any additional recording artists.

DJ shows at Kelly's were very popular with the local fans from the neighboring counties. As music was changing in the '80s, live shows with a recording artist at Kelly's Nite Limit were often a big financial risk. Mr. Kelly continued to invest primarily in tour packages at larger Florida venues with his business partners. Investing in tour packages was most profitable for him during this time.

THE 1980S: THE KELLYS STANDING TOGETHER

Clifford Kelly Jr.: My Cristina, Back in Love Again

In 1983, after his employment concluded in London, Clifford Kelly Jr. returned to Los Angeles, where he met the love of his life, Ms. Cristina Jo'Lan. She's the daughter of Pablo Jo Lan and Shui Ting Jo Lan (Teresa Leon) of Mexicali, Baja, Mexico. On September 10, 1983, Clifford Kelly Jr. and Cristina Joleon were married in Las Vegas at the Imperial Hotel and Resort. The newlyweds made their home in Los Angeles, San Bernardino County, California. They had two children: a son named Christopher Lee Kelley and a daughter named Jacqueline JoLan Kelley.

Photograph of Mr. and Mrs. Clifford Kelly Jr. was provided from the collection of Mrs. Margurie Williams Kelley

THE 1980S: THE KELLYS STANDING TOGETHER

Photograph: Kelly's Curb Masters Construction: Clifford Kelly on the far right with a few of his Laborers

As always, Clifford Kelly Sr. maintained his rigorous work schedule between Kelly's Nite Limit and Kelly's Curb Master Construction. He continued to work Monday through Friday in Central Florida on various construction sites. Clifford Kelly Sr. always worked hands on with his laborers for all of his subcontracting projects. Kelly's Nite Limit was still open on Friday, Saturday, and Sunday nights only. Mrs. Kelly worked 12–14 hours primarily at the nightclub from 2:00 p.m. to 4:00 a.m. Not to mention the preparation for shows, other events and shopping for supplies during the week.

Music was changing and Clifford Kelly Sr. tried to adapt. He even purchased and wore a Thriller Jacket. His wife Margurie referred to the jacket as "The Michael Jackson Coat." Mrs. Kelly was always embarrassed whenever her husband wore it. Clifford Sr. was proud of his red leather jacket, which he wore regardless of the weather for about two years. Business was very slow at times. Primarily because Kelly's still did not have a liquor license. People wanted to drink liquor while playing 8 ball, pinball or while listening to the jukebox. There were always a few dedicated customers who came to buy their favorite bone-in sandwiches with a fruit flavored soft drink. Mrs. Kelly prepared the sandwiches cooked to order, always hot and fresh, topped with iceberg lettuce, tomato, mayonnaise and a tap of seasoning.

Photograph of Kelly's Nite Limit provided by Harriette Davis Tyson

Kelly's Nite Limit and Muff Security

It was the 1980s and still there was no landline telephone, electric cash register or security system installed at Kelly's Nite Limit. For whatever reason, Mrs. Kelly refused to even allow a public phone booth to be installed on the property near the curb by Highway 225.

Mrs. Margurie Kelly was the boss; she was feisty and set in her ways to the core. She utilized a manual cash register, a cordless phone, and security guards when needed at Kelly's Nite Limit. For decades, Clifford Kelly Sr. consulted with Mr. Ulysee Muff, Founder & Owner of Muff Guard and Patrol Agency (Muff Security Inc.) of Jacksonville, Florida. The company was established in 1970. For fifty years, Muff Security Inc. provided services for the City of Jacksonville, Duval County Schools as well as a multitude of entrepreneurs and private engagements.

Ulysee Muff remembered the quintessential soul-singer Sam Cooke performing live at Kelly's Nite Limit around 1963. For Keen, and RCA records, the six time Grammy Award nominee Sam Cooke had five #1 Billboard R&B Chart hits titled "You Send Me" (1958), "Another Saturday Night" (1963), "Twistin the Night Away" (1962), "Good News" (1964), and "Good Times" (1964). He scored thirty-four Top 40 Pop and R&B Hits over the course of his career.

Sam Cooke is best known for his civil rights anthem "A Change Is Gonna Come." The recording peaked at #9 on Billboard's R&B Chart in February 1965.

However, it would be a few years before Ulysee Muff established his security company or met Clifford Kelly Sr. personally. Ulysee Muff and Clifford Kelly Sr. met initially at one of the clubs on Soutel Drive in Jacksonville during the early 1970s. Their business-friendship would evolve over the next thirty-five years. One night a fight broke out at Kelly's Nite Limit between female patrons arguing over a picture of HI Records recording artist Sly Johnson. He's the father of three time Grammy-nominated R&B songstress Syleena Johnson, who's best known for her collaboration on the hit recording "All Falls Down" by Kanye West. At the time of his performance at Kelly's Nite Limit, Sly Johnson was riding the wave of his hit recording "Take Me to the River." The song reached #7 on Billboard's R&B Chart in 1975. He was a gifted soul-singer and musician who scored twelve Billboard R&B Top 40 hits. His recording titled "Different Strokes" has been sampled multiple times by recording artists, namely Public Enemy, Kanye, JayZ, Wu Tang Clan, NWA, and hundreds more. After his performance at Kelly's Nite Limit, a hostile incident broke out among the women. The other customers were in total disbelief by the brawl among them. One female managed to snatch and grab the photograph of Syl Johnson off the wall and ran out the door with it. For years, promotional pictures lined the walls for all the recording artists that performed at Kelly's Nite Limit. Yet, after this incident, Mrs. Kelly decided to remove all the photographs.

A show at Kelly's Nite Limit started primarily at 10:00 p.m. If authorities had to be called, they came from Starke, Florida, which

Memorabilia: Promotional portraits & original recording (HI Records & Twilight Records) for Sly Johnson provided by Kelly's Nite Limit

is seven miles south of Lawtey. Fighting was not ongoing at Kelly's Nite Limit. However, this was not the first nor only time a serious life-threatening occurrence happened at the venue. Clifford Kelly was advised to have his own security team on site for emergencies.

Mr. Ulysee Muff, founder of Muff Security Inc. (MG&PA), was also a Driver for the City of Jacksonville for twenty-two years. In 1981, Ulysee Muff and his wife Mary Frances Drummond were also the owners of two restaurants named Mom's Kitchen. One diner was located in Plains, Georgia. The other diner was located in Preston, Georgia. For thirty-nine years, each Sunday after church, U.S. President Jimmy Carter ate dinner at Mom's Kitchen located in his hometown of Plains, Georgia. The former President lived a few blocks away from the diner in a brick home as Ulysee Muff recalled. It was common for members of President Carter's congregation to eat at Mom's Kitchen as well. Mr. and Mrs. Muff reserved a special section inside the diner for the President and his wife First Lady Roselyn Carter to eat privately.

THE 1980S: THE KELLYS STANDING TOGETHER

From left to right: Ulysse Muff, George Crimes, President Jimmy Carter, Maggie Muff-Crimes and First Lady Roselyn Carter in Preston, Georgia, February 2003. The President and First Lady attended the repast for Mrs. Evelyn C. Holley- (-mother of Ulysse and Maggie) Photograph provided by Ulysse Muff Sr.

From left to right: Ulysse Muff Sr, Maggie Muff-Crimes, President Jimmy Carter, First Lady Roselyn Carter and Mrs. Mary Frances Muff were photographed at their family home in Preston, Georgia.

THE 1980S: THE KELLYS STANDING TOGETHER

Although the majority of ticket buyers at Kelly's Nite Limit conducted themselves as mature adults, the times were changing. Clifford Kelly would often call on the Muff Guard and Patrol Agency for security services. Mr. Kelly wanted to ensure the safety of everyone inside the juke joint as well as "the cash box" located at the front entrance. Ulysee Muff vividly remembered Clifford Kelly saying: "He would call me up and say, "Ulysee, bring me four guards."" Ulysee Muff knew right away that if Clifford Kelly needed four guards, there was going to be a big show coming to town.

Photographed at Kelly's Nite Limit: Muff Security Inc./Muff Guard and Patrol Agency (L-R): Ulysee Muff with Security Officers: Alfonzo King, Rose Parker, and Daniel Brown. Photograph provided by Ulysee Muff Sr.

Clifford Kelly Sr. Founder of Kelly's Nite Limit. Photograph provided by Emma Kelly Strong

Ulysee Muff would dispatch the officers to Kelly's Nite Limit. "Two on the Lot, one at the front entrance and one at the stage." All officers were certified by the State of Florida and licensed to carry a firearm. The guards assigned to the parking lot would set up traffic cones and direct drivers where to park their vehicles. Ulysee Muff (the company's founder) sat with the officer at the front entrance to collect and exchange show tickets with the customers. This process ensured orderly entry or re-entry of patrons at the venue. The fifth officer remained "In the Back" during the entire show, primarily to protect the artist on stage. Ulysee and Schoolboy became good friends over the years. Ulysee Muff remembered this: whenever Clifford Kelly put on a suit, it was a big show in town. "When Clifford Kelly dressed up in that white suit he would have as much fun as anybody." "He knew how to make a dollar and he always paid me." "He was a good man as far as I knew."

Eighties Music at Kelly's Nite Limit

During the 1980s, Mrs. Kelly would spend a lot of hours just sitting inside Kelly's Nite Limit alone. She had a TV, an electric heater to keep her legs and knees warm, plus a cordless phone for her personal use. The phone with its 12-inch antennae was a gift from her son Clifford Jr. She was just head over heels proud of it. The customers were impressed too whenever they saw Mrs. Kelly using her new phone.

Pictured in 1980 from left to right are the sons of Mr. and Mrs. Clifford Kelly Sr.: Jerome Sims Kelly, Bobby King Kelly, and Clifford Lee Kelley Jr. Photograph provided by Marylou Kelly

A landline phone was still the primary source of communication for most families and businesses. The use of cordless technology was rather uncommon in a business setting at the time. If a customer needed to make a phone call, Mrs. Kelly would let them use her cordless phone while sitting at the counter. If they needed privacy, they could simply walk across the parking lot to her house, and use the phone in the kitchen while sitting at the bar table. A standard procedure for every recording artist her husband ever promoted at Kelly's Nite Limit. Mrs. Kelly continued to work only on Friday, Saturday, and Sunday. Most of the locals went to Thompkins or "The Lounge" down the road where liquor was available. After Thompkins closed for the night, all the customers would head down to Kelly's Nite Limit to play 8 ball, listen to the jukebox, and eat bone-in sandwiches until 4:00 a.m.

The high school students would pack the building primarily after BHS homecoming and on graduation night. The local DJs were Alvaughn Golden, Mickey Slocum, Nathan Mack, and Errol Brown. DJs Slocum, Mack, and Brown played a lot of regional and popular rap music. Alvaughn Golden played all Top 40 R&B Jams. Whenever Alvaughn was the featured DJ, the young people came out in droves to dance at Kelly's Nite Limit.

As for recording artists in the 1980s, Clifford Kelly and his son Bobby Kelly promoted a variety of artists. Clifford Kelly continued to book and promote blues artists he preferred from decades past. Bobby Kelly booked and promoted new rap artists he preferred. Among the 1980's roster of Blues, Soul, R&B, and Rap Artists were:

Bobby Blue Bland (MCA Records). Agency: (ABC) Associated Booking Corporation, 1995 Broadway, Suite 501, New York, New NY 10023 Agent: Phil Friedensohn.

ZZ Hill (Malaco Records), Agency: Rodgers Redding and Associates, POB 4603, Macon, Georgia 31208.

Confunkshun (Mercury Records), Agent: Nowag & Williams Talent Agency, 5094 Alrose Avenue, Memphis, Tennessee 34117.

Larry Graham (Warner Brothers Records), Agent: Regency Artists LTD, 9200 Sunset Blvd Suite, 823 Los Angeles, California 90069.

Paulette Reeves (DASH Records), T&K Productions, 495 South East 10th Court Hialeah, Florida 33010.

Tony Troutman (T. Main Records), 1449 Lucile Avenue, SW Atlanta, Georgia 30310.

Denise LaSalle (Malaco Records), Agency: Rodgers Redding and Associates, POB 4603, Macon, Georgia 31208

2 Live Crew (Luke Records) Agency: ICM International Creative Management, 10250 Constellation Place, Los Angeles, California 90067. Agent: Peter Seitz

JJ Fad (Ruthless Records), 21860 Burbank Blvd, Suite 100, Los Angeles, California 90211.

Get Fresh Girls (Breakaway Records), 38 NE 167th St, Miami, FL 33162.

Chill Deal Boyz (Pump Records), 8484 Wilshire Blvd, Los Angeles, CA. 90211

Icey Jaye (JBM-Arista Records) MC Jaye McGowan and C.C. Orange, 6 West 57th Street, New York, NY 10019. Management: Fred Frank and Jayne Wilson of Coast to Coast Music.

Mamado & SHE (WTG-Epic Records) Attitude Records, 5214 North Pearl Street, Jacksonville, Florida 32208.

Tyrone Davis (Malaco Records), Agent: Rodgers Redding and Associates, POB 4603, Macon, Georgia 31208.

Clarence Carter (Ichiban Records), Agent: Rodgers Redding and Associates, POB 4603, Macon, Georgia 31208.

Marvin Sease (London-Polygram Records), Agent: Rodgers Redding and Associates, POB 4603 Macon, Georgia 31208.

Benny Latimore (Malaco Records), Agent: Rodgers Redding and Associates, POB 4603 Macon, Georgia 31208.

The Chill Crew (Big Tyme Records). Agent: Big Tyme Entertainment, 22 West University Blvd, Gainesville, Florida 32601.

2 Smooth: Independent marketing and representation.

Love Maze: Independent marketing and representation.

Technic Posse: Independent marketing and representation.

THE 1980S: THE KELLYS STANDING TOGETHER

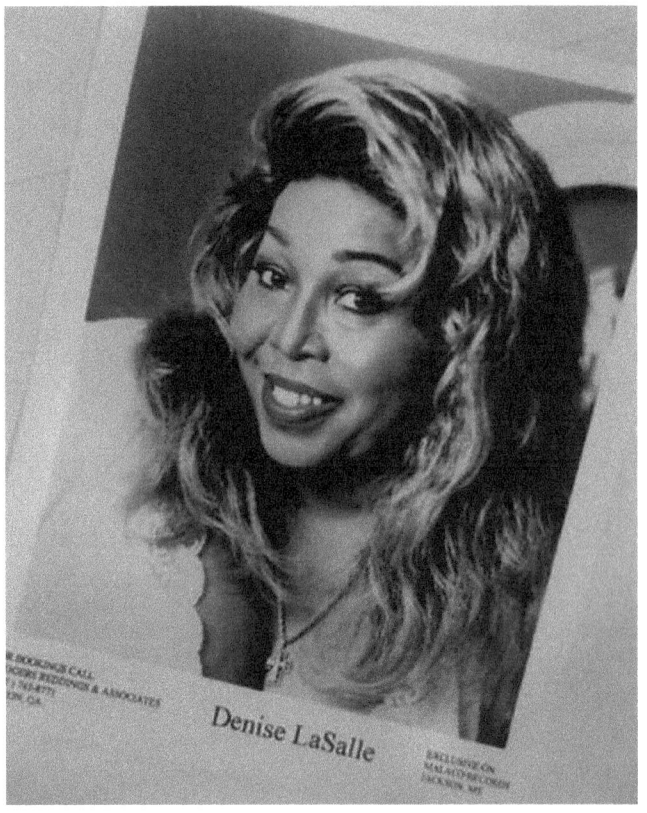

Denise LaSalle was one of the last recording artists that Clifford Kelly promoted in Lawtey just prior to his wife's retirement. Ms. LaSalle's current R&B Top 40 album on Billboard was titled "Right Place, Right Time" On the night of the show, it was as if Kelly's Nite Limit returned to its heyday. An unbelievable maximum full capacity crowd packed "The Place" out in 1984 for Denise LaSalle's sassy wit and blues revue.

Then, after thirty-one years of self-employment, Mrs. Margurie Williams Kelly (co-owner and co-founder) retired from her very own Kelly's Nite Limit in July of 1985. A few weeks later, The Kellys returned to Los Angeles, Las Vegas, and Tijuana, Mexico for a much needed vacation. Clifford Kelly took his little sister, Harridelle Bright, along with him for this trip. The Kellys took this same vacation six times within twenty-five years.

THE 1980S: THE KELLYS STANDING TOGETHER

Clifford Kelly at the marketplace in Tijuana, Baja, Mexico August 1985

Margure Kelly, Clifford Kelly Sr. and Harridelle Taylor Bright Walking the strip in Las Vegas

Clifford Kelly Sr. and his sister Harridelle Taylor Bright photographed in front of Mann's Chinese Theater in Los Angeles. (August 1985)

All photographs provided by the Collection of Margurie Williams Kelly

THE 1980S: THE KELLYS STANDING TOGETHER

Photograph of Willie Brown (R) & Truman Strong (L) at Kelly's provided by Mrs. Patricia Brown) (Photographs of 2 Live Crew at Kelly's Nite Limit provided by Willie and Patricia Brown

Starting in the Fall of 1985, Kelly's Nite Limit was managed by Willie "Cooter" Brown and his wife Patricia "Bonnie" Brown of Lawtey. For the next nineteen years, the Browns managed "The Place" for the regular patrons who grew up in Bradford County and the next generation. Clifford Kelly was always amazed and confounded at the size of the crowd who frequented his place during the Rap-Hip Hop Era. The rap era was still in its infancy. Most of the rap artists at Kelly's did not have a major record deal, but some of them had a growing and loyal following of enthusiastic fans. A new upcoming rap group named 2 Live Crew from Miami, Florida performed at Kelly's Nite Limit. Their albums "This Is Who We Are (1986)" and "Move Somethin' (1988)" were certified gold by the Recording Industry Association of America (RIAA). Mr. Kelly's grandson Tony Jones and his fiancée Lori were in the audience. It was a wild night, and Kelly's Nite Limit was packed, packed, packed!!! Rap music was becoming more popular and profitable. Yet, it was a genre that Mr. Schoolboy was not able to comprehend. Of course, he would have made a lot more money promoting hip hop artists than ever before. Nevertheless, Clifford Kelly Sr. simply could not relate to rap music nor wanted to engage with some of the rude and juvenile attitudes of a new generation. He detested smug ass remarks by some of the 19- or 20-year-olds rolling their eyes and sucking their teeth at him. Therefore, whenever he wanted to have a live show at Kelly's, he booked and promoted blues recording artists only.

Clarence Carter Live at Kelly's Nite Limit on September 26, 1987. Promoted by Clifford Kelly Sr. Photograph provided by Ulysee Muff Sr.

Memorabilia: A Kelly's Nite Limit promotional flyer for the Rap Artist Showcase featuring Chill Deal, Icey Jaye and 2 Smooth on 11/25/1988, promoted by Bobby Kelly. C.C. Lemonhead and Jay Ski of Chill Deal achieved success writing and producing for Icey Jaye and as members of 95 South, Sixty Nine Boyz, and Quad City DJ's. On Billboard's Hot Rap Chart, the 3x platinum **"Whoot There It Is"** *by 95 South went to #3. Their 2 X platinum hit* **"Tootsee Roll"** *by The Sixty Nine Boys went to #1. Both recordings were certified multi-platinum by the RIAA.*

THE 1980S: THE KELLYS STANDING TOGETHER

Memorabilia: In March 1990 Icey Jaye also performed at the Tasco Teen Dance Party in a series of events at the St. Petersburg Coliseum. A musical extravaganza initially established in 1924

Promotional portrait for Icey Jaye (Arista Records) provided by Kelly's Nite Limit

Portrait Author: Arista

Memorabilia: A promotional portrait and original recording (WTG Records) for Mamado & She provided by Kelly's Nite Limit. The rap group performed at Kelly's on December 31, 1988 along with guest artist TECHNIC Posse. The event was promoted by Bobby Kelley

Memorabilia: Promotional portrait (Malaco Music) and contract (Rodgers Redding and Associates) for Benny Latimore at Kelly's Nite Limit on April 15, 1989. The event was promoted by Clifford Kelly. Portrait provided by Kelly's Nite Limit. Contract provided by Emma Kelly Strong

CHAPTER 10

The 1990s
The Kelly's 50th Wedding Anniversary

Although Clifford Kelly Sr. promoted a vast cohort of recording artists, the pinnacle of his legacy at Kelly's Nite Limit was his 50th Wedding Anniversary. Mrs. Kelly wanted to have a real wedding this time. As she noted, the first time they were married was at the courthouse in Starke, Florida. This time, she wanted to walk down the aisle and have their son Clifford Jr. give her away.

It was also during this time that Clifford Kelly implemented a complete makeover for the dance hall area usually referred to as (The Back) at Kelly's Nite Limit. Total square footage of the building was 8,220 sq. ft. The dance hall area covered over 5,000 sq. ft. After his vacation in Las Vegas five years prior, it was Clifford Kelly's dream to bring Las Vegas to Lawtey, so to speak. He wanted to add a touch of upscale glitter to his nightclub decor. Once again, Clifford Kelly hired an all indigenous team of residents from Lawtey for the project. His son in law Benjamin Strong was among those commissioned to renovate and revamp the structure along with Archie Kittles Sr., Jeremiah Johnson, and Master Painter Oscar Williams all of Lawtey.

The ceiling was replaced with new plywood and painted royal blue. Mr. Williams painted the walls with a dual color of half pink at the top and half blue at the bottom. He painted three rows of pink stars encompassing two of the four walls' horizons like a border. For the first time ever, carpet was installed by Mr. James Griffis for all four seating sections of the dance hall. The dance floor was decked like a checkerboard with royal blue & gold tiles. The stage wall was painted blue with pink stars interwoven with the initials KNL (short form of Kelly's Nite Limit) in capital letters. The stage guard rail was painted burnt orange. A border was added to the ceiling above the stage, which was painted blue with pink stars also. Multicolored lamps were installed at the top of all twelve poles of the first section seating area. A string line of white lights were positioned like crown molding around the inner perimeter of the entire ceiling. Fluorescent black light tubes were aligned on both sides of the ceiling's outer perimeter. Mr. Kelly was well pleased with the outcome of his design. Kelly's Nite Limit was squeaky clean and glistening for his upcoming anniversary.

A week before the ceremony, Clifford Kelly Jr. and his family arrived in Lawtey from Los Angeles, driving their beautiful new 1990 Mercedes 500. Throughout the week, the extended Kelly family rolled up their sleeves to decorate Kelly's Nite Limit which was always affectionately called "the place" by CIifford and Margurie Kelley. He and his wife Margurie, always referred to the dance hall area as "the back". The back was adorned with a 50th anniversary theme utilizing ivory and gold colored event supplies and equipment. Down by the stage, Benjamin Strong transported seven buffet tables and about fifty gallons of assorted fruit beverages. One table for the bride, one table for the champagne fountain, four tables for food/appetizers, and one table for gifts. The gift table was placed at the other end of the dance floor near the Piccolo (Juke box).

THE 1990S: THE KELLY'S 50TH WEDDING ANNIVERSARY

On May 26, 1990 (Memorial Day Weekend), four hundred guests attended the Kelly's 50th Wedding Anniversary nuptials and reception in Lawtey. The ceremony was held at Philadelphia Baptist Church. The nuptials were officiated by Pastor W.G. Mayberry. Mrs. Everlina Kittles was the Mistress of Ceremonies. Mrs. Harriedell Bright was the Matron of Honor. Robert Austin Sr. was the Best Man. Mrs. Aretha Denefield served as Mother of the Bride. Musical selections were provided by Helen Franklin, Shirley E. Johnson, and Steve Marshall. Mrs. Willie Mae Randolph was the Pianist. Derek Alvarez was the official wedding photographer. Mrs. Edna Bell Allen and Mrs. Clementine White both of Lawtey, accepted and organized the gifts as guests arrived at Kelly's Nite Limit for the reception.

The Kelly family could not agree about the dinner menu. Therefore, the meal was a mix of appetizers, deviled eggs, gourmet sandwiches, and cake. For drinks, a table was centered by a gold champagne fountain that dispensed assorted fruit punch. The bride's table featured a four-tier wedding cake, a floral bouquet, and two golden long-stem candle holders with white candles. Clifford Kelly wasn't having it with just finger foods. He went left and had the reception catered with BBQ and a fish fry. His sister, the Matron of Honor Mrs. Harridelle Bright, cooked an oversized lobster pot full of her delicious poultry seasoned Chicken 'n Rice. Somehow, that great big pot of savory rice managed to take center stage at the bride's table. A large piece of plywood was placed over one of the pool tables to carve up a slow-roasted barbecued goat. Clifford Kelly booked a DJ and a local band named The Rackety Roches from Jacksonville, Florida, to entertain the guests.

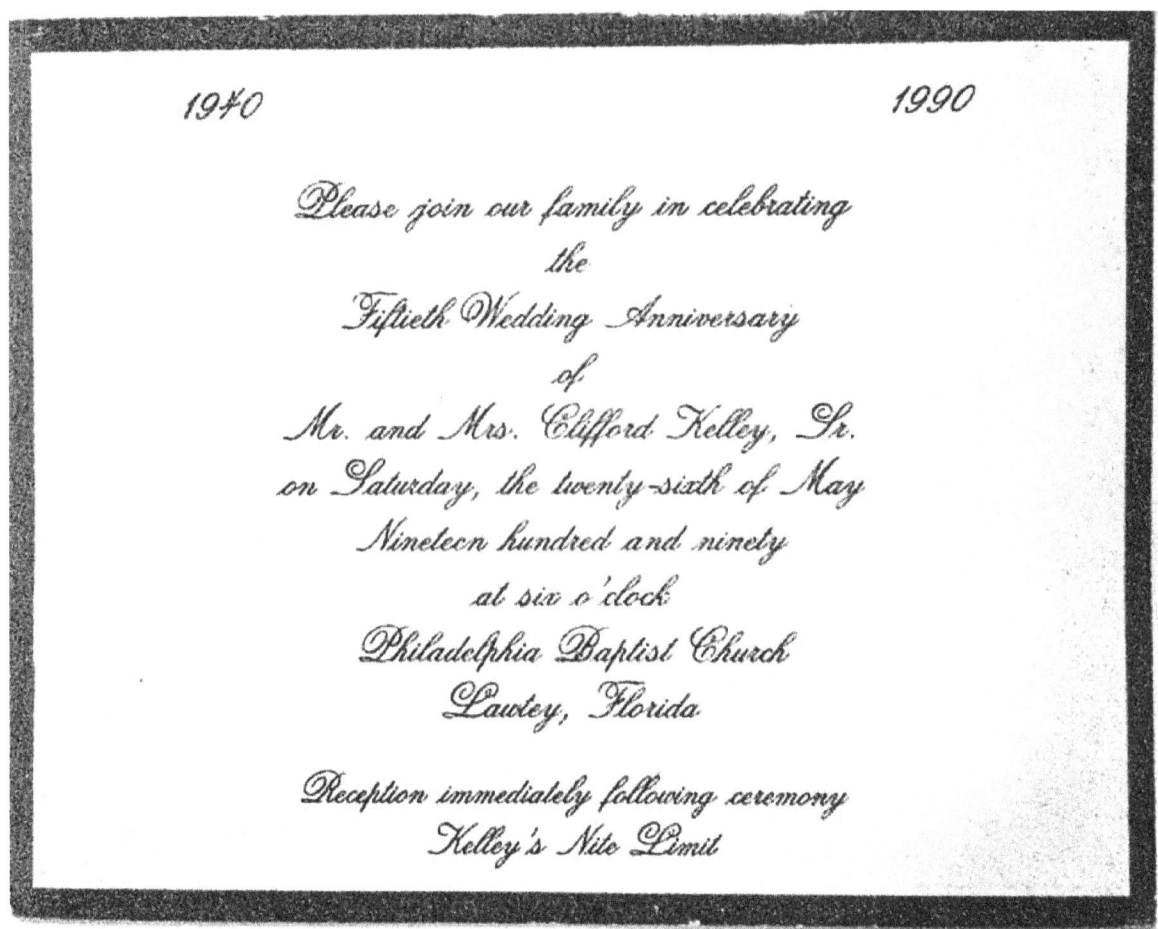

The 50th Wedding Anniversary Invitation of Mr. and Mrs. Clifford Kelly Sr.

THE 1990S: THE KELLY'S 50TH WEDDING ANNIVERSARY

The Groom: Mr. Clifford Lee Kelly Sr.

THE 1990S: THE KELLY'S 50TH WEDDING ANNIVERSARY

The Bride: Mrs. Margurie Williams Kelly.

THE 1990S: THE KELLY'S 50TH WEDDING ANNIVERSARY

Mr. and Mrs. Clifford Kelly Sr.: 50th Wedding Anniversary Reception at Kelly's Nite Limit in Lawtey, Florida May 26, 1990

THE 1990S: THE KELLY'S 50TH WEDDING ANNIVERSARY

The Bride's Table

THE 1990S: THE KELLY'S 50TH WEDDING ANNIVERSARY

Mr. and Mrs. Clifford Kelly Sr.

To the Bride and Groom!

THE 1990S: THE KELLY'S 50TH WEDDING ANNIVERSARY

Golden Anniversary, Golden Smiles: Mr. Kelly wore gold caps on his teeth. Mrs. Kelly wore a diamond solitaire and gold crowns on her teeth too!

THE 1990S: THE KELLY'S 50TH WEDDING ANNIVERSARY

Happy Anniversary!

THE 1990S: THE KELLY'S 50TH WEDDING ANNIVERSARY

We are gathered here today to reaffirm the wedding vows of Mr. and Mrs. Clifford Kelly Sr.

THE 1990S: THE KELLY'S 50TH WEDDING ANNIVERSARY

Place the ring on the Bride's finger

You may kiss the Bride!

THE 1990S: THE KELLY'S 50TH WEDDING ANNIVERSARY

Kiss her again!

THE 1990S: THE KELLY'S 50TH WEDDING ANNIVERSARY

Our Wedding Day

Harridelle Taylor Bright (Matron of Honor)

Robert Austin Sr. (Best Man)

Margurie Williams Kelly (Bride), Clifford Kelly Sr. (Groom)

Aretha Lee Denefield (Step Mother of the Bride)

THE 1990S: THE KELLY'S 50TH WEDDING ANNIVERSARY

Mrs. Harridelle Bright, Mr. and Mrs. Kelly and Mr. Robert Austin Sr.

THE 1990S: THE KELLY'S 50TH WEDDING ANNIVERSARY

Our Family: James Jackson Jr. (Cousin), Ferniece Jackson (Cousin), Margurie Kelly (Bride), Clifford Kelly Sr. (Groom), Willie Mae Jordan (Niece), and Willie Mae Cromity–Randolph (Organist and Family Friend)

THE 1990S: THE KELLY'S 50TH WEDDING ANNIVERSARY

The Kelly Family: Marylou Kelly, Emma Kelly Strong, Margurie Kelly, Clifford Kelly Jr., Clifford Kelly Sr., Margaret Jean Kelly Copeland, and Aretha Lee Denefield

THE 1990S: THE KELLY'S 50TH WEDDING ANNIVERSARY

Mr. and Mrs. Clifford Kelly Sr.

50th Wedding Anniversary

May 26, 1990

Lawtey, Florida

The festivities were featured on the cover of the African American newspaper "The Jacksonville Free Press" (est 1986). The publication was established by Rita Carter. She was a close friend of Mrs. Kelly and photographed the event personally for the newspaper. Suggested wording: Rita Carter was an activist and General Manager of radio stations WZAZ, WERD, WPDQ, and several other radio stations in Jacksonville, Florida. Mrs. Rita Carter-Perry was also a former executive for Motown Records and the first female founding publisher in the State of Florida.

Photograph: Blues Legend Clarence Carter at Kelly's Nite Limit provided by Ulysse Muff

Also, in 1990, another generation became of age and Clifford Kelly Sr. was now over 70 years of age himself. Despite the overwhelming popularity and attendance for Rap/Hip Hop music artists at Kelly's Nite Limit, Mr. Schoolboy continued to book the blues and soul music recording artists he loved the most. During the 1990s for multiple performances, Clifford Kelly Sr. continued to promote Bobby Blue Bland, Clarence Carter, Tyrone Davis, Marvin Sease, Chuck Roberson, Roy C., and Betty Wright to perform live at his place in Lawtey.

Bobby Blue Bland returned to the Kelly's Nite Limit Stage on December 10, 1994. The blues legend was inducted into the Rock 'n Roll Hall of Fame presented by B.B. King at the Waldorf Astoria in New York just two years prior to his latest performance in Lawtey, Florida. It was an all too familiar routine as fans called the Kelly home to reserve their tables. On the night of the show, Ulysee Muff, owner of Muff Security Inc., was at the front entrance coordinating the ticket exchange. Clifford Kelly's granddaughter, Sibyl Kelley (aged thirty), sold show tickets at the door, just like her aunt Jean Kelly did in years past. Silas Jenkins Sr. of Lawtey had the best table in the house at center stage with his family and friends. Gerald Pettyway and Alton Moore of Starke had front row seats as well at table #3 on the far right side of the stage. On this mild December night at Kelly's Nite Limit, just over one-third of the seats were filled. Under four hundred fans came to see the show that night. Mr. Bobby Blue Bland, the consummate professional, stepped off his custom tour bus and hit the stage and sat down on a comfy bar seat. Mr. Bland's musicians, particularly the horn section, looked impressive with their printed sheet music and orchestra stands positioned on the Kelly's Nite Limit Stage. It was clear, the musicians were reading the musical score as they flipped the pages of their sheet music during the live performance. At age 64, Bobby Blue Bland performed sitting down on a bar seat. His fans clapped, laughed joyfully, and gleamed with adulation as they witnessed an authentic blues icon perform live at Kelly's Nite Limit…again.

Blues Music Icon Bobby Blue Bland on stage at Kelly's Nite Limit (December 10, 1994). Photograph provided by Ulysee Muff Sr.

THE 1990S: THE KELLY'S 50TH WEDDING ANNIVERSARY

The Legendary Bobby Blue Bland live at Kelly's Nite Limit in Lawtey Florida on December 10, 1994. Photograph provided by Ulysee Muff Sr.

Mr. Bland traveled the world entertaining audiences in ninety countries. On February 25, 1997, he was honored with the Lifetime Achievement Award at the 39th Grammy Nominee & Award Reception. The award is for performers who, during their lifetime, have made creative contributions of outstanding artistic significance to the field of recording.

(Memorabilia: ABC Booking Corporation Press Kit: Promotional portrait, press release (Malaco Records) press release (The Recording Academy) provided from the Collection of Mrs. Margurie Williams Kelly. The press kit included a total of thirty-four pages

THE 1990S: THE KELLY'S 50TH WEDDING ANNIVERSARY

Photograph: Clifford Kelly Sr. and family provided by Marylou Kelly Williams

As the 1990s progressed, Kelly Nite Limit thrived under the management of Willie "Cooter" Brown. Bookings and promotions for live DJ shows, and private events continued to increase at the venue. Under his management, heyday size crowds of young fans ventured out to Kelly's Nite Limit to see new and upcoming Rap artists such as The Chill Crew, Get Fresh Girls and JJ FAD. Clifford Kelly maintained his connections with Rodgers Redding & Associates whenever he decided to promote another show and dance. As always Mr. Ulysee Muff Sr. was at the front entrance coordinating the ticket exchange at Kelly's Nite Limit. Kelly's Curb Masters was no longer in Central Florida. Clifford Kelly would bid on construction development in North Florida primarily in Fleming Island, Pace Island, Orange Park, and St. Augustine.

The Kelly's spent their latter years attending events for their adult grandchildren, great grandchildren, and extended family. The great and great-great grandchildren of Clifford and Margurie Kelly born in the 1990s and beyond are: Tiaira, Destiny, Nykeria, Savannah, Ekiyah, Steve, Shania. Jayden, E'lasiah, Myanna, Josiah, Mia, Naomi, Brice, Milaik, Katelyn, Jamiaya, Christian, Kylie, Braydon, Amari, Taven, Toren, Tailyn, Connor, Cameron, Destinee, Anthony J., Antonio Jr., Larissa, Kiyoami, Aubryettah, Amaria, William, Bryan, and Maryah.

THE 1990S: THE KELLY'S 50TH WEDDING ANNIVERSARY

Clifford Kelly Sr. pictured with his brother Robert Willie Jordan on the left

Photograph provided by Marylou Kelly Williams

Graduation Night for FCCJ at the Times Union Center for the Performing Arts in Jacksonville, Florida (1991–1992)

Pictured L-R: Emma Kelly Strong, Toika Strong, **Sibyl Kelley**, Britany Highland, Margurie Kelly and Clifford Kelly Sr.

THE 1990S: THE KELLY'S 50TH WEDDING ANNIVERSARY

Granddaughter of Clifford & Margurie Kelly, Miss Toika L. Strong

Senior Year 1993–1994

Bradford County High School

Starke, Florida

Clifford Kelly Sr. with his grandson Frank A. Green Jr.

Graduation Day for
Andrew Jackson High School

Jacksonville, Florida. (1997–1998)

THE 1990S: THE KELLY'S 50TH WEDDING ANNIVERSARY

Miss Vakela L. Kelly, Granddaughter of Mr. and Mrs. Clifford Kelly Sr.

Westover Comprehensive High School Albany, Georgia Class of 1998

Mrs. Margurie Kelly and her grandson Bobby Kelly Jr. Graduation Day at First Coast High School Jacksonville, Florida (1995–1996)

A Special Evening for a Doting Fan at Kelly's Nite Limit

Marvin Sease, from Vicksburg, Mississippi was the embodiment of risque soulful blues. Clifford Kelly booked and promoted Marvin Sease to perform on multiple occasions at Kelly's Nite Limit. Mr. Sease had a loyal female following around the U.S. nightclub scene and was always a popular Blues-Jazz Fest favorite.

Mrs. Beverly Turner of Jacksonville, Florida, remembered Mr. Sease performing in Lawtey. It was on November 1, 1997 that Marvin Sease was promoted for another show and dance at Kelly's Nite Limit. Lawtey was still a tiny rural North Florida community without a hotel. Under contract, Clifford Kelly reserved seven hotel rooms for Mr. Sease, and his fourteen musicians at the Days Inn in Starke, Florida. Just seven miles south of Lawtey.

Beverly Turner was at Kelly's Nite Limit for the live show and dance. On that November evening in 1997, Beverly Turner recalled what she wore on the night of the show. Beverly wore a stylish dress-casual denim outfit by Fredrick's of Hollywood. She drove down to Lawtey, Florida in her 1995 burgundy and black ragtop Cadillac DeVille. It was rare that customers

Photograph of Beverly and Marvin at Kelly's Nite Limit was provided by Mrs. Beverly Drummond Turner

brought a camera with them for a show at Kelly's Nite Limit. Mr. Kelly always had a photographer on site for fans who wanted to capture the moment before or after the dance. Beverly Turner was fortunate to take a picture with one of her favorite entertainers Mr. Marvin Sease. He placed his arm around her and touched her hand for the picture. Mrs. Turner remembered Marvin Sease performing his calling card, his signature recording titled—C@ndy L*ck'r—live on the Kelly's Nite Limit stage. The song received national attention on Billboard's R&B Chart back in 1987. Over the course of his career, twelve of his recordings reached the Top 100 on Billboard's R&B Hip Hop Albums Chart. Mrs. Turner, a stylish energetic woman, has fond memories of the shows she attended. Mrs. Turner believes that as you get older it does not change who you are. "Your body will change, but inside, you are still who you are." She continues to wear blonde highlights and stylish fitted clothing to this day. Just like countless cohorts of mature adult women of the era, Mrs. Beverly Turner was a doting fan of Mr. Marvin Sease as well.

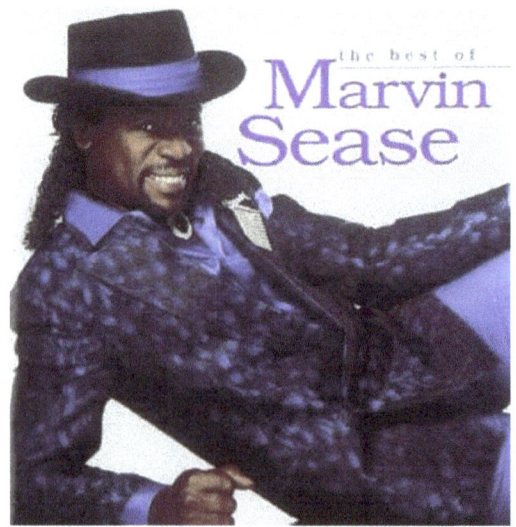

On YouTube Marvin Sease received 8.4 million views for "Please Take Me." "Stuck In the Middle" & "Is It Over" both downloads received 2.9 million views each presented by Malacomg (Malaco Music). His recording "Ghetto Man" (20th Anniversary Collection) received 10 million views (Malaco Music). Digital Image by Malacomg

CHAPTER 11

Y2Ks: Kelly's Nite Limit and the Digital Blues

In the year 2000, Clifford Kelly Sr. turned 82 years old. He was still unapologetically a self-employed Blues Artist Promoter to his soul. Through the decades he continued to utilize the booking agency of Rodgers Redding & Associates. As technology transitioned, Clifford Kelly remained loyal and faithful to his cultural blues music. In the final years, he continued to book and promote Clarence Carter, Mel Waiters, and Roy C. to perform at Kelly's Nite Limit.

On May 13, 2000, Alabama blues boy native Clarence Carter, a veteran of the stage for more than 30 years, performed a Mother's Day special at Kelly's Nite Limit. Clarence Carter was booked and promoted to perform at Kelly's at least three to four times per decade since the late 1960s. He was always a fan favorite at Kelly's Nite Limit. Clifford Kelly was a diehard fan who enjoyed the music of Clarence Carter immensely. He loved the music so much that he could count the number of Clarence Carter's performances in Lawtey, Florida on both hands.

Photograph of Clarence Carter originally published by The Encyclopedia of Alabama

Clarence Carter, a 1960 graduate of Alabama State University earned a bachelor of science degree in music. He was inducted into the Alabama Music Hall of Fame (AMHOF) in 2003. His C. Carter-Topic & Playlist "A Touch of the Blues" presented by YouTube received over 12 Million views.

On May 18, 2002, the soulful blues balladeer Mel Waiters performed all of his hit recordings at Kelly's Nite Limit.

After twenty years in the business, Mel Waiters from San Antonio, Texas was among the younger class of blues recording artists. His most successful hit recording "Got My Whiskey" went to #11 on Billboard's Blues Album Chart in 1997.

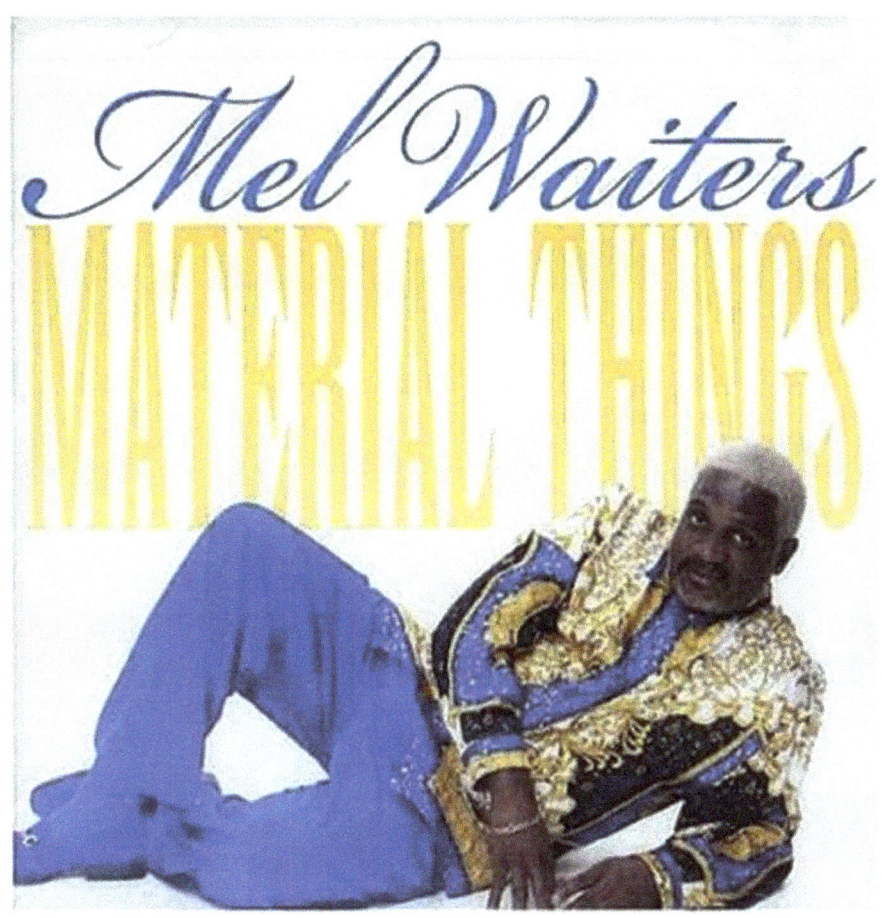

On YouTube, Mel Waiters "Got My Whiskey" received 21 million views. His recording titled "Hole in the Wall" received 14 million views. His discography and digital image are presented by Malacog (Malaco Music).

Roy C. Pioneer of the Breakbeat

Memorabilia: Promotional portrait of Roy C by (Rodgers Redding & Associates provided from the Collection of Emma Kelly Strong. Digital Image of Roy C provided by Three Gems Records

By the time Roy Charles Hammond (aka Roy C.) performed at Kelly's Nite Limit, his career spanned well over forty years. Roy C. was a gifted singer, songwriter, producer, promoter, and entrepreneur.

He owned and founded three record labels: Alagra, Hammond, and Three Gems Records. Over the course of his career, he released thirty-six singles and eleven albums.

Better late than never, as Clifford Kelly finally booked Roy C. from Allendale, South Carolina to perform at Kelly's Nite Limit. Emma Kelly Strong and Beverly Drummond Turner remembered his performance in Lawtey. His down home country blues vocal style was well received among blues fans.

His recording titled "Shotgun Wedding" went #14 on Billboard's R&B Chart in 1965. The song went to #6 on the UK Singles Chart in 1966. Roy C. was also a pioneer in modern music. He wrote and produced a song titled "Impeach the President" by The Honey Drippers. The song was recorded during the 1973 Watergate Era and released on his very own Alagra Records label.

Digital image of Roy C., provided by Three Gems Records

The drum beat he created has been sampled numerous times by various singers and rap artists namely LL Cool J "Around the Way Girl," Notorious B.I.G. "Unbelievable," N.W.A: "Gangsta Gangsta," 2PAC: "I Get Around," Nas: "The Message," Janet Jackson "That's the Way Love Goes," and hundreds more. After 1986, every artist and recording that utilized the drumbeat (technic breakbeat) pioneered by Mr. Roy C. was a hit. It was his drumbeat that revolutionized the sound of New York Rap forever. Most blues artists of Roy C.'s caliber, pedigree, and talent were primarily overlooked by the industry, fading into the horizon. Yet, thanks to YouTube, all Blues artists of yesteryear continue to inspire the next generation. Roy C. received 1.1 million views for his recording "If

I Could Love You Forever" and 1.4 million views for "Don't Blame the Man" both recordings were presented by CD Baby. He received 1.5 million views for "Peepin" Through the Window on Roy C-Topic, plus millions more on individual YouTube channels and playlists.

Mr. Roy C. Hammond was a genuine blues musician, singer, songwriter, producer, promoter, and entrepreneur ahead of his time. He was among the very last recording artists to perform live at Kelly's Nite Limit in Lawtey, Florida.

The Kelly's Nite Limit Business Card

CHAPTER 12

A Personal Heritage and Legacy

In the summer of 2004, the last hoorah finally arrived. Mr. Clifford "Schoolboy" Kelly, an 86-year-old self-employed Concert Promoter and Concrete Finisher for fifty years shut the front door and closed down Kelly's Nite Limit. It was once said that when you saw Clifford Kelly Sr., you saw his father John Wesley Garrer. In some ways, this is true. He modeled himself after his father's sense of style: always well dressed and committed to self-employment. John Garrer was a big and tall man with smooth hands and fabled as a really good cook as he often prepared steak and eggs for the family. On the other hand, Clifford Kelly Sr. barely cooked anything. There was nothing soft about him. He was aggressive, abrupt, evasive, headstrong, short-tempered, boisterous, domineering, temperamental, laid back, humorous, energetic, and very hardworking with incredible endurance. He relied heavily on his inherent raw instinct to navigate through the obstacles of everyday living. He would envision a plan, then execute to manifest his ideas. He was not an activist for social awareness or change. He was not political nor religious but served as a Trustee at his local church in Lawtey. Just like his father, Clifford Kelly Sr. was a big and tall man who liked to get dressed up in a three-piece suit and tie, a fedora, a diamond ring, gold chain, and a pair of Stacy Adams. He spoke using his own version of the Gullah Geechee dialect and terminology of clichés. The grandchildren thought it was hilarious at times, but his wife always understood every word. Clifford Kelly would say: "Don't forget the bridge that brought you across." Unknown to the grandchildren, there were *icons in the yard*. He had some of his own catch phrases too. He would say: "Git-thah-Checkbook!" or his animated household phrase "Git-thah-Shotgun!" Which Mr. Kelly did, as he went after some street dogs who entered his property and mauled his three-year-old Pekingese poodle named Dallas Kelly.

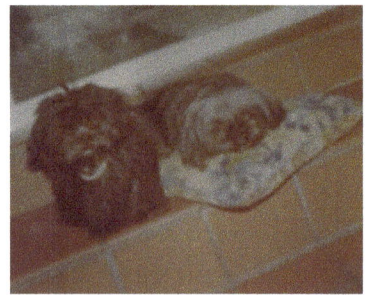

Ebony Jones Kelly on the pillow
(1975–1992)

Dallas Kelly
(February 1982–February 1985)

His home office became nothing more than a nice storage room with a brass and white-laced daybed. So how did a man with a limited education maintain two businesses for five decades? His managerial policy consisted primarily as a Mom'n Pop, Five & Dime, Cash'n Carry acumen. Clifford Kelly always utilized the services of a professional agency to book recording artists. Any executive duties or tasks were outlined and processed by an agency. He also relied heavily on his wife and children to assist him with reading and writing. Most booking contracts signed in his name were actually signed by Mrs. Kelly. His children and even grandchildren would write down information he wanted for a project. He'd take the document to a vendor for professional reproduction or duplication as needed. His taxes were prepared by H and R Block. He banked with Community State Bank of Starke, First Union, and Citibank. He would listen to people in the community and ask questions. He was not a member of any exclusive clubs or auxiliaries. He was not an activist nor champion for social awareness or change. He had Kelly's Nite Limit as an extension or personal reflection of himself in the community. He dedicated most of his adult life to the promotion of recording artists of his own cultural background. His adoration and venue provision for blues and soul music artists spanned more than five decades. Although the author used certain terminology to highlight the era, Clifford Kelly Sr. never associated words or phrases such as chitlin circuit, blues club, juke joint, or juke house to describe Kelly's Nite Limit. Nor did he use such words to describe any other venue where he promoted live entertainment. For him, Kelly's Nite Limit was always referred to as "the place" or "my place." When referring to a different venue, he'd state the name of the business, the location, or simply say the name of the nightclub owner.

It was no secret that he could not read or write very well at all. Nonetheless, Clifford Kelly Sr. was intuitive enough to hire and retain former Florida House Representative Eugene Shaw of District 16 as his personal attorney for decades. After an unconventional childhood and adolescence, Clifford Kelly Sr. believed that he made a name for himself. Over 120 recording artists performed live at his very own Kelly's Nite Limit. He was satisfied with his personal achievements for Kelly's Curb Master Construction as well. The businesses were his personal contribution to the economy and society.

Photograph: The children of John Wesley Garrer: (L-R) Ray Garrer, Harridelle Bright, Clifford Kelly Sr. and Eva Jean Evans on June 3, 2006-Lawtey, Fla

Clifford Kelly Sr. at home in Lawtey, Florida June 3, 2006

He had to say goodbye to three of his children: (***Vernon Lee Kelly: 1945-1946***) (***Jerome Sims Kelly: 1952-1985***) (***Margaret Jean Kelly Copeland: 1950-2003***)

After more than six-and-a-half decades of marriage, he said farewell to his bride Margurie Williams Kelly (Jan 16, 1921–May 25, 2006). Although she was in hospice, it was Clifford Kelly's last wish that his wife would live until their wedding anniversary. Margurie Kelly lived for 90 minutes and passed away on their sixty-sixth wedding anniversary. Nine weeks later, they were reunited. Although his education was limited, there was one thing Mr. Schoolboy understood perfectly about reading and writing. At the end of the day, with pen in hand, the only thing Clifford Kelly Sr. knew how to truly read and write was a check.

"You Run Your Mouth, I'll Run My Business!"

Clifford Kelly Sr.

(1918–2006)

Owner and Founder

Kelly's Nite Limit (1954–2004)

Kelly's Curb Masters Construction (1960–2006)

Lawtey, Bradford, Florida, USA

A PERSONAL HERITAGE AND LEGACY

The Florida Times Union

August 11, 2006

References

1. Academic Accelerator (1918) Age of Consent Reform, State of Georgia (academic-accelerator.com).

2. American Railroad Labor and The Genesis of The New Deal, 1919–1935 (https://www.jstor.org).

3. Ancestry DNA Testing Services (Ancestry.com).

4. Associated Booking Corporation (1980) May 3, Correspondence

    (1974) June 3, Correspondence

5. Austin, Robert Jr. (2023) July 31 and August 10, Correspondence, Entrepreneur, Educator, Bradford County Schools.

6. Billboard.com

7. Billboard Magazine (1968) July 27, B. Wright, Page 11.

    (1968) November 2, C. Carter Vol. 88, No#44

    (1970) March 28, J. Simon, Page 105.

    (1973) October 20, B. Bland, Page 23.

8. Bradford CountyTelegraph (1900) Augusta 10, Volume XXII, No. 8, page 1.

9. Bright, Harridelle Taylor (2011) Entrepreneur, Samuel Proctor Oral History Program, University of Florida.

REFERENCES

10. Brown Willie and Patricia (2024) March 4, Business Associates, Correspondence.

11. Camp Blanding Museum (Campblandingmuseum.org).

12. Cashbox Magazine (1968) November 30, T. Davis, Page 25.

    (1976) August 21, T. Davis, Page 2.

13. Circuit Court for Bradford County Florida (1982) March 29, Civil Action Case, Cleosie Daniel, Name Change Petition and Order.

14. Encyclopedia Britannica (Britannica.com)

15. Encyclopedia of Alabama (https://encyclopediaofalabama.org/)

16. Evans, Eva (2023) March 30, Entrepreneur: phone interview and correspondence.

17. Florida Department of Business Regulation (1970) November 23, (Beverage Division) Recommendation and Order, Pages 1–3.

18. Florida Memory (1938) State Library and Archives of Florida (Manuscript Copy of the Florida Negro by the Florida Writers Project ca. 1938) (floridamemory.com)

19. Florida Postal History Society Journal (2014) January, Vol. 21, No.1, page 9.

20. Gainesville Sun (1985) October 3, Anderson Honored for 40 Years of Teaching, by Sherry Sapp, page 2B.

21. Gainesville Sun (1989) June 26, Retired Educator Leaves Indelible Mark, by Lisa Trei, pages 1d and 3d.

22. Globeatmica.com, Globe Collection and Press at MICA.

23. Grammy.com

REFERENCES

24. Historic Images 6073 Mount Moriah Road Suite 12 Memphis, TN 38115 (Historic Images.com)

25. History.com

26. History.delaware.gov, Delaware History and Cultural Affairs: African American Participation in WWI.

27. Jacksonville Public Library (Main Library) North Laura St and (San Marco Branch) LaSalle Street, Jacksonville, Florida.

28. Jordan, Willie Mae (2023) March 20, 22, 23, 24, 25, 26, June 25, Phone Interview and Correspondence, Educator, Richmond County Schools.

29. Kelly, Bobby K. (2023) August 27 Interview, Veteran U.S. Navy.

30. Kelley, Clifford L. Jr. (2023) March 28, 2023, April 5, 2023, June 29, 2023, July 24, 2023, and July 27, Phone Interview and Correspondence Entrepreneur, Veteran U.S. Air Force.

31. Kelly, Mary Lou (2022) December 8, Interview, Retired Therapist.

32. Miller, Donna J. Garrer (2022) October 31 and November 27, Phone Interview.

33. MTV/Viacom.com

34. MyFamilySearch.com

35. Muff, Ulysse Sr. (2023) April 27, June 19, Interview, Business Associate, Entrepreneur: Muff Security Inc.

36. Parker, Lee (2023) February 12, Business Associate, Entrepreneur: Down Home Blues Festival & Brimstone Records. Phone Interview.

37. Recording Industry Association of America (RIAA.com)

REFERENCES

38. Roberson, Chuck (2023) August 7, Recording Artist, Entrepreneur CEO of Desert Sound Records. Phone Interview.

39. Rodgers Redding & Associates, P.O. Box 4603 Macon, Georgia 31208.

40. Rollingstone.com

41. Rolling Stone Magazine (1973) August 30, L. Milton, Page 21.

42. Ross, Cynthia S. (2022) July 30, Memories Lawtey-Peetsville "Come Together Day."

43. Smith, William W. (1836) Sketch of the Seminole War: Sketches During A Campaign. Page 25.

44. Strong, Benjamin (2020) January 1, Retiree-Dupont Industries, Interview and Family Meeting.

45. Strong, Emma L. (2020) January 1, Family Meeting, Retiree-Educator Bradford County Schools.

46. The Jacksonville Free Press (1990) May 26, Page 1. Photographer: Rita Carter.

47. The New York Times (2021) September 21, Roy Hammond, Soul Singer Who Birthed a Hip Hop Heartbeat (nytimes.com).

48. The Savannah Tribune (2009) May 6, The Georgia Funeral Service Practitioners Association to Convene, by Staff. Savannah (Tribune.com).

49. Timeline of Events Important to Prohibition (Triblive.com).

50. Twenty Three and Me (2018) DNA Testing Service (23&me.com).

51. Turner, Beverly D., Interview January 9, 2024 and Correspondence January 14, 2024.

REFERENCES

52. University of Florida (2011) Samuel Proctor Oral History Program (http://oral.history.ufl.edu).

53. University of North Florida (2009) Digital Commons: George Lansing Taylor Collection.

54. U.S. Department of Labor (DOL.gov).

55. U.S. Social Security Administration (SSA.gov).

56. Walden, Phil Artists and Promotions 1019 Walnut Street Macon, Georgia 31201.

57. West, Jerry (2023) February 2, and August 8, Interview, Business Associate, Entrepreneur, DJs Record Shop.

58. Wikipedia, Wikimedia Common and the World Wide Web.

Index

A

Action Talent, 88
African Americans. *See* Black Americans
age of consent (AOC), 1918, 5–8
alcohol selling, 26, 54, 110, 111, 115, 130, 131
alcoholic policy, 54
Alexander, Laura, 215
Allen, Carla, 10
Allen, Edna Belle, 253, 317
Allen, Enoch, 54
Allen, Ester Marie, 133–134
Allen, Georgie, 10
Allen, Kenny, 10
Allen, Peter Jr., 10
Allen, Richard, 46, 112, 113
Allen, Tess Laquell, 134
Allen, Tracy, 10
Alvarez, Derek, 317
ancestry testing (Ancestry.com), viii, x, xv, 7, 8, 11, 18, 19, 24, 25, 29
Anderson, Alice Strong, 22
Anderson, Annie B., 22
Anderson, Charles C., 21, 22
Anderson, Raymond, 38
Application for Marriage License in 1940, 23, 24
Archie Bell & The Drells, 219
Armstrong, Louis, 56
Ashley, E., 194
Associated Booking Corporation (ABC), 56, 60, 84, 147, 160, 185, 202, 206, 247, 280, 305
Atlantic Recording Corporation, 203
Austin, Aretha, 258, 260
Austin, Robert (Bobby), 258–260, 317, 330, 331

B

Bagley, Mildred, 17
Bar Kays, 87, 121
Barber, Earl, 45
Barnes, Pearl, 2
Bass, Fontella, 87, 91
Battle at Burke County Jail in 1779, x
Battle of Brier Creek 1779, x
Battle of Waynesboro in 1864, x
Bauer, D. J., 193
Baylor, Johnny, 204
Beary, R. E., 193
B.E.E. The Black Exotics, 205
Bell, Alavan Walker, 28, 29, 34, 35, 38
Bell, Archie, 202
Bell, Mae, 40
Bell, William, 206, 246, 250–252
Ben Waller's Enterprises, 83
Benson, Jo Jo, 87
Berger, Bettye, 84, 142
beverage license, 55, 69, 111, 115, 131, 270, 297
Bickmeyer, Walter, 278
Big Maybelle, 83
Big Spring Ball, 100, 103
Big Tyme Entertainment, 307
Billboard Magazine, 129, 199, 200, 229, 231, 243

INDEX

Billboard's R&B Chart, 60–67, 70, 71, 117–120, 122, 123, 129, 130, 200, 201, 208, 217, 221, 224, 225, 228, 250, 254, 261, 263, 269, 292, 299, 344, 349
Birdsong, Larry, v, 57, 58
Black Americans, xiv, 2, 4, 8, 12–14, 20, 24, 26–27, 34, 39, 46, 102, 104, 105, 135
Black Code Laws of 1740, x, 20
Black Exotics Enterprises, 205
Bland, Bobby (Blue), 84, 91, 206, 220, 233, 241, 242, 243, 247–250, 257, 280, 301, 305, 336, 336, 337, 338
Blount, Ellie Peterson, 2
Blount, Emma Jones, xi, 1
Blount, John Jr., xi, 1, 2
Blount, John Sr., xi, 1
Bluebird Records, 68
Blunt III, John, xi, 1–4
Bobby Williams & The MarKings, 203
Bobo, Lonnie, 204
Boggs Academy, 12
Booker T. & The MGs, 86, 119, 121, 123
Boone, Jessie, 204
bootlegging, 9, 26, 55, 69, 112
Bostick, Desmer, 10
Bradford County Occupational License, 195
Brass Construction, 207, 271, 272
Bright, Deborah S., 51
Bright, Emmett Jr., 50–52, 248
Bright, Emmett Sr., 50
Bright, Florence Jackson, 50
Bright, Harridelle Taylor, 10, 29–31, 50–53, 95, 308, 309, 310, 317, 330, 331, 352
Bright, Judith Maria (Judy), 51, 216
Bright, Mischel Lucretia, 51, 216
Britt, Joseph Sr., 39, 40, 259
Britt, Willie Mae, 39
Brown, Charles, 83
Brown, Daniel, 302
Brown, Eddie, xv, 19
Brown, Errol, 270, 305
Brown, James, 57, 67, 95, 128, 207, 256, 263–268
Brown, Jerry, 2
Brown, Ruth, 84
Brown, Shirley, 205, 255
Brown, Susie Wilson, 17
Brown v. Board of Education of Topeka Kansas, 43–44
Brown, Willie, 311
BT Express, 206
Buffalo Booking Agency, 84, 85, 176, 204
Burke, Solomon, 85
Butler, Jerry, 86

C

C. & S. Productions, 205
CAMIL Productions, 204
Camp Blanding, 25
Campbell, James Milton, 228
Cantor, Phil, 84
Cape Canaveral, 210
Carter, Clarence, 130, 198, 202, 208, 209, 233, 241, 257, 278–279, 306, 312, 336, 345, 346
Carter, Jimmy, 263, 300, 301
Carter, Maxie, 292
Carter, Rita, 335
Carter, Roselyn, 300, 301
Carter, Russ, 165
Cashbox Magazine, 225, 227
Chandler, Gene, 84
Charles C. Anderson Junior High School, 22, 43–44, 109, 135, 136
Charles, Ray, 83, 128, 257
Cherokee War of 1759, x
The ChiLites, 205
The Chill Crew, 307
Chill Deal Boyz, 306, 312
Christon, John, 2
Chubby Checker, 84
Circle Artists Corporation, 85, 162, 163
Civil Rights Act of 1964, 104, 135

INDEX

Civil Rights Movement, 104–109
civil unrest, 128
Civil War 1861–1865, x, xii, 14, 34
Clark, Marie Jenkins, 262
Clay, Otis, 246
Cleveland Stadium, 48, 49
Club Eaton, 226
Collins, Bootsy, 207
Concept Productions Inc., 88
ConFunkShun, 271, 272, 305
Conley, Arthur, 202, 208, 209
Continental Artists Inc., 203
Continental Can Company, 27
Convay, Don, 246
Cooke, Sam, 83, 128, 298, 299
Copeland, Brian, 235, 262
Copeland Construction Company, 234, 235
Copeland, Ernest, 125, 234, 235, 237, 248
Copeland, Kenny, 235, 280
Couch, Tom, 205
Cox, John, xiii
cradle of education, 12–13
Crawford, Dave, 203
Cromity-Randolph, Willie Mae, 332
Cross, Charlie Jr., 205
Cunningham, Eva Jean, 2, 3, 35, 96–98, 352
Cunningham, Geraldine, 35, 96
Curtis, King, 87

D

DAKAR-Cotillion, 190
Daniel, Annie Bell, 27
Daniel, Cleosie, 5–7, 282–291. *See also* Kelly, Clifford (Cleo)
Daniel, Emma Kate, v, 5, 6, 13, 15, 16, 26, 28, 92–94, 127, 282
Daniel, Grady Lee, v, 6, 7, 13, 15, 16, 25–28, 47, 95
Daniel, Issac, 6
Daniel, Joshua, 5, 7, 26, 27, 47
Daniel, Lula, 5

Davis, Carl Sr., 87
Davis, Clora, 70
Davis, Tyrone, 87, 205, 208, 209, 220, 225, 227, 229, 233, 246, 257, 306, 336
De Noia, Carmine, 186
The Dells, 84
Delta Blues, 68
Denefield, Areatha Lee, 23–24, 95, 317, 330, 333
Denefield, Edward R., 23–24
Denefield, James E., 23
DeNoia, Carmine, 88
The Devastations, 204
The Dick Boone Agency, 86
Diddley, Bo, 85
digital blues, 345–350
Dock Productions Inc., 206
Doggett, Bill, 86
Domino, Fats, 82
Doster, Donneil Anthony, Jr., 99
Doster, Tony, 210, 216, 219, 265
Drayton, Richard, 134
The Drells, 202
The Drifters, v, 57, 64
Drummond, Mary Frances, 300

E

Ellerson, Robert, 20
employment, 7, 14, 16, 21, 25, 27, 93, 104, 133, 258, 276, 277, 282, 295
The Enchanters, 85
Environmental Protection Agency (EPA), 278
Evans, James, 87
exclusionary laws, 4

F

Fair Labor Standards Act of 1938, 15
family business expansion, 34–38
The Famous Flames, 67, 83
farming, xi–xiii, xv, 2, 3, 7, 9, 10, 12, 15
Fifteenth Census of the United States 1930, 11, 18

Floyd, Eddie, 203, 208, 209
Floyd, King, 203, 216–219, 246
Floyd, Milton, 44
Ford-Strong, Maxie Belle, 235
Franklin, Aretha, 87
Franklin, Helen, 317
Frazier, Skipper Lee, 202

G
Gaines, Roy, v, 57, 61
Galaxy Artist Management, 87
The Gale Agency, 56, 64, 140, 143
Gamble, Kenny, 223
Garrer, Alavan, 96, 126
Garrer, Cornelia Walker, 6, 7
Garrer, Elizabeth, xii, 1–3
Garrer, Ida Belle, 35, 96, 126
Garrer, John, 5, 6, 8, 9–13, 26, 28, 29, 34–38, 41, 55, 79–80, 96, 110, 126, 351, 352. *See also* Blunt III, John
Garrer, Lillie Belle, 2
Garrer, Prince, xii, 1–3
Garrer, Ray, 352
Garrer, Sarah, 3
Garrer, Tamer, 1–4
Garrer, Warner, 2, 3
Garrer's Blue Flame, 34, 35
General Artists Corporation (GAC), 83, 84, 138, 153, 156
Georgia Funeral Service Practitioners Association, 79
Get Fresh Girls, 306
Gilmore, Mary, 42, 43
Gilmore, Odessa, 42
Gilmore, Taft, 42
Golden, Alvaughn, 270, 305
Goodman, Shirley, 71–78, 83
Gordy, Berry Jr., 155, 183
Graham, Larry, 305
Great Depression, 12, 14, 15
Green, Frank A., Jr., 280, 341
Griffis, James, 316
grown folks business, 13

H
Haines Normal and Industrial Institute (est 1886), 2
Halling, Dorothy, 278
Halling, Jane Marie, 277
Halling, Richard Earl, 277, 278
Hamilton, Jessie, 54
Hammond, Roy C., 345, 347–350
Hampton, Lionel, 128
Hampton, W.H., 21
haplogroup E-V38 (E1b1a), vii, viii
Harris, Ernest, 2
Haywood, Leon, 246
Henderson, Louis, 54
Hendrix, Pattie, 205
Herald Attractions Inc., 66, 85, 146
Highland, Britany, 280, 340
Hill, Z.Z., 204, 220, 222, 229, 245, 305
Hinton, Joe, 85
Hippie, Harry, 261
Holey, Nellie, 5
Holley, Evelyn C., 301
Holmes, Mamie Key, 29, 30
Huff, Leon, 223
Hughes, Jimmy, 86, 112
Hunter, Ivory Joe, 84

I
Icey Jaye, 306, 312, 313
ICM International Creative Management, 306
Imperial Records, 82
Importation of Slaves, x
The Impressions, 203
Ingram, Luther, 204
International Talent Management Inc., 84, 86, 183, 203

J
Jackson, Ferniece, 332
Jackson III, James, 43
Jackson, James Jr., 18, 41–43, 332
Jackson, James Sr., 18, 19, 42

INDEX

Jackson, Jennifer, 43
Jackson, Josephine Wilson, 18
Jackson, Melvin, 247
Jackson, Mildred Virginia, 256
Jackson, Millie, 205, 246, 256, 257, 293
Jackson, Samuel, xiii–xv, xiv, 18
James Brown Enterprises, 207
James, Etta, 70, 83, 130, 219
Jarrett, Theodore R., 58
Jenkins, A.O. Sr., 21
Jenkins, Silas, 336
Jim Crow era, 38
JJ Fad, 306
Jo Lan, Pablo, 295
Jo Lan, Shui Ting, 295
John, Willie, 83
Johnson, Evelyn, 84
Johnson, Fred, xiv
Johnson, Jeremiah Sr., 315
Johnson, Margaret, 17
Johnson, Mary Wilson, 17, 23
Johnson, Shirley E., 317
Johnson, Syl, 206, 246
Johnson, Syleena, 299, 300
Joleon, Cristina, 295–297
Jones, Charlie, 2, 3
Jones, David Antonio, 116, 210, 216, 219, 265
Jones, David Jr., 116
Jones, David Sr., 116, 196
Jones, Ebony, 274–275
Jones, Emily, 29
Jones, Lewis, 29
Jones, Luther Henry Sr., 29, 36
Jones, Luther Jr., 37
Jones, Margot, 37
Jones, Pamela, 37
Jones, Peggy Ann, 29
Jones, Rhodia, 37
Jones, Rosemary, 37
Jones, Tia, 280
Jones, Tony, 311
Jones, Willie Bell, 36
Jordan, Alwena, 92, 93

Jordan, Andriette Dionne, 93, 94
Jordan, Bobby Jr., 94
Jordan, Cathy Veronica, 94
Jordan, Hazel Turner, 27, 92–94
Jordan, John Willie, 13
Jordan, Robert Willie, 12, 13, 15, 26, 27, 92, 94, 240, 340
Jordan, Willie Mae, 27, 92–94, 332
Jr. Walker & The All Stars, 203

K

Kelley, Brandon Lee, 262, 277
Kelley, Christopher, 280, 295
Kelley, Clifford (Cleo), v, viii, x–xii, xv, 11–13, 15–17, 19–21, 23–38, 41, 42, 45–50, 53–56, 69, 70, 81, 82–192, 194–198, 202, 208, 210, 211, 214, 216, 217, 218, 220, 226, 229, 230, 233–240, 242, 244–250, 253, 256, 258–262, 268–271, 273–278, 280–344, 345, 349, 351–357
Kelley, Clifford Jr., viii–x, 11, 28, 33, 54, 69–70, 80–81, 98, 102–103, 124, 132–134
Kelley, Jacqueline, 280, 295
Kelley, John Jr, v, 5, 6, 282
Kelley, Lee, 11, 12
Kelley, Nellie, v, 11, 282
Kelley, Sibyl, 210, 216, 219, 265, 266, 277, 284, 336
Kelley, Sibyl Denise, 102
Kelly, Anthony, 262
Kelly, Bobby King, 49, 72, 90, 98, 113–115, 121, 123, 124, 130, 196, 212–215, 261, 262, 265, 282, 304, 312, 314, 342
Kelly, Bobby Jr, 342
Kelly, Clifford Sr, 282, 283
Kelly, Emma, 26–28, 33, 36, 41, 53, 54, 71–78, 95, 98, 99, 124, 199, 214, 219, 234, 235, 236, 258, 282, 303, 314, 333, 347, 349
Kelly, Jerome Anthony, 215
Kelly, Jerome Sims (Ronnie), 37, 72, 90, 98, 113–115, 124, 125, 212, 213, 252, 282, 304, 354

INDEX

Kelly, Justin, 280
Kelly, Margaret Jean, 35, 36, 43, 44, 48, 72, 90, 98, 113, 114, 123–125, 233, 234, 235, 236, 282, 333, 336, 354
Kelly, Margurie Williams, v, xv, 17–21, 23, 25–29, 31–33, 35, 37, 38, 40–42, 44–47, 49, 50, 52, 53, 56, 67, 68, 69, 71–73, 77, 79, 90, 95, 98, 100, 103–107, 112, 115, 116, 124, 127, 134, 193–279, 280, 281, 282, 291, 295, 298, 308, 309, 310, 316, 320, 330, 332, 333, 338, 339–342, 353, 355
Kelly, Ronnie, 280
Kelly, Vakela Lynette, 215, 262, 280, 342
Kelly, Vernon Lee, 28, 354
Kelly's Curb Master Construction Company, 80–81, 210, 283, 296
Kelly's Nite Limit, v, 54, 56–72, 82–192, 194–200, 202, 208, 216, 217, 218, 219, 220, 221–223, 225, 226, 228, 229, 231, 233, 235, 239, 241–257, 261, 262, 264–266, 268–271, 273, 279, 280, 288, 291, 293, 294, 296–300, 302–317, 321, 336–339, 343–344, 345–350, 351, 353, 354
Kelly's Restaurant, 45–46, 50, 51, 54
Kennedy, John F., 99, 100
King, B.B., v, 34, 57, 59, 91, 128, 257, 336
King, Ben E., 85
King Davis, 206
King, Martin Luther Jr., 104
King Setnakhte, viii
Kittles, Everlina, 317
Knight, Gladys, 86
Knight, Jean, 204

L

LaBelle, Pattie, 85
Land of Judah, viii, ix
Lane, Jeff, 207
Laney, Lucy Craft, 2
LaSalle, Denise, 204, 220, 221, 229, 257, 306, 308

Latimore, Benny, 206, 220, 224, 229, 257, 307, 314
Lawtey Training School, 20–22, 43–44
Leaner, George, 204
Lee, Aretha, 49
Lee, Leonard, 71–78, 83
Lee Taylor Productions, 203
Little Anthony, 84
Little Johnny Taylor, 86
Little Milton, 204, 220
Little Richard, 57, 66, 85, 106, 113
Little Walter, 83
2 Live Crew, 306, 311
Love Maze, 307

M

Mack, Nathan, 270, 305
Mamado & SHE, 306
Margo, Nat, 86
Marie, Jane, 277
Marine Corps, 4
Mark IV, 207, 246
marriage certificate, 29
marriage license, 24
Marshall Brevetz and Associates, 206
Marshall, Steve, 317
Martin, Willie, 197
Mason, Barbara, 86
Matassa, Cosimo, 83
Mayberry, W.G., 317
McCrae, George, 206, 248, 249, 250
McCrae, Gwen, 206, 249
McPhatter, Clyde, 83
Mel and Tim, 86
Mendelsohn, Freddie, 83
Merritt, Condor, 226
Merritt Island, 210
The Midnighters, 82
migration, v, x, xiii, 14–22, 27
Miles, Buddy, 88
military registration, 8
Miller, Donna Garrer, 29, 38, 79, 96, 109, 126
Miller, Elizabeth, 20, 40

INDEX

Mims, Garnet, 85
Mims, Spencer, 4
Misty Blue, 253, 254
Mitchell, McKinley, 204
Moondock Productions, 207
Moore, Alton, 336
Moore, Dorothy, 205, 253, 254
Moore, Jackie, 203
Moore, Minnie Pearl, 44
Moore, Rosa Lee, 77
Morris, Ella, 28
Muff, Guard, 302
Muff, Mary Frances, 301
Muff Security Inc., 298–303, 336
Muff, Ulysee, 298–303, 336–339

N
NASA, 210
National Industrial Recovery Act, 15
Navy Hospital Corps, 212
Negro Travelers' Green Book, 46, 47
Nelson, Sonny Boy, 68
New Deal, 15–20
Newton, Margaret Johnson, 291
Newton, Nate, 291
Newton, Tim, 291
Nowag & Williams Talent Agency, 305

O
The Ohio Players, 88

P
Palmer, Gertrude, 4
Papin, Walter, 135
Paragon Agency, 202, 203, 204, 205, 206, 207, 208, 209, 217, 245, 246
Paramount Artists Group, 85, 168
Parker, Lee, 220–232, 248, 257
Parker, Rose, 302
"Patches," 200
Patrol Agency, 302
peacetime draft (WWII), 24–26
Peaches & Herb, 84

Penguin Artists Management, 86, 175
Personality Productions Inc., 60
Pettyway, Gerald, 336
Phelps, John Lawrence, 12
Phil Walden Artists and Promotions, 85, 86, 87, 112–113, 117, 172, 178, 180, 184, 187–189, 192
Pickett, Wilson, 87
Pierce, Attorney G.H., 194
The Pips, 86
The Platters, v, 57, 60
Ponder, Beverly, 94
Ponder, Jean, 94
Progressive Era (1890–1917), 1–4
Prohibition era, 1920s, 9–13
Prohibition Law violation, 26, 28
Purple Heart, 10

Q
Queen Booking Corporation (QBC), 84, 87, 167, 174, 181, 205
Queen Tiye Merenese, viii

R
racial discrimination, 4, 27, 104
Ramesses III, Pharaoh, vi–viii
Rand, Jess, 83
Randolph, Willie Mae, 317
RCA Victor, 164
Reconstruction Era (1865-1877), xi–xv
Recording Industry Association of America (RIAA), 221, 223, 225, 231, 256, 268, 311
Redding, Otis, 87, 120, 121, 123, 202, 245
Redding, Rodgers, 202, 203, 204, 205, 206, 207, 246
Redding, Velma, 204, 245
Reed, Robert R., 79
Reeves, Paulette, 306
Regency Artists LTD, 305
registration day (WWII), 26–33
road trips, 46–49
Roberson, Chuck, 204, 256–257, 336

INDEX

Robertson, Willie Mae, 4
Robinson, Emory, 220
Robinson, James, 20
Robinson Jenkins Ellerson (RJE) High School, 20, 44, 72–76, 80, 125, 133
Robinson, Martha (Aunt Maude), 17–20, 37, 42
Robinson, Sinclair, xiv, 17, 18
Rodgers Redding and Associates, 305, 306, 307, 339, 345
Rolling Stone Magazine, 228
Roosevelt, Franklin D., 14, 15
Roy, C., 336
The 5 Royales, v, 57, 63
Rush, Bobby, 88

S

Sam and Dave, 86
Sample III, Walter A., 93
Sample, Reginald A., 93
Sample, Walter Allen, 93
Scott, Abbie E., 2, 126
Scott, Agnes, 2
Scott, Freddie, 88
Scott, Freddy, 4
Scott, Harold, 4
Scott, Harriett Parker, 2
Scott, Ina Belle, 2, 126
Scott, Madison, 1, 2, 4
Scott, Maggie, 2
Scott, Odessa, 4
Scott, Peggy, 87
Scott, Samuel, 2
Seaboard Airline Railway, 17, 20, 25, 39
Sease, Marvin, 307, 336, 343, 344
Selective Service Act, 4, 24, 26
Sergeant First Class, 10
Shanks, Peter, 10
Sharp, Dee Dee, 85
Shaw, E., 194
Shaw Artists Corporation, 56, 59, 61, 65, 82, 83, 84, 85, 86, 87, 139, 141, 145, 148–150, 154, 157, 166

Shelton, Roscoe, 85, 122, 123
Sherman, Hermia Thompkins, 131
Siege of Augusta in 1781, x
Sikes Coal and Wood Company, 13
Simon, Joe, 87, 122, 123, 198, 204, 220, 223, 229, 233, 234, 239, 253
Singleton, Charlie, 128
Skarning, T.B., 206
Sledge, Percy, 203, 208, 209
Slocum, Mickey, 270, 305
Small, Nat, 128
Smathers, George Armistead, 105–106
Smith, Don, 197
Smith, Sherry, 206
2 Smooth, 307, 312
Social Security Act, 14
Social Security Administration, 14, 282
Sound Alternative Inc., 88
Southside Movement, 207
Spann, Maggie, 132, 133, 211
SRO Artist Inc., 85
State of Florida Department of Business Regulation License, 195
Staton, Candi, 205, 208, 209
Stax Records Company, 119
stock market crash, 9
Strong, Barrett, 84
Strong, Benjamin Franklin, 235, 315, 316
Strong, Enoch Jr., 235
Strong, Toika L., 262, 340, 341
Stroud, James, 205
Sullivan Enterprises, 84
Swann, Bettye, 202, 246

T

Talent Consultants Internationals Ltd., 88
Taylor, Bill, 10
Taylor, Evelena Wilson, 18
Taylor, Johnnie, 86, 263
Taylor, Johnny, 257
Taylor, Mamie Key, 10
Taylor, Ted, 88, 204
Taylor, Willie Belle, 10, 29, 32

INDEX

Technic Posse, 307
Terry, Johnny, 256, 257
Tex, Joe, 203, 268
Thomas, Bobby, 205
Thomas, Carla, 85, 117, 118, 121, 123
Thomas, Rufus, 117, 203
Tisdale, Mollie Davis, xiii
Tisdale, Peter, xiii
T&K Productions, 205, 206, 248, 249, 306
TRAMA, 205
Troutman, Tony, 292, 293, 306
Turner, Beverly Drummond, 343, 344, 349
Turner, Ike, 84, 87, 89–91, 95, 173
Turner, Tina, 84, 89–91, 95
Tyson, Harriette Davis, 297

U

Universal Attractions Inc., 56, 62, 63, 67, 82, 83, 85, 87, 88, 144, 151, 152, 158, 161, 169–171, 177, 182, 191, 202, 203, 204
U.S. Air Force, 4, 102–103, 211, 277, 278
U.S. Army, 4, 10, 21, 23, 25, 29, 102, 213
U.S. Navy, 4, 25, 28, 212, 261
U.S. Secretary of Labor, 15, 114
U.S. World War I Draft. *See* Selective Service Act

V

Vanleer, J.R., 207
Vastola, Tommy, 205
Vietnam War, 42, 234

W

wages, 14, 15, 18–21, 56, 92–94, 96
Waiters, Mel, 345–347
"The Wall," 198, 252
Walt Disney World, 210
War of 1812, x
Warren, E., 44
Warren, J.F., Jr., 193
Warrick, Dionne, 84
Washington, Dinah, v, 57, 62, 128
Waters, Muddy, v, 57, 65, 95

Welty, R.E., 282
West, Jerry, 220–232
West, Kanye, 299
The Whalers, 54–56
White, Clementine, 317
White, Ted, 87
William Morris Agency Inc., 83–85, 179
Williams, Bobby, 244
Williams, Charles H., xv
Williams, Clarence, xv
Williams, Ferniece, 43
Williams, Fred, 16
Williams, Lizzie Stuart, xv
Williams, Marylou Kelly, 29, 33, 36, 48, 72, 73, 90, 98–100, 109–116, 125, 131, 194, 213, 252, 274, 304, 333, 340
Williams, Otto, 54
Willie "Cooter" Brown, 311
Willis, Chuck, v, 57, 61
Wilson, Catherine, xiii–xv, 21
Wilson, Dave, xiii
Wilson, Jackie, 128
Wilson, Josephine, xiv
Wilson, Margaret Dixon, xiii
Wilson, Martha, xiv
Wilson, Mary, xiv
Wilson, Samuel, 21
Wilson, Susie, xv
Womack, Bobby, 206, 261, 262
World War I (WWI), v, 3, 7, 8, 9, 14, 34
World War II (WWII), v, 24–26
Wright, Albert, 205
Wright, Betty, 128–129, 198, 201, 203, 206, 246, 336
Wright, O.V., 204
Wynn, Chester, 134
Wynn, Deloris, 102, 134, 135
Wynn, Rodney, 134
Wynn, Tracy Faulkner, 200, 227

Y

Yamassee Indian War of 1715, x
York, Tiny, 128

www.ingramcontent.com/pod-product-compliance
Lightning Source LLC
Chambersburg PA
CBHW042358030426
42337CB00032B/5137